# Creatability

## Creative Arts for Preschool Children with Special Needs

by Fran Herman, RMT, MTA, CCW, and
James C. Smith, B.A., AOCA

Foreword by Ayala Manolson
Founder and Director of the Hanen Early Language Parent Program

Illustrations by James Smith
Photographs by Richard Loveszy

**Communication
Skill Builders** ®

3838 E. Bellevue/P.O. Box 42050
Tucson, Arizona 85733
(602) 323-7500

Music Credits

- ASCAP for permission to reprint "Truck," by Jim Newton, from the Celebration Shop Cassette, "Friends of the Family." © 1988 by ASCAP.

- Anne Bindernagel for "Hey! Do You Have Something to Say?" and "Halloween Song."

- The Birch Tree Group, Ltd., for "Halloween," by Marcia Berman. From the Folkways Record #7525 "Activity Songs for Children." Used by permission of Folkways Records/Smithsonian.

- Caroline Fynney for "Seed Song" and "Daddies Are Special."

- Gabi Music for permission to reprint "Love Is the Word," by Deborah Dunleavy. © 1984 by Jibbery Jive KRL 1015, Kids' Records, Toronto.

- Homeland Publishing for permission to reprint "Shake My Sillies Out," by Raffi and B. and B. Simpson. © 1977 by Troubadour Records.

- Nancy Minden for permission to reprint "Hug Your Baby," "Telephone Song," and "Cleanin' the House." © 1987 by Nancy Minden.

- Paulo for "Feelings." © 1987 by Paul Finkleman (CAPAC). Reprinted by permission.

- Robert Sutherland for copying the music.

Published by

**Communication Skill Builders, Inc.** ®
3838 E. Bellevue/P.O. Box 42050
Tucson, Arizona 85733
(602) 323-7500

ISBN 0-88450-577-4          Catalog No. 7748

10 9 8 7 6 5 4 3 2
Printed in the United States of America

For information about our audio and/or video products, write us at:
Communication Skill Builders, P.O. Box 42050, Tucson, AZ 85733.

# Dedication

By Fran Herman

To the memory of my parents, Rebecca and Harry Korson, and to Carl and Eve, who are always with me.

By James Smith

With love to my ever supportive family.

By both authors

To all those who provide a tapestry of caring and nurturing for special children everywhere.

# Acknowledgments

Our appreciation and thanks to:

- Our first readers, Drs. David Berbrayer, Darcy Fehlings, Yuen Chua, and Donal O'Leary, for their medical input.

- Judith Bowles for support and editorial advice.

- Everett Campbell for photographs in Appendix A.

- Nancy Cole, Heidi Pattendon, and Renee Hiltz for their willingness to experiment in the arts with young children, and Julie Nicks, who does the same with sensory stimulation.

- Paul Hogan for the concept of the Harvest Festival as a fitting end to summer.

- Dr. Eva Kalman for her model of prevention.

- Rebecca Loveszy for her enthusiasm and caring.

- Richard Loveszy for photographs that speak to us all.

- Eileen Purdie and Harriet Fried for helping us gain understanding of children with hearing impairments.

- Janet Quintal for sharing thoughts on the preschool child.

- The Hugh MacMillan Centre School and Play Haven (for medically fragile children) and Easter Seals Pre-School Program for granting permission to take photographs.

- Our colleagues at The Hugh MacMillan Centre for their willingness to share and to the Creative Arts Department for inspiration and creativity.

- Our families for enduring and tolerating the ever-mounting collection of books, papers, and drawings, and our preoccupation with the tasks at hand.

# About the Authors

This is the second book by Fran Herman and James C. Smith, who also wrote *Accentuate the Positive! Expressive Arts for Children with Disabilities* (1988, Toronto: Jimani Publications).

**Fran Herman,** RMT, MTA, CCW, is Director of the Creative Arts Department at The Hugh MacMillan Rehabilitation Centre, a pediatric facility in Toronto, Canada. She has been an active clinical practitioner and proponent for music therapy in Canada, and has served as President of the Canadian Association for Music Therapy.

Mrs. Herman is internationally known for her work with children with severe disabilities. As an advocate for them, she has lectured and given demonstrations at many universities in Canada and abroad. She is the creator and director of the Toronto Wheelchair Players, a company of young people with chronic disabilities who produced the acclaimed film, *The Emperor's Nightingale.*

**James C. Smith,** B.A., AOCA, is a sculptor and remedial art instructor. He has worked with young offenders and emotionally and behaviorally disturbed children. For the past several years, he has worked at The Hugh MacMillan Rehabilitation Centre with children who have physical disabilities. He strives to gain broader recognition for the value of creative arts in the lives of special persons through giving workshops and seminars for teachers, therapists, life-skill coaches, and other health-care professionals.

# Contents

# Foreword

A Toronto facility for children with disabilities, where I worked as a speech-language pathologist some twenty-five years ago, was the last place I expected to feel pure joy. The joy emanated from a production of "Snow White and the Seven Dwarfs" by a cast in wheelchairs. The warm memories surrounding that happy event have remained with me.

Why was this production so memorable? First, children with special needs are seldom given the opportunity to participate in the creative arts. From conception to performance, this "Snow White" was a thrilling, fulfilling experience. Second, the emotions felt by the children involved were contagious and unforgettable. The inspiration behind this production and innumerable other creative opportunities for children with special needs was Music Therapist Fran Herman. She has shared with colleagues and children her enthusiasm and skill for enriching children's lives by involving them in creative activities. I was fortunate to be one of those colleagues.

Helping children express themselves in creative ways has become a major thrust in the Hanen Early Language Parent Programs. Throughout the country and abroad, we have found that creative activities offer the best opportunities for children to acquire language. The processes of sharing experiences and creating foster the richest and most natural environment for learning.

We desperately need specific ideas and directions to let young children with special needs express themselves through the creative arts. Fran Herman and colleague/artist James Smith have responded to that need, sharing their wisdom and experience from years of innovative and successful work with children.

The information Fran and James have compiled in this book will give children with special needs the freedom and opportunity to participate in creative activities and express their ideas and feelings. I am sure this book will contribute significantly to the joy that professionals, parents, and children can experience from sharing and creating together.

Ayala Manolson

Founder and Director of the Hanen Early Language Parent Program

December 1990

# Preface

"I could kiss you for writing that book," the woman said. "That book" was *Accentuate the Positive!,* our 1988 effort on creative arts for children with disabilities.

"It's what I've always needed for my little boy," she said. "He has cerebral palsy and is nonspeaking, and I've been tearing my hair out trying to find activities that would help to draw him out. My only complaint with it is . . . that it doesn't go far enough. Why didn't you start with the very young child and go from there? You still can, you know."

We thought about her comments for a long time. We dug into the literature on exceptional children, but found very little on the arts and their potential to empower young children. Very little, even though we know that the early years are crucial, that they include the period when a child's emotional patterning begins, when personality is most pliant and learning tools can make the greatest impact.

*Creatability* advocates use of the arts—music, art, puppetry, movement, and play—to enrich learning for children from infancy through six who have physical disabilities, developmental delays, or behavioral difficulties. It is intended for teachers, therapists, parents, and child-care workers who want to explore every avenue for promoting and supporting children's self-awareness. We hope it will guide those who may be unsure how to address the arts with children with disabilities, as well as supporting practitioners who seek to explore new avenues to learning.

Our approach must always be holistic, sensitive, and flexible. One must believe that interaction of some kind is possible for all children; that disability need not bar artistic expression; that all children can be participants, not just spectators; and that the arts can and will help children express their innermost thoughts and feelings.

Our book's design and presentation will, we hope, facilitate activity, supply ideas, suggest adaptations, and advance approaches for creative self-expression. Each of the book's four parts present explorations and activities targeted for specific ages and sensory systems. Appendix A presents detailed descriptions of adaptive devices, tools, and instruments mentioned throughout the main text. Appendix B lists additional readings. By necessity, the book's organization is sometimes arbitrary, and some of the information overlaps. Readers are encouraged to cross-refer for guidance for a particular child.

The activities and explorations encompass language development, sensory awareness, gross and fine motor development, visual and auditory discrimination, and social/personal growth. All activities and explorations have been fieldtested by the authors or their colleagues in both mainstream and special-education facilities with children with mild to severe disabilities.

These activities and explorations are designed to be adapted to meet diverse needs. Some are traditional, others are innovative; all are directed toward helping a child to function creatively while developing the whole child, not just a specific skill area.

**Note:** Assumptions inherent in our language can perpetuate ignorance. Thus, we prefer to refer to "a child with epilepsy" rather than labeling the disability by saying "the epileptic child." The former phrase suggests we consider the child first and the disability second.

# Introduction

*Creatability . . .*

There's no such word. At least, you won't find it in the dictionary.

We joined together *create*—to cause, to make, to bring into existence—with *ability*—natural talent or acquired proficiency. What we came up with was *creatability,* a talent which everyone has to some degree. That's what this book celebrates.

*Creativity* is a special way of thinking, understanding, and learning. Being creative does not mean that one must produce works of art; instead, it means that one applies mental processes to make order out of chaos and to bring meaning out of special events. Creativity means the ability to play with whatever comes to hand, to invent and transform. Institutionalization, be it in a hospital or in a school, can rob children of creativity. They work to please and display, rather than to express themselves and discover the infinite realms of their imaginations.

*Ability* exists in every child, in various and profound ways, no matter how severe the disability: the ability to create, the ability to respond to aesthetic experiences, the ability to learn from self-expression.

## Nurturing: The Most Important Job

We believe there is no more creative and important job in the world than nurturing the growth of children. Our future depends on the quality of relationships, development, and discipline experienced by our children. We must determine the nurturing options that best reinforce the growth and development of the children with whom we work.

There is a delicate balance between guiding a child and following the child's lead, and each therapist or teacher finds a personal style that strikes this balance. We must allow children to use their own initiative in presenting their expression of feelings. If our approaches stay flexible, children will develop inner controls *without losing* the joy that accompanies experimentation and discovery. Children can profit enormously from exposure to the arts that offers activity instead of passivity and from opportunities to stress abilities instead of disabilities. Young children involved in creative efforts will be excited and enlivened as they explore and come to terms with their world, master new skills, and learn to express themselves in a variety of ways.

1

Self-esteem is a precious and critical part of nurturing. An interesting view of self-esteem comes from Virginia Satir, the noted pioneer in family therapy. In her book *The New People Making* (Science and Behavior Books, Inc., 1988, 21), Satir calls self-esteem "a concept, an attitude, a feeling, an image, . . . represented by behavior." Satir explains self-esteem through "pot symbolism," a term she first used with a client family struggling to articulate how they felt about themselves. Satir told them about an old family pot that had had many uses. They caught her meaning and began talking about their individual "pots," and whether they contained feelings of worth or guilt, of shame or usefulness.

Those of us who work with and care for children with disabilities must find ways of "filling up their pots" with experiences that are fulfilling and contribute to growth. There are many techniques to foster expression through the creative arts, but the critical factor, no matter what technique is used, is to maintain unconditional acceptance and a nonjudgmental attitude. Regardless of what you and the children do at any one time, the purpose remains the same: to nurture the children and to help them become aware of themselves and of their place in this world.

## Taking Care of Ourselves

The world is in a dark place right now. We find ourselves bombarded by daily reports of violence and corruption, all reminding us that humans have the potential to be lethal. But we also have the potential to be nurturing. The challenge of today and the hope for all generations to come is to bring out our nurturing capabilities. We make the choice. And when we do, we must keep in mind the four "C"s: *Concern, Caring, Connection,* and *Commitment.*

We must remember, though, that change is gradual; we sometimes become so involved in helping others that we forget we have nothing to share if we are fully spent. If we "burn out," it may be because we have allowed no time for peaceful moments, enjoyment of self, and personal regeneration. As nurturers, we must get in touch with that "child within us" and resolve to balance each day to allow room for ourselves. We must give ourselves permission to become friendly with our feelings so that they work for, not against, us. Only by nurturing ourselves can we nurture the children with whom we work.

## Supporting the Arts

The arts call for a special commitment. Despite tangible gains in education and treatment for people with disabilities, there is no concerted effort to make the arts an integral part of the school curriculum. Remedial or therapeutic creative arts programs have made striking contributions to the education of children with special needs, but these programs still are not seen as essential or as having the same importance as other core subjects.

This reluctance may stem from society's tendency to reward cognitive accomplishments rather than activities that promote the affective, or "feeling," domain of the child. Compared with computer science or math, learning in the arts may seem nebulous. Achievements in work with clay, painting, and movement cannot be easily measured, and thus the arts often are perceived as "busy work" used to fill time or for manual or vocational training. The limited funding and training available for those working in the arts perpetuate such a view. Yet for many exceptional children, the affective side is just as important—if not more important—than cognitive development. Unfortunately, the number of children who can be helped by arts programs falls far short of the number who need such help but do not receive it. This shortfall is often due to a severe shortage of resources as well as to a lack of understanding of the real potential of arts programs.

One apparent advantage of arts for the young child is that one can make contact with the whole child. The child is treated as an individual, not as a student, client, or patient. Thus children who have little control of many aspects of their lives can take control, if only in the way they dab paint on a piece of paper, mold a piece of clay, or respond to songs.

Health, education, and welfare systems—all programs serving children—must help children develop to their maximum potential. Educational programs must be reorganized to make a child's worth the focal point for all activities. We must also avoid watered-down arts programs that pander to trendy educational ideas. Instead, we must make the arts part and parcel of the children's everyday experiences to ensure that they have real-life relevance and application.

We must always remember that the children we work with require respect, caring, freedom, and the knowledge that they are both unique and similar to everyone else. Finally, we must nurture ourselves and thus foster our abilities to help children maximize their senses, imagination, and talents.

It all begins with us!

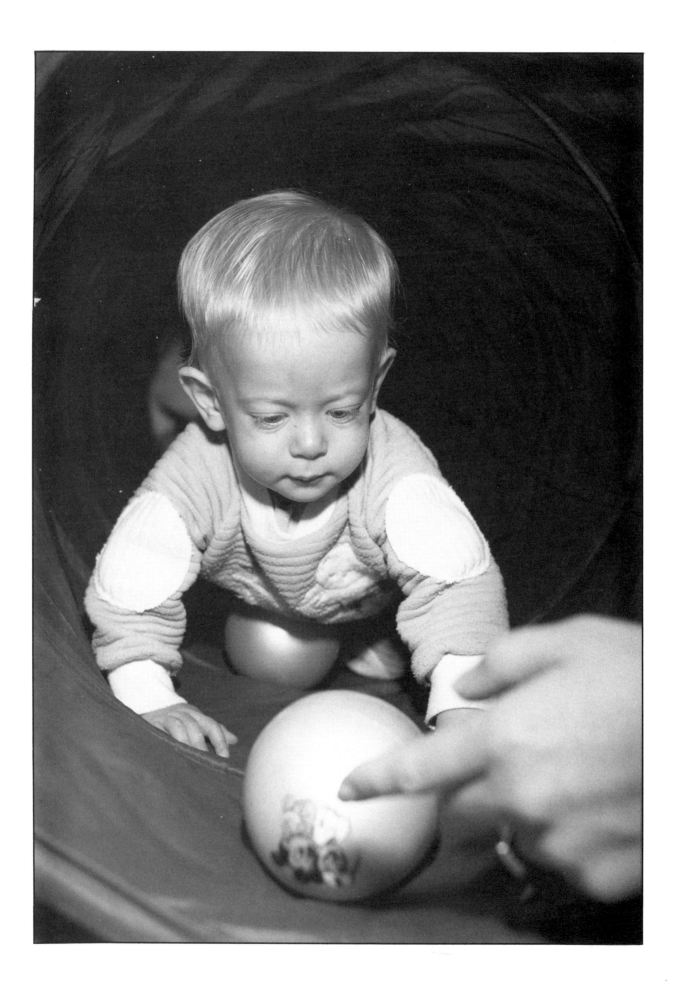

# Babies and Toddlers: Awakening the Senses

*Evie sat in the middle of the kitchen floor, just as she had since she was plunked down an hour earlier. At 16 months, Evie could not crawl, stand, or roll over. Because she could not move around to explore the world, the world had to come to her. So there she sat, surrounded by pots, pans, and wooden spoons, creating her own symphony of sounds. Another time, she had plastic containers of large dried beans, acorns, and walnuts, as well as little boxes into which to put these varied treasures. The next day, a container of big colored buttons or a box of tissues held her interest.*

*One day I was somewhat harassed, so I simply handed Evie a roll of toilet paper. As any curious child would do, she began pulling it, watching it unroll. Soon she began to see the effect of what she was doing. In minutes she was swathed in toilet paper, jabbering away delightedly. I sat down beside her to demonstrate how to tear the paper at the perforated lines. She began ripping and playing with small pieces. Some were crunched in her hand; others she let lie. Next she began piling larger sheets, one on top of the other. She was experimenting and satisfying her curiosity—surely, the core of creativity.*

## GOALS

Part I focuses on the use of creative experiences that help babies and toddlers—

- To recognize and coordinate different parts of the body
- To maintain a state of quiet alertness and deal with stress
- To engage in vocal play
- To increase attentiveness to new sounds
- To develop self-awareness
- To discover new things about their surroundings
- To interact with people
- To play games involving imitation and anticipation
- To focus on and visually distinguish objects and movements

We know well that the sensory system is the doorway to all learning and creativity, a direct passageway to the brain, where information is gathered and processed. If that passageway is wide open, children can see, hear, taste, touch, and smell. If the passageway closes, children are closed off from their full potential.

We may, however, get an early start in opening that passageway by helping children explore the senses through the expressive arts. Through this exploration, we can help children cultivate their desire for active participation rather than passive dependency—a tool they will need to cope with the often-rocky road ahead.

It all begins in infancy. We know that all babies need objects nearby to stimulate sight and hearing. Playthings put near the baby in the first few months nourish the baby's cognitive appetite and enhance physical and mental development. The sooner the baby is actively using hearing, seeing, and touching, the sooner active learning begins.

**THEME ONE**

# With Our Bodies

The integration that occurs as infants and babies learn to move, coordinate movements, get up from the floor, and walk is critical to all future learning. Children begin to form a self-image as they reach out, touch, and explore, experiencing new sensations and new motor behaviors. Once children become aware of their bodies and of their constantly changing abilities and limitations, they become capable of interacting with other people and with objects.

**UNIT 1**

## Developing Body and Tactile Awareness in Babies

It is important to develop body and tactile awareness from infancy. Infants who kick their feet, gaze at their hands, or touch your face with their fingers are making discoveries about their body and its capabilities. There are many simple things we can do to encourage body and tactile awareness as the baby grows. Babies want to touch what they see, and hands are the most versatile tools for touching, grasping, and manipulating objects. Babies will repeat these motions in response to a ring, jingle, or rattle. Remember that textures, shapes, temperatures, and spatial arrangements can all be felt by the tactile receptors in the skin.

By three months, babies typically have the physical coordination to reach and grasp a toy. As they approach five months, they become more intent on using (rather than just watching) their hands. Up to six months or so, the baby will be working on "visually directed reaching," the ability to reach out and grasp an object at arm's length. Mastery of this hand movement is considered a landmark in cognitive development.

### EXPLORATIONS

An infant should not just while away waking time. To keep infants involved, make sure the crib or playpen includes reachable objects with interesting shapes, colors, and textures.

**Bath time.** Bath time is an excellent opportunity to increase body awareness: massage arms, legs, fingers, and toes while toweling the baby dry.

**Tickle, tickle.** Tickle the baby with your fingertips, stroke the baby with a soft brush, wiggle the baby's toes, or blow on the baby's tummy or back.

**Body sensations.** Provide tactile stimulation to different areas of the baby's body. For example, to create different sensations, touch the baby's hands with feathers, differently textured brushes, toys that vibrate, objects with varying temperatures (such as cool milk or warm water), a wet sponge, or a dry cloth.

**I touch, you touch.** Touch part of the baby's body, then encourage the baby to do the same. Give praise if the baby responds.

*A spoon friend.*

**With bells on.** Bells sewn on an elastic band can be put on the baby's wrist or ankle to provide opportunities for cause-effect experimentation. These bracelets hasten the pleasant discovery of a baby's "built-in" playthings—the hands and feet.

**Sweet strokes.** Babies love to stroke different textures with their fingers. The satin edge of a baby's blanket may be one of the first objects the baby discovers. To encourage investigation of these fingertip sensations, make a small sampler of fabrics with different textures: silk, satin, fur, wool, cotton, terry cloth, and corduroy are possible choices. A narrow sampler can be attached to the baby's car seat or across a stroller. Larger swatches make interesting scarves for babies to play with or touch to their faces.

**Spoon friend.** As babies learn to bring their hands together at midline, they learn to hold objects, first with both hands and then shifting from one hand to the other. Soft textured shapes are good at this stage, as is a "spoon friend." To make a spoon friend, take a wooden baking spoon with a short handle and draw faces on the front and back with nontoxic paints or permanent markers. You can glue yarn to the spoon for hair and add whatever your imagination suggests, avoiding toxic materials or small items a baby might choke on. Babies love faces; this fascinating toy also provides them opportunities to use their hands and mouth to feel hardness and shape.

**Food fun.** At around six months of age, the baby should begin feeling food textures and temperatures. Put the baby in a baby seat or high chair and place a small helping of warm mashed potatoes on the tray. Let the baby mush them around; don't worry if the baby samples a bit. Cooked pastas, cereals, puddings, and whipped cream are among many other possibilities for the baby's research. Playing with water or a melting ice cube can also enhance awareness of the surrounding world. (Supervise play with ice cubes closely, of course, to make sure the baby doesn't swallow them.)

*This baby is exploring modeling dough made from potato flakes, a few drops of oil, and a little water.*

**UNIT 2** "Difficult" Babies

The term "difficult" describes babies who, for many different reasons, are very sensitive to various stimuli and stresses. These babies can be very difficult to care for, and their lives must be difficult for them to live as well.

Some babies are difficult to soothe almost from birth. Even minimal changes in routine or levels of stimulation disturb them. They seem more susceptible to environmental stress (noise, hunger, fatigue) and can be highly irritable, sensitive, and difficult to manage. These characteristics are often seen in babies with prenatal drug exposure.

*Tactile defensiveness* (hypersensitivity to being touched), which is often present in "difficult" babies, can occur in babies who are premature or have cerebral palsy or other types of neurological involvement. These babies may be agitated by being held or touched, by contact with your clothing, or by feeling the water in the bath.

Bear in mind that babies with specific handicapping conditions may react negatively to certain types of stimulation. Babies with cerebral palsy may have whole-body startle reflexes that are triggered by sudden sounds or quick movements. Babies who are hearing impaired will be upset if touched by someone who approaches from behind and takes them by surprise. Similarly, babies with visual impairments will react to being handled if they haven't heard your voice or footsteps moving closer.

## Reducing Tactile Defensiveness

At best, daily routines such as bathing, feeding, and putting the baby down to sleep present real difficulties if the infant has tactile defensiveness. Overcoming these difficulties demands time and patience, but this care is critical in nurturing the baby's trust. It is best to introduce new sensations slowly. As the baby's comfort level increases, you can gradually add other stimuli.

### EXPLORATIONS

**Holding.** During feeding, hold the baby next to the skin or a soft fabric. Place the baby's hand against the chest or face for short periods of time each day until this sensation can be tolerated. Men shouldn't hold the baby against their face because facial hairs can be scratchy; instead, they can use the underside of their forearm to cradle or touch the baby's face or hands.

**Stroking.** Spend some time stroking the baby with a soft makeup brush. Start with the hands and feet, and eventually involve the arms, legs, belly, and back as the baby's tolerance to touch increases.

**Massaging.** Some babies enjoy being massaged gently with a little oil, especially after bathtime, while other babies will tolerate firm, constant pressure better than light stroking. Be sensitive to signals that the baby has had enough (usually indicated by turning away or closing the eyes, and then by increasing signs of distress).

**Baths.** Baths can be one of many routines that are not easy for babies with tactile difficulties. To reassure these babies, try putting their hands in tepid water until they are calm, or gently rub their body with water instead of immersing them. Singing or talking softly as you proceed may also help.

**Clothes and bedding.** Getting dressed may provoke outbursts. If the baby cannot tolerate the touch of unfamiliar fabrics, it may be wise to wash all new clothing a few times to eliminate stiffness. Putting new clothing in the crib may also help by giving the baby an opportunity to feel the clothing and get used to it.

It is probably best to use soft cotton sheets for these babies rather than sheets that contain polyester or other synthetic fibers. Cotton clothing is also recommended.

**Playtime.** Laying the baby on a multicolored textured quilt or blanket that you know the baby can tolerate may be a good tactile and visual stimulus. Put plastic or soft cloth sheets on the floor or ground to keep toys and playthings clean. Cleanliness is very important. Washing toys and playthings regularly is, of course, a wise precaution.

**Toys.** Give only soft toys to babies who are hypersensitive to touch until other textures can be tolerated. The baby may respond negatively to a particular sensation, and it may take some detective work to find a texture the baby will accept. Put pieces of different fabrics up to the baby's face, or leave them in the crib as playthings to give the baby an opportunity to become familiar with these fabrics and, thus, more likely to play with toys made from them.

With noise-making toys, it is best to give these babies a toy with a chime or bell sound rather than one that squeaks.

**Food.** Food presents many sensations. When the baby can sit in a high chair, it becomes important to learn to accept the feel and texture of solid foods. Give the baby time to taste and play with food put on the high-chair tray—to get messy, hold the food, squeeze it, and feel the different tactile possibilities (see page 8). Watch the baby play: you may discover a preference for something warm over something cold, or something firm over something squishy.

**New sensations.** As the baby develops an increased tolerance for textures, introduce new tactile sensations. You can ease these experiences in by rubbing the baby's arms, legs, and feet with materials that create varied feelings: soft cloths; water; whipping cream or pudding; dry substances, such as puffed wheat or cornmeal; mushy materials, such as mashed potatoes, cooked pasta, or bread dough; and firmer textures, such as modeling clay. Little by little, these experiences help the baby overcome a hypersensitive sensory system and discover the desire to explore.

### Trying to Calm Distressed Babies

Babies may signal that they are becoming stressed through one or more of the following behaviors: avoiding eye contact, arching the back or trunk, holding the legs straight up in the air, breathing shallowly and rapidly, or uttering piercing cries. It is important that all baby's caregivers learn to recognize these early distress signals so they can cease the stimulation before the baby completely loses control.

A baby's main means of communication is, of course, crying. Try to relieve the distress signaled by crying. Sound, motion, physical contact, or changing the baby's environment are time-honored techniques for soothing a baby. First, though, determine what upsets the baby. If the baby is bothered by bright lights, dim them. If curtains blowing in the window produce a quivering reaction, keep the window closed. If numerous or sudden noises intrude, take care not to startle. If there is a negative response to rough fabrics such as wool or linen, wear soft clothing when holding or nursing the baby.

Give agitated babies time to become quiet on their own. Remain calm and quiet, and turn your face away (eye contact is too much for some babies to handle). Offer a finger or a pacifier for sucking. Try such comforting techniques as tenderly patting the baby's abdomen with your hand, holding the baby's hands together at midline, changing the baby's position in the crib or on your shoulder, or introducing low monotonous music or a ticking clock.

Sometimes babies react to a new sound and will calm down to listen. Beautiful sounds made by tapping glass (especially the cut-glass variety), plucking guitar strings, or playing a few notes on a piano may also be effective.

Some babies require a concerted attempt to reduce stimulation before they can relax. Tuck the baby in bed with a favorite blanket, darken the room, speak tenderly while stroking the baby, croon a little song, and hope for the best. If the baby does not quiet down, it may be best to let the baby cry, knowing that sleep will come eventually.

**Calm is restored.** Signs that the baby is ready for interaction and stimulation include eye contact, a quiet and alert manner, and hands held toward the midline of the body or the mouth. At that point, you can gradually intervene with songs, quiet talk, rocking, or walking to a gentle rhythm. Place the baby face down on your lap while gently rocking or bouncing the baby up and down to a definite rhythm.

Your voice is very important: the human voice introduces interaction whether you sing or talk. If you sing softly while rocking the baby, sing in the same rhythm as the rocking. Even though your words are not understood, the sounds and tone of your voice help to establish a relationship.

## UNIT 3  The Medically Fragile Baby

The "medically fragile" label may apply to babies born prematurely or with low birth weight, cardiac conditions, or other severe medical anomalies. This label is applied when the condition significantly hinders the child's developmental processes. The range and symptomatology of medical fragility is diverse, but these babies share a characteristic set of needs. Careful adjustment to these needs can help facilitate healthy adjustment of the child and family to the condition involved.

*Wanna play ball? Age-appropriate activities are essential for a child who is medically fragile.*

Like any child, children who are medically fragile need a normal, structured environment that includes age-appropriate activities and interaction with significant others. Children who are medically fragile demonstrate areas of normal development and maturation, but developmental delays can result from limited opportunities to participate in activities and social interaction as well as from long hospitalizations. The developmental delays and differences caused by serious illness are compounded when the child is treated differently from other children. Providing the most normal environment possible allows these children to grow and develop at their own rates. It is important to treat the child like any other child and not to emphasize the child's fragility or illness in the daily course of child management.

*A gentle rocking motion to some quiet music makes for a great ride!*

## Music and Sounds

The sensory organization of premature or "at risk" babies is not as good as that of healthy, full-term babies. These babies may be easily overwhelmed by stimuli and may need extra time to adjust to new situations.

Sound awareness and music can be two of the most consistently useful vehicles for nurturing and development; they should be explored almost from birth. Crooning, rocking, and body contact are essential to early bonding between the baby and parents. Parents often feel apprehensive and tense during the first few months of the baby's life, particularly if the baby has been labeled "at risk" and has had a long post-birth hospitalization. Singing to and rocking the baby may help to relax the adult as well as the baby. Singing gently or playing music may also encourage the baby to move.

As the baby grows, responses to music will continue if used throughout daily routines. Music can either stimulate or soothe, so use music appropriate to the baby's needs. To settle the baby down, use a ticking clock or restful and rhythmic music because these are reminiscent of the mother's heartbeat in the womb.

## Visual Images

Visual images are important, too. Babies can distinguish between light and dark and are fascinated by brightly colored mobiles, pictures taped to the wall near the crib, patterned curtains, or shadows cast on the wall by a lamp.

Mirrors can become entertaining and important learning tools: an unbreakable and accurate mirror attached to the crib will tempt the baby to look, smile, perform, and be utterly intrigued. Later on, a larger mirror secured to a wall can be a great learning tool. As you and the baby sit together facing the mirror, wave to the baby, touch and identify body parts, make funny faces, or eat together.

## Hypersensitivity

Many medically fragile babies are hypersensitive to touch, sounds, visual stimuli, and other sensations. See the preceding section ("'Difficult' Babies") for guidance here.

## Play Programs

The growing awareness of the needs of babies who are medically fragile has initiated programs that provide play experiences in safe surroundings. A parent or caregiver usually accompanies the baby, reinforcing the adventure of interaction. There is no doubt that children thrive and develop through opportunities to be involved with the outer world. These opportunities help children become more self-reliant. Through rolling a ball back and forth or playing "peek-a-boo" or "hide-and-seek," they learn to sequence events and take turns in interaction, as well as recognizing relationships with others and beginning to appreciate the feeling of play.

*Play is the work of children, and children thwarted in this work are at a serious disadvantage.*

| UNIT 4 |

# Developing Body and Tactile Awareness in Toddlers

Children nearing two years of age show increasing interest in manipulating and controlling small objects. Toddlers also show an increased interest in their bodies and how they work. However, they need tactile sensations to understand this: toddlers cannot tell whether an object is hot or cold, soft or hard, smooth or fuzzy merely by looking at it. Touching objects is part of their growing skills. Children also like and need to be touched. The touch of an adult relieves fear and builds confidence. Developing a "touching repertoire" in children begins with imitation.

*A young child needs to explore by touch, as well as sight and hearing.*

## EXPLORATIONS

**Clap like me.** Put on some highly rhythmic music. Clap to the rhythm of the music and wait for the children to do the same. When the children show interest, pat parts of your body that young children typically learn to name, calling each by name. Begin with body parts the children are likely to know. The children may imitate touching these parts on their own bodies. If not, you can go around the circle touching each child's leg or foot and so on. You can play this game many ways, becoming more sophisticated as the children learn what their bodies can do.

**Making faces.** Sit with the children on the floor in front of a mirror. Talk about and demonstrate things your face can do: chewing, laughing, and licking, for example. Demonstrate facial expressions: angry, happy, surprised, or silly. Make faces: all squashed up, or very big with a wide-open mouth and eyes. Encourage the children to join in the activity.

**Variation.** With the children, explore opening and closing eyes, mouth, and hands. Ask the children to touch these parts as you name them.

## Painting

General tips on painting play with toddlers:

1. Use fat stubby crayons that are easy to grasp.

2. Tape coloring paper down at the corners to prevent sliding.

3. When painting, use nontoxic paints, preferably with short, thick brushes for better control.

4. Children can paint horizontally at tables, or vertically at an easel or on paper taped to walls at the appropriate height.

## EXPLORATIONS

**Finger-painting.** Most toddlers enjoy finger-painting, which can be done on a table covered with oilcloth or plastic. Initially, it is best to use just one bright color. Avoid red because a child may be reminded of blood and become fearful. After several enjoyable experiences with finger painting, add a few other colors. You can also add new textures by adding coarse salt, rice, or coffee grounds to the mixture.

Some toddlers hesitate to finger-paint, finding it too messy. In this case, start painting with them, exclaiming how much fun it is to slide the paint all over the paper and making clear that it's okay to get one's fingers all squishy with paint. If the children remain resistant, "painting" with pudding or a gelatin dessert may be more appealing.

**Paint bags.** This alternative to finger-painting is easy to make. Take self-sealing sandwich bags reinforced on all four sides with tape. In each bag, put a dollop of one of the following: ketchup; mustard; mayonnaise tinted blue, green, or yellow: an orange-colored baby food; or a mashed vegetable. Tape the bag to the table at all four corners so that the children can slide their fingers across the bag, enjoying the patterns that result.

Here's another good paint bag trick: use a larger bag (such as a freezer bag), reinforce the sides, put in mineral oil and food coloring, and tape to the table. This creates a quite different visual effect.

**Sponge printing.** Tape paper to the table. Then, using a sponge and thick paint, show the children how to dip the sponge into the paint and print all over the paper. The children can either hold the sponge or use a clothespin clipped to the center of the sponge as a handle. Using several colors makes this even more interesting.

**Block printing.** Block printing is similar to sponge printing. Take halved potatoes or cucumbers, cut decorative shapes into them, dip them into the paint, and print on the paper. You can make beautiful gift wrap this way. Empty spools, erasers, keys, or pieces of wood also work well for block printing.

**Hand and foot printing.** For hand printing, the children put their hands into tempera paint and then imprint the paper. For foot printing, the children step into a paint tray and then walk across mural paper. Children who cannot walk can have the soles of their feet painted and then held down on paper.

**Variation.** Here's a fun alternative: Tape paper to a wall. Then have the children lie on their backs on the floor or be held near the paper and stamp or "walk" a print. Lots of giggles will accompany this trick.

### Modeling

Toddlers love to take things apart and change them around, to poke and squeeze things. Modeling clay lends itself well to such activities because of the way it feels and changes shape. There is no limit to what children can do with modeling clay.

You can also use bread dough, letting the children participate as much as possible by choosing colors and odors to add to the dough and squishing the dough around. (This activity may be especially helpful for children with cerebral palsy; encourage poking with each finger and thumb as a means of developing individual finger extension.) Let the children knead the clay or dough, exploring it by poking holes in it, rolling it into balls, or pricking it with kitchen utensils.

## EXPLORATIONS

**Pancakes.** Demonstrate how to pound clay or dough until it is flat like a big pancake. Use plastic cookie cutters to cut out shapes; add buttons, macaroni, and pipe cleaners as decorations.

**Snakes.** Show the children how to roll the clay or dough into long snakes. If help is needed, hold the child's hand and roll together. You can then make a bracelet by joining the ends of the snake together.

**Variation.** An alternative is to give the children plastic or butter knives to cut the snakes into little pieces.

### Water Play

Children love to play with water; it's fascinating and soothing, which is why we often use water play when youngsters are tired or fussy. Water play also encourages children's curiosity to explore the physical world, and can be both creative and educational.

## EXPLORATIONS

**Pouring.** Let the youngsters have lots of plastic vessels to practice pouring from one container to another. Learning to pour liquids involves a number of complex motions, and mastering them is a step toward independence. Adding soapsuds to the water means plastic dishes and toys can be washed, which is fascinating play for children.

**Water, water everywhere.** Take advantage of nearby water spots: take children to parks with small wading pools and fountains, to lakes and winding creeks, to ponds, or to the seashore. Give them opportunities to interact with water by wading, sailing little boats, throwing pebbles, splashing, and filling or pouring.

*Children love to interact with water. These activities can be creative and educational.*

*Intent on scooping up water.*

| UNIT 5 | The Toddler with Physical Difficulties |

Mobility is important to sensory development. Children who must be wheeled or carried are at a disadvantage unless care is taken to place them in different surroundings throughout the day, thereby stimulating their curiosity.

Put children near a window to observe what may be happening outside: snowflakes falling, trees blowing in the wind, rain hitting the windowpane, or wind chimes tinkling. A colorful windsock hung outside to catch the breeze can be a cheerful stimulant that promotes visual awareness.

The kitchen, laundry room, bedroom, and den all provide interesting opportunities for discovery through sound, sight, and touch. Give the children pots, pans, and spoons to make sounds with; potatoes, onions, and oranges to roll; small towels to help fold. Fill a few dresser and kitchen drawers near the floor with small interesting objects. Allow children to discover them, take them out, and hide other treasures in these drawers.

Let children watch other people doing things: working in the garage, raking leaves, making dinner, vacuuming, or dusting. It is very important to involve children in these daily activities by telling them what things are called and how they are used. Stimulate children who are visually impaired with descriptive language and with sounds and textures. With toddlers who are hearing impaired, incorporate consistent gestures and visual cues to arouse interest and curiosity.

## Adapting Toys

Toys must be adapted to let toddlers with little mobility and coordination explore and gain experience with the world. A simple change to a difficult-to-handle (and therefore frustrating) toy can make the difference between success and failure.

Cause and effect can be explored when the child touches the disk which, in turn, makes the music play.

**Grasping knobs.** Tiny knobs on simple wooden puzzles are easily replaced with larger knobs from the hardware store. Similarly, putting a larger turning knob on a jack-in-the-box lets children with physical difficulties activate the toy.

**Choosing easily manipulated toys.** It is especially helpful if manipulative toys have a built-in tolerance for error—for example, puzzles that fit together although they don't match perfectly, or blocks with strips of hook-and-loop fastener (such as Velcro®) attached for easier building.

**Controlling battery-operated toys.** Some children are unable to play with any commercial toys despite such adaptations. Fortunately, in recent years the toy industry has produced a wide array of battery-operated toys. Children previously unable to control anything in their environment can now control a toy by touching or batting a large toggle switch with any part of their hand. By selecting toys with a wide range of actions, you enable the children to experience play, make choices, and use imagination.

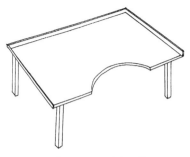

*A cutout table offers good forearm support from elbow to wrist.*

## Adapting Play and Work Areas

Adaptations may also be necessary for play or work both inside and outside. The degree and number of adaptations depend on the child's specific physical limitations. An occupational or physical therapist is an excellent resource for identifying appropriate and possible adaptations for an individual youngster.

**Cutout tables.** Possible adaptations include tables with semicircular sections cut out, letting children sit closer to the work space. The tabletop on either side supports the children's arms and keeps objects from being easily knocked off the table. Tables used for sand and water activities may be raised for children in standing braces or wheelchairs, or lowered for children seated on the floor.

**Adaptations for art and music.** Use large crayons, marking pens, and chalks for easier gripping. For many children, paintbrushes should be built up by winding foam around the handle.

You can adapt musical instruments if children have difficulties holding them. A mitten with a drumstick glued to it or attached with strips of hook-and-loop fasteners (such as Velcro®) can make the difference that lets a child beat a drum. Holding the drum at just the right angle ensures the child's success. Finger cymbals are usually grasped by small knobs, but are easier to hold with elastic bands that go around the hand. (See Appendix A for more information on adapting arts tools and instruments.)

## EXPLORATIONS

**Encouraging exploration.** Mounting toys on a wall at standing height promotes grasping, hand coordination, and balance. Children in standing braces need this kind of incentive to explore.

**Painting.** Children in standing braces can paint at a large upright easel or on large sheets of paper taped to a wall.

**Tossing, catching, and rolling.** These skills need to be practiced by children with physical difficulties. Large beach balls (slightly deflated), balloons, foam balls, table-tennis balls, and balls made of wool or tinfoil are good. Each has different and intriguing properties—one wobbles, another rolls, while a table-tennis ball makes a staccato sound on a tile floor. Children can also try tossing beanbags into large containers or into a ring on the floor.

*Your turn next!*

**Hand dancing.** Hand dancing promotes gross motor movement for children in wheelchairs; adding music stimulates interest. If you let the children lie on the floor, they can experience rolling over, swaying from side to side, crawling, kicking, and bicycling in the air.

## Improving Fine Motor Skills and Eye-Hand Coordination

**Paper corner.** Make a "paper corner" in the room, supplied with a variety of papers. Tissue, cellophane, newspapers, magazines, discarded envelopes, junk mail, and gift wrap are all potential toys for toddlers.

Paper is an inexpensive medium for expression, perfect for a toddler's creativity and energy. It can be crushed, torn, rattled, sorted (as to same and different, for example), folded and unfolded, and put into containers of all sizes (open or closed). It can also be scribbled on or pasted into collages.

**All kinds of containers.** Containers with indentations or compartments let children practice grasp-and-release movements as their curiosity dictates. Giving a choice of three different containers makes things even more interesting. Ice-cube trays, muffin tins, egg cartons, and plastic makeup trays are all intriguing. Large buttons, beads, pegs, poker chips, and pasta are excellent items for picking up, transferring, and manipulating. (**Note:** Closely supervise children who might swallow these items.)

**Modeling clay and dough.** Soft modeling clay or bread dough is a good manipulative medium, especially for children whose muscles are not strong. Encourage play with cookie cutters or small rolling pins.

**Stringing along.** Have the children try stringing large objects—for example, big beads, buttons, macaroni, or even napkin rings—onto a large shoelace. This is good for eye-hand coordination. Make sure the objects are too big to be swallowed.

**Open up!** Give the children plastic jars with lids that are partially unscrewed. Inside each jar put a "prize"—perhaps a miniature toy, food item, pebble, or bell—as an incentive to try to unscrew the lid. The children may need help replacing the lids; help when required so as not to frustrate. This activity helps fine motor control while encouraging development of the concepts *off* and *on* and *in* and *out*.

**Book time.** Using books made of cloth, firm paper, or cardboard, encourage children to turn the pages as the story progresses and to look at the pictures. Bright, simple illustrations are best for toddlers.

# With Our Ears

**UNIT 1**   ## Developing Auditory Awareness in Babies

Hearing is extremely important in developing communication, and parents are the baby's first teachers, greatly influencing the acquisition of auditory skills. Even before birth, babies respond to the comforting rhythms of their mother's bodies. In all cultures throughout the ages, parents have soothed their babies by rocking them in their arms while singing or crooning softly. (Crooning is a soft half-speaking, half-singing sound that rises and falls with each breath.) These songs are enjoyed by both parent and baby, and eventually give rise to the baby's response of babbling and cooing.

### Talking and Singing

It is essential that you talk softly or sing while caring for newborns. Your words and singing ability are not important here, but rather the tone and feelings you convey. Such communication, even at this early age, encourages a baby to listen and begin to develop auditory skills. Initially the baby may make few responses, but gradually the sounds heard will encourage the baby to move and react in some way.

Your voice and facial expressions in response to the baby's efforts at communication are vital in helping to make the baby a social being. Experts on child development stress the importance of parents enjoying their infant by cuddling, talking, laughing, singing, of parents and infants playing with and looking at each other; all are crucial to the baby's intellectual and social growth.

In the early months, babies may be startled by sudden noises, lights, or movements: call the baby's name as you approach. Most babies will turn their head toward a sound and look up when they hear a familiar voice. Reinforce this auditory awareness by touching or picking them up when they respond to your voice. If there is no acknowledgment, touch the baby's face as you talk and repeat his or her name; reward any response.

When you sing, have the baby focus on your mouth, turning his or her head if necessary. When the baby is focused on you, move your face slowly from right to left and help the baby follow the sound. You can also try moving your face up and down. Bring another sound, such as a tuning fork or rattle, into the baby's line of vision, and help the baby locate the source of the sound.

### Music

Playing music benefits both parent and child. Choose music that has a definite beat but is not too intrusive. Folk songs sung by one or two persons with minimal accompaniment are recommended, but you can use any type of music that seems appropriate. At bedtime, quiet music or a signature lullaby can help settle the baby down.

It is important to remember that babies will lose interest in music played continuously, and the potential here for cultivating listening skills will be lost.

*Soft singing keeps these little ones involved.*

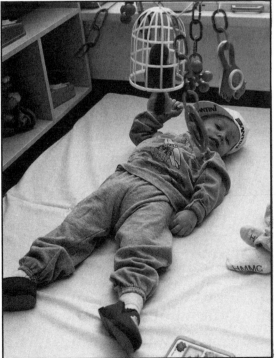

*A young child bats at objects overhead, gradually becoming more precise.*

## Crib Toys

Babies love to play with crib gyms hung overhead. By three months, a baby will reach for any toy dangling at the side of the crib, especially if it makes a noise. If the toy makes a pleasant sound when it is hit or pulled, the baby may be persuaded to activate the object, thus discovering the rudiments of cause and effect.

Similarly, babies who can kick their feet enjoy a "kicking gym." This toy is easy to make. Put rattles and bells on an elastic strip, tying the ends securely to two sturdy chairs that will not topple and are about three feet apart. Make sure the elastic is low enough to let the baby kick at the dangling objects when lying face up on the floor between the chairs. The sounds made by kicking the objects will keep the baby happily occupied and will become more rhythmic as the baby's kicking becomes more proficient. Watch to make sure the baby's feet don't get caught.

### Growing Responses to Sound

As babies become more sociable, they will respond to people by looking at them as they speak. They may hold up their arms and make a noise to indicate that they want to be lifted. They also show a growing interest in words, sounds, and music, listening intently as you produce sounds by hitting bells, playing an instrument or pinging a tuning fork. Babies generally prefer low-pitched sounds; a higher pitch sometimes startles them or causes tensing.

Beginning at six months, babies need sturdy pleasant-sounding toys: a few soft balls with chimes inside, rattles with different tones, metal bells, or wooden spoons. Within a few months, hard cardboard rolls to drum on are appropriate. "Banging" is an important part of babies' play. Much of this play will be difficult at first, but they will gradually begin to experiment. These early attempts to make sounds are also helpful in the ongoing development of coordination.

Songs and chants that you sing will become familiar, and the baby will derive enjoyment from joining in and trying to sing along. Don't drop this music; familiar things contribute to a child's sense of security. The baby will begin to participate more actively in games such as "patty cake," "pop goes the weasel," and "peek-a-boo."

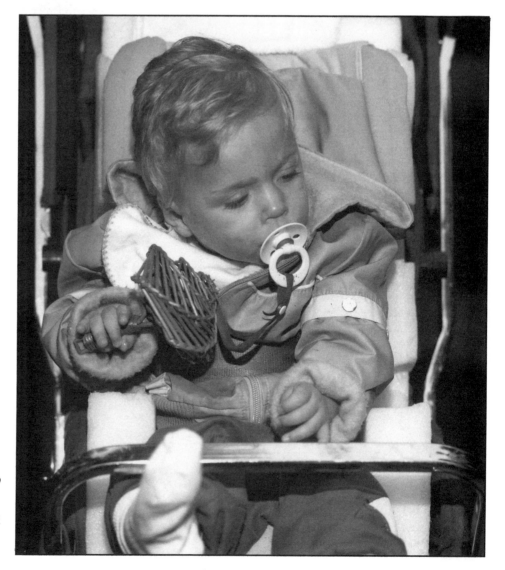

*Reed rattles are easy to hold and shake. Little pebbles in this one make a pleasant sound.*

**UNIT 2**

# The Baby with Hearing Needs

Babies with hearing impairments present difficult challenges to parents. Hearing impairments interfere with both the reception and expression of spoken language. Because language influences almost every aspect of development, a baby with hearing impairments must make tremendous social and learning adjustments.

For example, babies with normal hearing learn very early on that they can attract attention by making noise. Children who are hearing impaired are not as apt to make vocal sounds to attract attention, primarily because they may not be aware such sounds exist. However, the baby can come to recognize the usefulness of sounds for attracting attention as caregivers respond to the baby's nonpurposeful vocalizations. Calling out the baby's name and consistently wearing one brand of cologne or aftershave will help the baby recognize an approaching caregiver by fragrance.

If hearing aids are fitted early on, realize that it may take time for the child to become used to keeping them in. Some babies keep taking them out and playing with them, even putting them in their mouths, just as they explore other toys and body parts.

Always minimize extraneous noises when interacting with the baby. If you can use a quiet room with a rug on the floor, so much the better. During baths, the bathroom often provides a lovely small enclosure with natural amplification.

Early identification of a hearing impairment results in early intervention to enhance development of sensory and communicative skills. Emphasis is often put on vision and touch, because these are important senses for the baby with impaired hearing.

## Talking and Singing

It is crucial to talk to the baby, even if there is little or no response, because it is difficult to know how much residual hearing is present. Talking is important to helping the baby learn to focus attention. Your face is also important: the baby might not understand the content of what you say, but may still learn from your facial expressions. Always establish eye contact when talking so that the baby can see your lips. (Women who wear lipstick can use bright colors to encourage this.) If the baby breaks eye contact, pat the head or hold the baby's hand to try and keep attention on you.

When the baby is alert and quiet, try talking with your lips close to the baby's ear. For some babies, this works almost like a hearing aid and should be tried in both ears. Sing or hum a tune with your lips against the baby's head so the baby feels the vibrations and turns to you.

Sing a simple song while holding the child, occasionally putting the baby's hand over your mouth. This is a signal for you to stop singing. Take the hand off your mouth and continue singing. If the baby stops looking your way, keep singing and watch whether the baby searches for you.

## Emphasizing Sounds

There are many ways to emphasize sounds: put the baby's hand on your mouth or the front of your neck as you begin to speak or sing. Move in a rhythm while swaying or rocking the baby in your arms. When playing games, such as dandling the baby on your lap, sing or chant to help the baby sense the rhythm in your speech.

### Rhythm Work

Play with percussive elements, such as a drum, sticks, wood blocks, or a tambourine. Play a simple pattern repeatedly (perhaps the syllables in the child's name). Hand over hand, beat the pattern of the word or name together, saying it all the while. You can "play" other words, such as hel-lo, good-bye, Ma-ma, Da-da.

Our lives are based on rhythmical sequences—day and night, sound and silence, sleeping and waking—but children with hearing impairments have difficulties sensing auditory rhythms. These exercises may help them gain a feeling of the natural rhythms in the sounds around them.

### Visual Aspects

From first knowledge of a child's hearing impairment, it is important to plan activities that require visual responses. Hang gaily colored scarves, ribbons, and toys where the baby can grab them, or put them on a fan so they will blow in the breeze. You can also hang ribbon streamers in front of a window to ripple in the wind, or add bunches of streamers to the kicking gym (see "Crib Toys" on page 21) to encourage the baby to make the streamers flutter by kicking.

It is helpful for the baby to see and feel objects as adults use sounds and words to describe them. While holding a ball in your hand, say "ball, ball" several times, then put the ball in a basket. Let the baby hold the ball, then establish eye contact while repeating "ball, ball." Together, put the ball in the basket.

In a similar exercise, hold a toy animal and repeatedly make the sound associated with the animal. Hold a toy dog and say "woof, woof," a duck and "quack," a cow and "moo," a cat and "meow." To add visual reinforcement, use a picture with each toy as you speak. You can also put pictures of these objects around the house. Little by little the baby will begin to connect the object with the word your lips are forming. If functional hearing is present, the auditory association will be reinforced.

By approximately two years of age, it becomes important to direct the child's attention to where sounds originate. When a phone rings, point to it. Do the same for a doorbell, a flushing toilet, or music from a radio or stereo. If the baby wears a body hearing aid, hold the amplifying unit to a window during a hard rain, or near a dishwasher on the wash cycle.

Make popcorn with the child so that the child can see and hear the popping corn. Let the child see and listen to a pop-up toaster, frying bacon, an alarm clock, or jingling keys. Sit with the child outside during a thunderstorm or when firecrackers are exploding in the sky. Visit a farm or a zoo to hear the sounds of live animals.

**UNIT 3**

## Developing Auditory Awareness in Toddlers

Music, so important from the very beginning of a child's life, continues to play a key role for toddlers. One very good time to play music is when toddlers need time out to rest and relax from their characteristically tremendous output of energy. Listening to music together can be a peaceful time in the day for parents and caregivers as well as for children. Before you put the music on, show the record jacket or tape or compact disc cover to the children and tell them what the music is about. If the children like the music, they may ask for it on other occasions.

## Musical Routines

Having a music time each day is good; making music part of the day's routines is even better. Children thrive on routines for eating, sleeping, getting dressed, and washing, and music can help get things done faster and with less fuss. Music is also very convenient: you can clap, sing, and dance anytime, anywhere.

Make up lyrics to songs the child already knows to help get routines underway. A song with lyrics relevant to the activity helps make the children more willing to do as you ask. It also helps the children learn to listen and concentrate on

*Playing music together can be an enjoyable part of each day.*

what you are singing and to follow directions. Make sure there are fewer than 10 key words in the song. All of this adds to cognitive development. Here's an example using "Here We Go Round the Mulberry Bush":

> This is the way we comb our hair . . . (or)
> This is the way we brush our teeth . . . (or)
> This is the way we wash our hands . . .

> Using "Put Your Finger in the Air":
> Come and sit on the chair, on the chair,
> Come and sit on the chair, on the chair,
> Come and sit on the chair, and I will brush your hair,
> Come and sit on the chair, on the chair.

You can also use music to lessen a sticky situation. If the children are doing something you don't want them to do, try improvising a song to distract them and encourage cooperation. You probably can imagine situations where you might make up these songs:

> I have to put your splints on,
> Splints on, splints on.
> I have to put your splints on,
> So you can go and play.

> Let us count up to three,
> Then we will buckle them,
> You will see.
> Annie's going out today.
> She's going out to play.
> Now . . . 1-2-3-SKIDOO!

## Rhythm

You can also use rhythm to ease a potentially sticky situation. Imagine a child reluctant to come in for lunch:

> Hey, Juan, let's play train all the way to the kitchen. I'll be the engine, and you be the caboose. Remember, a caboose is the end of the train. You have to hold on to me. Ready? Chugga-chugga chug, chugga-chugga chug, our little train goes chugga-chugga chug.

Make this chanting as rhythmical as possible while moving toward and, eventually, through the door. Repeat the chanting until the child has washed and is ready for lunch. If other children are present, include them in this transition play.

Early songs for children should involve simple fingerplays that solidify understanding. Choose songs or rhymes such as "Row, Row, Row Your Boat," "Eensy-Weensy Spider," "Twinkle, Twinkle, Little Star," "Ring Around the Rosy," and "Pop Goes the Weasel." At first you will have to do much of the work, singing and helping the children do most of the motions. After many repetitions, however, when the children are ready, they will do more and more without help.

The most appealing songs for young children depict their daily lives and sounds. Toddlers love songs about taking baths or eating peanut butter sandwiches, or lyrics like "I roll the ball to Mommy, she rolls the ball to me." Very short songs or chants that you make up using children's known vocabulary stimulate children to express their explorations of the world around them.

Songs with special sounds are also enjoyable. "Old MacDonald Had a Farm" encourages children to imitate animal sounds. "Bingo" encourages children to sing the letters in the word. "When You're Happy and You Know It" can use a combination of actions and sounds: the children can shout "hooray," or put in words or sounds such as "say hello," "wave goodbye," or "kiss goodnight."

## Family Time

Finding activities the whole family enjoys can sometimes be difficult. Singing and dancing together can appeal to people of all ages, including toddlers. To get toddlers involved, include songs they can make motions for or sing along with.

Singing together can help pass the time during trips. Try singing or chanting about what is passing by as everyone looks out the windows:

I see some big cows, big cows, big cows, I see some big cows over there.

The big red truck is passing us, passing us, passing us, the big red truck is passing us on its way.

What's going to be over the hill, over the hill, over the hill? What's going to be over the hill? Let's wait and see.

Dancing lends itself beautifully to family participation as well as to one-on-one time with a toddler. Put some rhythmical music on and dance away with the child in your arms, holding hands with the child, or pushing the child's wheelchair. Dancing encourages a sense of rhythm, offers an opportunity for close body contact, and is fun!

## Homemade Instruments

Playing musical instruments presents new challenges to the toddler and helps develop muscle control and manual dexterity. For children this age, you can buy a few basic instruments, such as a drum, triangle, xylophone, or chimes. If you want the characteristic sounds of these instruments, keep in mind that many inexpensive toys look realistic but sound like tin cans.

*Let's dance.*

You can make instruments whose sounds are neither too harsh or high pitched. Make sure they are put together securely and don't have sharp edges. Part of making them can be decorating the outside with colorful nontoxic markers.

Here are some tips for making instruments that are safe and fun.

**Shakers.** Shakers or rattles are probably the easiest, and most satisfying, homemade instruments. Plastic eggs or small containers with lids are suitable. Fill the containers with various materials to create different sounds. Rice, dried lentils, small nuts, sand, and pebbles are all possibilities. Don't put in too much; leaving room makes the sound more distinct. Tape or glue the container together to make sure it stays closed.

**Drums.** Any pot will do. You can also use round containers from oatmeal or potato chips; for best results, cover both ends with heavy plastic or rubber from balloons and tape this covering down securely. For beaters, use a short wooden spoon or a dowel with a one-inch rubber ball attached to one end.

**Bells.** Attach bells to a dowel, a leather strap, or a piece of elastic that can be tied around ankles or wrists. For children who cannot grasp, try attaching the bells to a mitten.

Children like the sound of bells, and can play them to accompany a record, tape, or a song you sing. Bells can also be used to help children learn new concepts, such as listening to rhythms, imitating rhythms, and taking turns.

### EXPLORATIONS

**Go and stop.** This game involves skills that are excellent for a child to develop, but it can take time to comprehend because making sounds is so enjoyable. At first, sit and have the children listen to recorded music as you periodically turn the sound on and off. Then suggest that you and the children clap until the sound "disappears" again. Tell the toddlers this means "stop."

Suggest that the children tell you when to "go." When they do, turn the music on and all of you clap again. If the children do not understand that they are to stop when the music does, hold their hands when the music stops. Once the children understand the concept, you can try this game with instruments.

**Fast and slow.** This is much like "go and stop." Go fast and slow with clapping, with instruments, and eventually with walking around the room to a fast and slow beat on a percussive instrument.

**Soft and loud.** Try this after the children learn "go and stop" and "fast and slow." It involves a similar concept, calling for sound discrimination and concentration.

Let the children mimic a musical sound with clapping or on an instrument. Say, "Can you make a soft, tiny sound? That's it. That's lovely and soft. Now make a loud, loud sound." Practice until they understand what "loud" and "soft" mean.

Extend the concepts of loud and soft to the voice. "Can you say 'patty-cake' very softly? Let's do it together. Now let's talk to one another very softly." (Children love this "whisper time.") Once the children can speak softly, suggest that they speak loudly for a minute or two.

**Listening walk.** Go for a walk and listen to all the sounds along the way. Ask the children about what they hear:

> Elizabeth, can you hear the noise of that big jackhammer? Do you think it is a loud noise or a soft noise?

> Look at the fence, Billy, there's a bird. Let's listen to it chirp. Do you think the bird's chirp is soft or loud?

> As you make children aware of sounds in the environment, you are opening up their ears to the surrounding world.

---

**UNIT 4**  # The Toddler with Hearing Needs

You can do a number of things to enhance communication in children with hearing impairments. Make sure the children are looking at you and that the light is shining on your face, not in their eyes. Keep your face level with the children's by stooping to their eye level or by holding them on your lap. Some children may have a good bit of hearing, but its usefulness will be considerably diminished if you speak from a standing position. At first it may be difficult for the children to comprehend why they should look at you when you speak, but eventually it will become clear that you have something to say and that the expressions on your face are important in understanding the message. The children may initially have little understanding of what you are saying, but they will learn to associate words they hear with actions they see. When you speak to a child who is hearing impaired, avoid using words that have figurative meanings. Such words tend to add confusion for the child who is trying to read lips.

## Bringing the Music Back

Unfortunately, music and dancing frequently are omitted from the lives of children with hearing impairments. With time and patience, however, these children can enjoy and benefit from these activities.

We know that almost all children with compromised hearing have some residual hearing. They may hear some environmental noises or instrumental sounds better than others. This means you should add a visual component to musical activities such as "go and stop" or "fast and slow" (described on page 28). Here are some suggestions for adding a visual component to musical games:

- Add another aide to a game like "go and stop." If the children don't stop on your cue, the aide can hold their hands. With practice, the children will stop their movements when you do.

- Use motions to show when the music stops. (An aide can also be helpful here.) Motions that can be stopped and started include walking, shaking hands, and lying on one's back bicycling or kicking feet in the air.

- Try motions at different speeds once the children begin to listen and follow the tempo of the music. (For example, kicking feet in the air slowly, then quickly.)

- Choose activities that help develop a sense of balance, such as starting, stopping, and changing directions. Children with damage to the vestibular system in the inner ear may have difficulty maintaining their balance.

- Singing songs with others may be more difficult, but the children may be able to join in if there are motions or visual cues, or if finger plays can be imitated.

- Remove the front panel of an upright piano and let the children watch the hammers strike the strings. The children can also feel the piano's vibrations by putting an ear, hand, or foot on it or by sitting on it.

## Rhythm Games

Rhythm games become fun and useful as children near the age of three. A drum is useful; you can also use voices. The following exercises call for the children to both imitate and initiate rhythms. When the children imitate you, they are also learning to wait for a turn. Once they understand imitating a rhythm, they are ready to initiate a rhythm.

- Drum several beats, then stop. Ask the child to do likewise. Try to have a drum "conversation."

- Beat out the syllables in a child's name again and again ("Laur-el, Laur-el"). Then have the child do it. Beat out the names of people in the child's family, pets, or things the child likes to eat.

- Beat your drum twice and say "two." Repeat this several times, saying "two" each time. Have the child try two beats; when this is understood, try three beats, then four.

Once the children can follow a short rhythmical phrase, you can make this exercise more creative. The more beats, syllables, or words you use, the easier it is for the children to catch on to what you intend. Avoid using "one" until the concept of imitating rhythms is well understood.

**THEME THREE**

# With Our Eyes

**UNIT 1**

## Developing Visual Awareness in Babies

Babies may spend much of their time with their eyes closed, but visual stimulation is nonetheless very important in their development. Research shows that human faces and toys with faces are especially stimulating during early infancy. Thus a picture of a face attached to the side of the crib should be one of the first things an infant sees. You can draw a face on a paper plate, using strong colors and a simple design.

Another early visual stimulus for infants is a brightly colored toy attached to the side of the cradle or bed, seven to nine inches from the infant's face. At this age, infants turn their heads to one side when lying on their backs (usually the right), so it is important to change their position to vary their visual experiences. Change the positions of visual stimuli so that the infant will look in other directions. Move the crib; this lets the infant see light from varying directions. At the same time, change the infant's position in the crib to let the infant experience light coming from different angles.

Keep in mind that infants can distinguish light from dark and are sensitive to bright lights, closing their eyes frequently in bright light and opening them only when the lights are dimmed. Keep a dim light on when the baby is awake so that the baby will have something to see.

Help the baby learn to associate distances and directions both in sight and in hearing by talking to the baby from different places in the room, giving the baby a familiar moving target to watch and follow.

### Getting in Focus

Developing the ability to focus brings the need for new exercises. As infants approach three months, they can look straight up, watch a moving object presented within their line of vision, smile at familiar shapes nearby, and want to touch what they see. They lack the coordination to reach for and grasp a toy, but their movements gain precision as they become more purposeful.

Around this age, the baby will enjoy looking at objects hanging overhead (eight to twelve inches away). Mobiles with various shapes, preferably in black and white or other strong colors, will be the most effective.

Infants at this stage no longer always clench their hands and instead concentrate on them intently. To help infants watch their hands, try selecting sheets that are significantly darker or lighter than the infant's skin color to make the hands more distinguishable. The infant's fingers begin to meet over the tummy (the midline) at this stage, and some objects can be held briefly.

### Widening Discoveries

At about six months, foot watching takes on meaning. Babies begin to use their leg muscles more and more, kicking and holding their legs up so they can see and play with their feet. At this time, babies also begin to investigate small objects for their colors, shapes, textures, whether they are hard or soft, and whether they change when shaken or squeezed.

Throughout this stage, make sure the baby spends part of each day in environments that allow the best use of sight. Encourage visual discrimination by putting the baby on a patterned quilt or blanket on the floor, or in a playpen or crib where the baby can reach objects with interesting shapes or textures. Put the baby in places where she or he can observe the shadows of leaves flickering on the wall on a sunny day, the rain coming down a windowpane, the wind moving branches, the pattern of sunbeams on the floor. Wheeling the baby to a new environment (perhaps a grocery store or playground) can provide other animating moments.

You can enhance all of your efforts to develop visual awareness by giving the child names for things. A leaf, for example: "Look at the leaf. Isn't it pretty? It's green and smooth. Touch it. Smell it." Hold the leaf up for the baby's examination while you talk. Rub the leaf against the baby's hands and face. All of this encourages increased exploration. From eight months onwards, babies will actively explore their world and all its fascinating facets.

### Pretty Rooms (and Ceilings)

Room decorations can provide the visual variety critical to further stimulating babies and alerting them to discovering the world. Use your ingenuity to make the baby's room visually enriching. Don't forget the ceiling: as the baby grows, he or she will start to look up at it for hours, but many people forget that when they decorate. Bright overhead pictures of flowers, animals, birds, or simple designs will provide many moments of visual fascination. You can also hang gaily colored kites, balloons, mobiles, or other objects that turn with the slightest movement of air.

Phosphorescent stickers of stars, moons, and planets intrigue infants as well as older children. You can buy these stickers in children's science stores. Sizes range from three-quarters of an inch to two inches. Put them on the ceiling or upper walls: they are invisible in daylight, but glow for some time after the lights are turned off. The soft glow will not impede a child's sleep but can be comforting if the child lies awake for awhile.

---

**UNIT 2**

## The Baby with Visual Needs

Vision is very important in the establishment of human bonds. For infants with visual impairments, body play must take the place of eye play; this is particularly true in communicating concerns and love, which in turn promotes self-concept. Parents must give more than the usual amount of cuddling, holding, and touching to keep these babies from withdrawing from the outside world. Intensive interaction with these infants must start when they are very young.

This intensive interaction must emphasize the tactile, auditory, and olfactory experiences through which infants who are visually impaired learn. These experiences are critical to teaching these infants to focus on environmental clues and discover that they are part of the world, not a world within themselves.

You can emphasize these experiences every day:

- Hold and talk to babies during feeding or other routines.

- Guide their hands to different textures, thus stimulating tactile curiosity.

- Call the babies by name, letting them know they are part of the action.

## Talking

It's important to talk to the baby frequently, especially during the day's many routines. When you pick the baby up, say, "Up, up, up! Baby goes up!" If you are walking in the rain, let the baby's face feel the rain and say "Wet." If you have an ice cube, let the baby feel it and say, "This is cold, cold." Similarly, water in the bath goes "Splash," and a wooden spoon on a pot goes "Bang." Alter the inflection of your voice so the baby will learn what various intonations indicate.

You can expand on this constant communication to help the baby establish head control, which is important in tracking sounds and identifying objects that may be within reach. Babies will not keep their heads up or reach for an object unless they know its location, and infants with visual impairments know the location only if they can touch, smell, or hear whatever it is that may interest them.

Use play to encourage reaching and making contact. For example, when you give the baby an orange to play with, hold the orange up to the baby's nose first. Put the baby's hands on the fruit, saying, "This is an orange, it has a nice smell, it is round, you can eat it." To give a sense of what "round" means, say similar things when you show balls of wool, rubber balls, and other round objects to the baby.

## Special Measures

Because infants who are visually impaired receive few visual cues, special efforts must be made to prepare them for environmental changes. These babies learn object permanence through hands-on experience. To make their environment predictable, you must guard against things seeming to appear from and disappear into nowhere.

Start talking before you enter a room the baby is in; when you leave, talk as you go out. Wear perfume or cologne so that the baby can recognize you by your fragrance as well as by sound or touch. Shaving lotion will also be distinctive. Touch the baby's hand gently before you present an object. You can also develop patterns for regular activities, thus conditioning the infant to anticipate the activity and be less likely to be startled.

Learn to read the baby's total body for responsiveness, not just the eyes. These babies may not have yet established attachments to significant others, or even have come to understand that there are "others."

If the baby becomes fretful, hold him or her near tinkling wind chimes. Take the baby's hand and touch about your face, naming all the parts of your face. Gently massage the baby's body, describing the parts of the body while you do this. Let the baby feel warm strokes while becoming aware of his or her own body image.

### Smells

Smell is a potentially rich experience. Try filling small bottles with a variety of smells, from aromatic to pungent. Open each in front of the baby's nose, saying, "Oh, I like this, it smells sweet" or whatever. You can use lemon rind, vanilla, mint, mouthwash, perfume, cloves, onion, and countless other herbs and products.

### Playing Together

Playing and singing together become even more important as the baby spends more time awake. You can tie small bells to the baby's wrist and hang some noisemakers (such as chimes or bells) over the crib to encourage the baby to repeat small, random movements. Lower this crib gym when the baby is awake; to ensure safety, raise it during sleep.

You can spur the ability to hold things with both hands by playing "patty-cake" and other improvised games that bring the hands together repeatedly at midline. Games for the older baby can include rolling large multicolored beach balls or balls with bells inside back and forth.

Playing in the bath is also fun for older babies. The sound and feel of water is delightful and sensual, contributing to the babies' tactile experiences.

Here are some other ways to stimulate babies who are visually impaired:

- Make a tactile book, with a different texture on each page. Cotton, silk, wool, and burlap are just a few of the textures you might use. Be sure the materials are safe to be put into a baby's mouth.

- Let the baby play with hard wooden spoons, sponge balls, and little rag dolls, all of which are fun to hold and touch.

- Provide different sensations by blowing on the back of the baby's neck or tummy or tickling the baby's toes or soles of the feet.

- Play with the baby's fingers, wiggling each one while you encourage the baby to play with your hands.

---

**UNIT 3**    # Developing Visual Awareness in Toddlers

Throughout the day, toddlers observe and explore their environment. Make the most of that curiosity by involving the children in regular activities, telling them the names of things around them and how those things are used.

### Shapes

Verbal description is important to learning about shapes and sizes; children learn by listening to others as well as by seeing that things are big or little, square or round, short or tall.

- Make a brightly colored felt board and cut out circles, squares, and other basic shapes in a variety of textures and colors. Encourage the children to match shapes and colors during unsupervised play.

- Show the children a circle. Join them in a search to find other circles. As you go from room to room or outside, point out circle shapes. Be sure to include foods, such as round crackers, orange or tomato slices, and round slices of cheese. Coins, jar lids, clocks, and plates can also help reinforce the concept. Squares and triangles can be explored in the same way after the toddlers learn the concept of a circle.

- Take a plastic container with a cover. Make a round hole in the cover to drop in objects such as plastic poker chips, small balls, or round beads. Cut a hole in the bottom that is big enough for a child's hand; this lets the children retrieve the objects after they "disappear" through the hole in the top. Holes can be cut in other containers for dropping in cubes, triangles, or other shapes.

- Place plastic toy circles in the bathtub or wading pool and let toddlers collect the circles in a pail.

- Make round cookies and have the children help decorate them. If the children cannot handle a cookie cutter independently, let them help you cut out the cookies. They can also practice using cookie cutters when they play with modeling clay.

- Cut paper out in round shapes of various sizes, textures, and colors. Glue the shapes on a larger round background to make a circle collage. Multi-colored stickers in the shape of circles add to the fun.

- Put a piece of paper on an easel. Cut a large circle out of the middle of a big piece of corrugated cardboard, and tape the cardboard over the paper. Let the children cover the paper with paint; they will see the round shape as they paint. Taking the cardboard off, leaving a large unpainted circle, will fix the circle shape even more clearly in the children's minds.

- Take a large supply of round buttons in various sizes and colors and let the children sort the buttons in egg cartons. (Make sure you closely supervise children who tend to put things in their mouths.)

## Same and Different

Match-up games require cognitive skills. To play, toddlers must be able to compare objects and understand "same" and "different," at least nonverbally. To cultivate this understanding, point out and talk about things that are similar.

- Point out household objects that are the same and put them together (for example, oranges in a bag, crayons in a box, books on the bookshelf, flowers in a vase, or towels on a shelf). Outdoors, you can point to cars, cookies in a bakery window, or leaves on a tree. In a supermarket, point to displays of oranges, apples, heads of lettuce, and potatoes.

- Show the children some forks and spoons. Ask the children to put all the spoons in one pile and all the forks in another. Do the same with other objects to differentiate shapes and sizes.

- Let toddlers help you sort laundry. Make a game out of matching socks or sorting shirts from pants.

- Give toddlers beads or blocks that are two different colors. Have the children put one color in a box or pail, then the other color. As the toddlers progress, use more colors.

- Put red objects around the room. Give the children red bags to fill with all the red articles they can find. After the children learn to recognize red, play the same game with another primary color.

- Collect three pictures of familiar objects. Make sure that two of the pictures are the same. Show the pictures to the children and have them point either to the one that is different or to the two that are the same. This exercise can become the basis for a simple game of lotto.

- Lotto is a picture-matching game. It challenges a number of visual skills, such as identification and matching, as well as the cognitive skills of memory and categorization. Use just a few squares at first, then more as the children progress.

A lotto board is easy to make. Divide a piece of card stock into four squares. In each square, draw or paste a picture of an object the children recognize (such as a ball, banana, pail, or cat) in random order. Paste or draw a duplicate of each picture on separate index cards. Have the child match one picture at a time to the pictures on the lotto board by placing each picture card over its mate on the board.

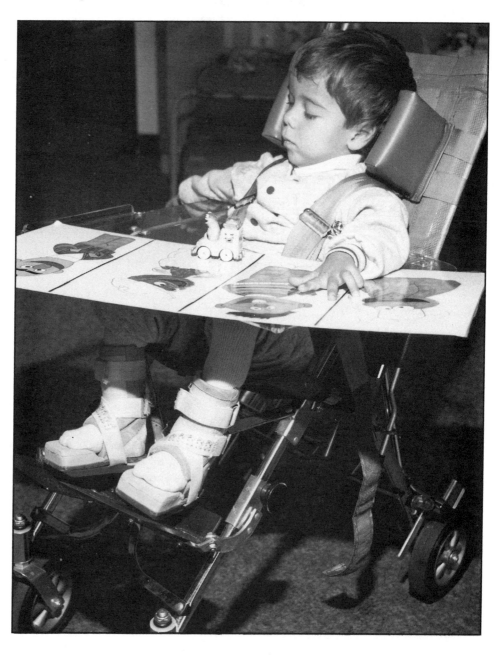

*Matching activities help a child's visual awareness.*

*Alike and different are part of the matching lotto game.*

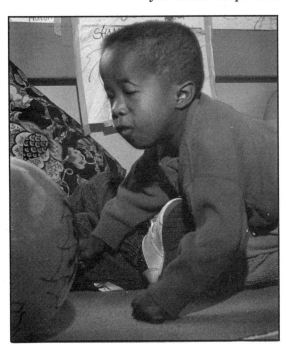

*A toddler with a visual impairment needs to explore his surroundings by touch and hearing.*

| UNIT 4 |

# The Toddler with Visual Needs

Toddlers who are visually impaired enjoy and benefit from many of the activities described in Unit 3 ("Developing Visual Awareness in Toddlers"). However, you must adapt those activities to stimulate touch, hearing, smell, or taste. These stimuli encourage children with visual impairments to investigate and discover their environment as fully as possible.

Here are some easy adaptations:

- In working with shapes, have the children touch a round cardboard form, as you explain that it is a circle. Give the children round objects to explore, such as buttons, jar tops, saucers, or rubber rings from preserves jars. Run the children's hands around the edge of a drinking cup, or have them feel the wheels on a toy or the roundness of an apple slice.

- Helping toddlers find similarities by touch calls for patience and ingenuity. For same-different games, always start out with large toys that are easy to hold (such as big spools, beads, pegs). Progress to smaller shapes that are similar (making sure, of course, that they can't be swallowed). Try similar games with objects of different shapes and textures. Eventually the children will begin to be able to sort objects by shape or texture. Then give the children two cardboard circles and a square. Ask them to identify the one that is not the same.

- Finger-painting is often enjoyed by these children. They may find it even more pleasurable if you give the paint texture by adding rice, sugar, or lentils. You can also use puddings as "paint" to add the dimension of taste to the fun.

- Children who cannot see color may get less out of painting. A pleasurable alternative could be to "paint" the floor or a door with water and a light two-inch brush.

- Play with bread dough or soft clay is especially helpful. Toddlers enjoy "squooshing" the clay or dough or making balls with it. They may need help understanding how to flatten or roll the material out (to make "snakes," for example), but the possibilities become fascinating once they catch on.

- Toys should stimulate hearing and touch as well as arousing curiosity (an effect many toys lack). It is important to choose sturdy toys because children with low vision manipulate toys in ways that may be more destructive than a sighted child's. Also, look for toys that meet one or more of these criteria:

  1. They have parts that fit inside other parts. (A variety of stacking toys are available.)
  2. They make noise.
  3. They open and close.
  4. They have different textures, sizes, and shapes.
  5. They have a smell that will enhance interest.
  6. They rock, shake, or rattle.
  7. They can be pushed, pulled, turned, rolled, sat upon, and crawled into.

# THEME FOUR

# With Our Mouths

## UNIT 1   Language Development in Babies

Communication is everywhere—in our work, our homes, and our play. We could not function without it. Most people think of communication as "speaking," but in fact, communication is much more complex. We communicate in many ways besides speech: through our facial expressions, our gestures, our body language, and our cries and laughter.

*Speech,* one mode of communication, refers to the physical production of sounds and combinations of sounds using the mouth and throat. *Language* is the code through which these sounds are combined to communicate meaning. For example, speakers of English recognize the combination of sounds "cat" as a word that stands for a four-legged pet; speakers of Spanish recognize this meaning in the sound combination "gato." People who are nonspeaking or have limited speech can express and understand language in a variety of other ways— through sign language, pointing to pictures, or reading and writing, to name a few.

Language can be broken into two components: receptive language and expressive language. *Receptive language* describes the language a person understands, and *expressive language,* the language a person can produce. In children, receptive language is usually more advanced than expressive language; they can follow directions and understand words that they do not yet use in speaking. Even as adults, we sometimes have the experience of understanding a word we read or hear (receptive language), but not being sure how to pronounce or use the word ourselves (expressive language).

The foundation for acquiring receptive and expressive language begins long before babies produce their first words. Receptive language begins with the information infants take in from what they hear all around them. Babies take in the sounds and language around them as they lie in their cribs. They begin to notice the sounds around them and recognize the meanings of environmental and speech sounds. Expressive communication actually begins with the first cry of the newborn. Babies spend many hours in "vocal play"—babbling, gurgling, and cooing—which is a precursor of expressive language.

Babies acquire early language through social interactions, expressing and experiencing a wide variety of communicative and vocal interchanges with their primary caregivers. Babies who have functional hearing will begin to imitate the sound sequences they hear you produce, without necessarily attaching meaning to them. As adults react with excitement to the sequences that resemble words, like "mama" and "dada," babies begin to attach meaning to those sequences and learn the power of words to influence the people around them.

Research has also shown that adults tend to use a particular style of language with infants and young children, coined "motherese." Some of the features of motherese are exaggerating the inflection—or rise and fall of one's voice—talking slowly, and repeating words or phrases often. These features are believed to direct a baby's attention to the adult's speech and foster language learning.

Here are some other ways you can enhance development of language and communication:

- At first, a baby can get attention only through crying and body movement. Respond by meeting the baby's needs. Babies thus learn that their vocalizations cause a reaction from the caregiver, that they have communicated successfully.

- Listen for the baby's random sounds and imitate them.

- Beginning at about six weeks of age, babies will chuckle or laugh in response to social stimuli. Play with the baby by making funny noises, tickling gently, or laughing out loud. By three to six months, the baby will vocalize and interact in response to sounds.

- Coo, sing, hum, and make finger and tongue noises to draw the baby's attention.

- Babies begin to babble and make other sounds as they start to explore what their voice can do. Pay attention to the baby's noises; smile at them, and repeat them.

- Sing or hum within the baby's hearing so that the baby experiences rhythm in music as well as in speech.

- Always use the baby's name when you speak to him or her. Call the name from different directions or from behind to help the baby learn to localize sounds.

- Shortly before one year of age babies begin to babble sound sequences that sound like words such as "Dada" or "Mama"—when left alone in the crib or at play. Because parents respond so positively to these sounds, babies continue to make them. Single words soon follow, and babies begin to acquire a vocabulary of real words.

## UNIT 2   Language Development in Toddlers

Young children use their first words in a variety of contexts, usually to label objects or interact socially. They use single words to encode what is important to them.

As children expand their vocabularies and their need for productive communication, they begin to use words in combination. First come two-word phrases, such as "My dolly," "Mommy come," or "Me go," then three- and four-word phrases. They also begin to imitate environmental sounds, such as animal, natural, or machine noises.

Here are some ways you can enhance toddlers' development of language and communication:

- During baths, name the child's body parts while you wash them. Ask the child where you should wash next.

- Use "I" (self-talk) to describe what you are doing: "I'm going to make your lunch. First, I'll make you a cheese sandwich."

- Use "you/I" (parallel talk) to describe what the child is doing: "You like to squeeze the modeling clay. Oh, you're smelling it now. I like the cinnamon smell. Do you like that cinnamon smell?"

- Use many adjectives and verbs when you do things with the toddler. Name objects and actions as you play. "Can you fold the brown bag?" "Look at your blue boat floating in the water!" "You like to cut round cookies. Let's bake the round cookies." Try using descriptive and action words when you play with clay, pick and smell a flower, or put on cologne.

- If children use words or grammar incorrectly, don't tell them they're wrong. Instead, paraphrase their intended message, but with the correct usage. Letting children hear you use words correctly is a natural and tactful way to teach.

- Go for a walk and point out environmental sounds. Together, try to imitate them. Try to make wind sounds, rain sounds, or even the roar of thunder.

- When you look at picture books together, talk to and ask the child about the pictures. Point to different objects in the book while you pronounce their names clearly. Ask, "What is this?" Add to the child's response: "Yes, that is a doggie. What sound does a doggie make?"

- Read simple stories the same way each time you read the book. Children desire and need the structure of familiar language and routines so their learning is reinforced and strengthened every time they hear the story exactly as they know it.

- Make a scrapbook with simple pictures that depict words the child knows (for example, a picture of a cat, a ball, a car, and so on). Similarly, make a book especially for the child with photographs of family members, pets, friends, and special places. Have the child name the various people, pets, and places in the book.

- As the child prepares for bed, review what the child did that day and will do tomorrow.

As language develops, activities popular with toddlers can promote continued interaction:

- Put some old clothes—old hats, scarves, vests, and such—beside the child while he or she sits in front of a mirror. See what the child does with the clothes, and talk about what's happening.

*Interaction is essential for emotional development.*

- Give the child an old purse to hold little treasures. Talk with the toddler when he or she shows you what the purse contains.

- Provide a set of small unbreakable plastic toy dishes. Suggest a tea party for the child's stuffed animals.

- The child may put a doll or teddy bear "to sleep" if you provide a blanket and box, small cradle, or basket. A toy baby bottle can suggest the idea of feeding and caring for dolls and stuffed animals.

- Children need to play the roles of parents, teachers, and other adults. Make simple dolls—the simpler, the better—part of the play area. Dolls that talk and walk leave little to the imagination. Give the child as much opportunity as possible to create and fantasize.

# The Toddler with Communication Difficulties

The development of language depends on a critical set of experiences as well as on maturation. These experiences include opportunities to hear and practice language in a meaningful context with a responsive adult. Many disabilities or impairments can delay the development of understanding and use of words. Communication difficulties can stem from hearing or visual deficits; physical, mental or perceptual handicaps; trauma; poor stimulation; or emotional problems. They can also affect children who display no other symptoms or impairments.

Children can communicate in many ways: nonverbally, through body language, nodding, signs, and picture boards, or verbally, through sounds, words, and phrases. Children who are language delayed or disordered may make infrequent attempts to communicate through any of these means. Even though many of their sounds and actions may seem random, try to deduce the child's intent and respond as if the event were communicative.

These tips embody communication goals and will help you enrich the child's learning environment:

- Make sure you are at the same level as the child when communicating with him or her. Your face will provide needed visual cues, and being close to the child gives you a better position from which to follow the child's lead.

- Respond to the child's initiations. Your response shows that you are aware and listening, and that the child has the power to affect you through communication. The child is more likely to learn when you follow her or his interests and concerns.

- Structure play so that you and the child take turns and are equally active. Understanding the concept of taking turns is a prerequisite to conversing.

- Imitate the child's actions, sounds, or words. Imitation confirms that you are interested and encourages the child to imitate you. This is another facet of taking turns.

- Name objects or actions that the child shows interest in but does not know how to label.

- Repeat words for familiar actions and objects frequently to increase vocabulary. Don't give up if the child doesn't use the word right away. Children may show an interest in an action and object many times and show signs that they understand the word before using it.

- Make books to help with naming. Use pictures cut out from magazines, picking simple pictures of objects and activities known to the child. You can include photographs of significant people, pets, and special events. Put the pictures in a large scrapbook. Clear plastic coating will make the scrapbook last longer, especially with a child who drools.

- Repeat favorite songs. Their familiarity gives the child confidence to progress to more advanced language goals, beginning with imitating gestures with the song, and progressing through sounds, words, and phrases.

- Sing to the child. Live singing fosters a more successful language learning experience than recordings do; many recordings are too fast and loud for children, while singing lets you use a slow tempo and thus emphasize words and pauses. Many youngsters also have difficulty in distinguishing foreground from background sounds. Children enjoy the rhythm in recordings, but may tune out if overstimulated.

- Tell traditional stories that use repetitive and predictable language with lots of action words and concrete adjectives. This repetition allows the child to participate with both words and actions. A good example from *The Three Little Pigs* is, "I'll huff and I'll puff and I'll blow your house down." Another example in *The Little Red Hen* is "'I won't,' said the dog, 'I won't,' said the cat."

*Water play is a great way to encourage sound and noise making. It is soothing and enjoyed by most children.*

- Make up stories that use the child's name. This may encourage the child to help tell the story. Keep the stories short and simple so that the child can mime the actions described and say some of words used.

- Games that spring from daily activities are especially suited to language learning. Encourage the toddler to help make the beds, put pens on the desk in a cup, sort laundry, or rake leaves, as you talk about the process. Helping makes the child feel important, try to learn the language of activities and objects, and try to imitate the motor skills involved.

- Encourage verbalization through water play. For example, when you bathe the child, play "hide and seek" with a water toy, splashing it, dunking it, or skimming it over the surface. Let the child hold the toy and do likewise, as you talk about what's happening:

"Where is Ducky? Oh, Ducky is in the water."

"Ducky likes the water. Does Paulo like the water?"

- Organize art activities so that the child has to ask for something, thus promoting language. For example:

  1. Put out only one color of paint, with other colors in sight but out of reach.

  2. Put crayons out of reach so that the child must ask for them.

  3. Tightly close the lid on a jar of paint so the child has to request help opening it.

  4. Provide paste, but no paste brush.

  5. Put out only a small portion of clay to encourage the child to ask for more.

- Use movement to increase body awareness and provide relaxation. Combining movement and sound can also be used as a transition from one activity to another; for example, "Fly like a bird and make bird sounds all the way to the playground."

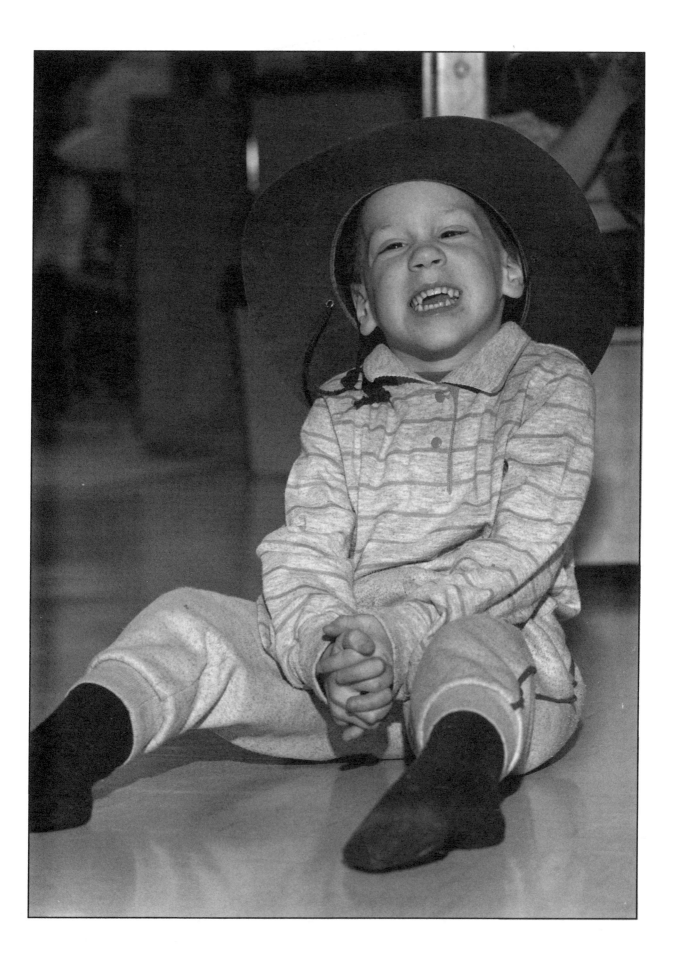

# PART II

# The Formative Years: Three to Six

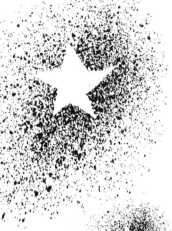

*Sara, almost four, sits quietly with head bowed. The therapist can tell she isn't feeling good today.*

*Therapist: Sara, tell me, how are you feeling today?*

*Sara: I'm sad today.*

*Therapist: Oh, dear me. Are you sad for a special reason?*

*Sara: I don't know. I think I might get happy if you play a song.*

*Therapist: Sounds good to me. What song would you like?*

*Sara: Twinkle Twinkle.*

*(The other children also enjoy this song. Together, the children sing and do motions to the song.)*

*Sara: Now I feel a teeney weeney bit happy. If you play another song, I might be whole happy.*

*Therapist: Why don't you tell us what else you would like to sing?*

*Sara: Skinnamarink.*

*(Again, the children sing and do motions along with the song. Now Sara is smiling.)*

*Sara: I'm whole happy now. I knew the music would stop my sad face.*

## GOALS

- To develop the creative potential of each child by helping the child appreciate and enjoy artistic endeavors

- To stimulate communication skills through involvement in activities appropriate to the child's age and abilities

- To foster self-confidence and motivation

- To encourage discovery, improvisation, and imagination as tools for learning as well as play

- To use artistic modalities as means of expressing and releasing feelings

45

The activities and explorations presented in Part II are designed to develop children's awareness of themselves in the world. Children must learn at an early age that there is a world that takes place *outside* as well as inside themselves. We can capitalize on their natural curiosity, their eagerness to learn, by welcoming and encouraging their efforts to reach out as well as within.

This section concentrates on expressive activities for children three to six years of age who have moderate to severe disabilities. These activities will also help the older delayed child grow and gain self-awareness. We have made a special effort to present activities for children functioning at a lower developmental level than their chronological ages.

Our exercises are based on group and individual activities used in the school of Toronto's Hugh MacMillan Rehabilitation Centre. Many of the children involved had cerebral palsy. Others had a wide variety of orthopedic and medical problems that were the result of serious infections, accidents, or congenital conditions such as spina bifida, arthrogryposis, spinal muscular atrophy, or sickle cell anemia.

Some of the children had some manual dexterity, but most of the children with cerebral palsy had severe motor difficulties. With these children, the term "involvement" (as in "seriously involved" children) describes the degree to which their bodies are affected. Possible associated problems for seriously involved children include perceptual and visual-motor disorders, speech and language deficiencies, oral and dental malformations, difficulties in swallowing and controlling drooling, hearing impairments, and learning disabilities.

## The Creative Experience

Our activities focus on the arts as an integral part of children's total learning experience. You can set the stage by providing art, music, movement, and play areas and activities that help free creative potential.

Self-esteem burgeons when young children feel that their efforts are successful. Creative activities shouldn't involve concepts of "right" and "wrong," but instead should allow the children to become immersed in textures, colors, shapes, smells, sounds, and rhythms. Stress process, sensory awareness, and participation. Don't judge the products: children should receive positive reinforcement for their efforts without the worry of trying to conform to an arbitrary standard.

When you plan activities, take into account the children's attention spans, the nature of their handicap(s), and their range of function. Keep in mind that children with disabilities need periods during the day when they can gain immediate satisfaction (for example, mastering a creative activity within a short time). Much of their learning and treatment is long and drawn out and daily tasks are laborious, which means that the children must work for a long time before they see any real progress. Programs that respond to their physical and emotional needs can offer the immediate satisfaction they need.

Remember to use a persuasive, flexible, nonthreatening, and sensitive approach. Most disabilities restrict or distort experiences in some way, and the children may be slow to comprehend or respond to what is being asked of them. Convince children who are hesitant that they will be successful.

It is also important to be verbally and visually explicit when you outline a process or procedure. Present simple, concrete instructions tailored to a given child's strengths and weaknesses. Follow through to see if the child understands and can apply the instructions.

*How* children learn is as significant as *what* they learn. Tell the children what you expect them to do:

- Enjoy themselves

- Not be afraid to try

- Ask questions

- Use their own ideas

## Setting the Stage

When you first present an activity, give the children every opportunity to discover and develop it for themselves. Tell them *what* they're going to do, but not *how* to do it. Take care not to impose your concepts. Children who are free from preconceived directions gradually acquire a repertoire of responses that become more appropriate with time. (There is an exception to this principle: children who are developmentally delayed often do need a visual model.)

For example, imagine that we put on slow, ponderous music and suggest that everyone walk like elephants. Adults will tend to put their arms together and down to portray an elephant's trunk. Young children, however, don't necessarily share that interpretation. What we would hope to see is the children reacting to the music in a way that shows they understand that elephants move heavily and slowly.

## Taking Cues from Experience

It's important to incorporate children's own experiences into the activities we present. To do that, we must be sensitive to cues the children may offer about what their experiences are. For example, if a child says, "Mommy had a new baby last night," you could do a session on babies and how they have to be nurtured. Throughout the session, you could improvise music (perhaps on a piano). Use very simple tunes with tempos and melodies appropriate to the topic (soft music for rocking the baby to sleep, or happy music for feeding the baby). The children can then move the way the music makes them feel. You could give each child in the group a doll or small toy animal, then ask the children what Mommy and Daddy do with little babies (answers might be feeding, rocking, diapering, bathing).

Try developing this theme:

- Have the children rock babies in their arms.

- Play and sing lullabies for the babies.

- Suggest that the babies are starting to cry. (Children will do this with great relish.)

- Ask, "Why do you think the baby is crying?" (Answers might be that the baby is hungry or wet.)

*I gotta feed the baby.*

- "Let's pretend we're feeding the baby." If small toy bottles are available, that's great. If not, see what happens if the children have to improvise.

- "What do we do after we feed the baby?" (The most likely answer is "burp it.")

You can have the children pretend to burp, change, or bathe their babies, all to improvised music to heighten their involvement. What is important is that you react to the children's excitement, explore their ideas, work with them, and expand on what they bring to you.

Another example: if a child comes into the room excited because she saw a fire engine going down the street, you can have a music session in which the children pretend they are firefighters. Again, you can improvise music. This session could go something like this:

- Ask what firefighters do in a fire station. (The children may not know. Suggest that the firefighters clean the fire engines, eat their lunch, rest, or read a paper. Children will mimic these activities.)

- Ring a "fire bell." The children must get dressed quickly: "Put on your boots, put on your hat. Put on your coat. Now zip it up!"

- Drive to the fire.

- Unroll the hoses. ("The water comes out "whooossshhhhh!")

- Hack the door down with your axes.

- Climb the ladder to save the little kitten.

- Climb down the ladder and roll up the hose.

- Drive back to the fire station.

- Hang up coats and hats and put boots away.

- "Now, what should the firefighters do next?" (Perhaps someone will suggest that the firefighters go to sleep. The children could then lie down on the floor and pretend to sleep—but the fire bell rings again, and the routine is repeated.)

This play lets children experience firefighters' work through mime and music, and thus gain a better understanding of what firefighters do and how busy they are. The session's overall impact will teach even four-year-olds about the subject at hand, as well as about themselves.

You can build many activities around children's love of mimicry and familiar things. Possible subjects include native animal and bird life, and inanimate objects, such as boats, steam shovels, trains, clocks, and typewriters. Children can discover the rhythms of coffee percolating, popcorn popping, water dripping, or telephones ringing, and respond to the sound of leaves trembling in the wind or rain as it hits the windowpane.

## Transitions

It is often necessary to help children make the transition from one activity to another. Transitions are especially difficult for children who are insecure or lack self-confidence. Common problem transitions are those between playing and stopping for lunch, between indoor and outdoor play, or on arrival at the nursery school or play group. If a child is having trouble making a transition, give him or her time to adjust to the new surroundings or activity. Don't rush the child: being asked to do or begin something new can be threatening to a child who resists change.

You can help children accept change by reassuring them, planning schedules with them, and talking with them about the new experience. A particularly successful technique is to tie a proposed activity to the children's personal experiences. For example, a trip to the zoo provides a familiar, enjoyable experience from which to launch other activities. Recycling the pleasant memory also gives you and the children the opportunity to reflect on and analyze the experience. This revisiting develops abilities to define, communicate, evaluate, and judge.

Using familiar experiences as a springboard for new activities provides another important advantage: it gives children a sense of control because it involves memories that are exclusively and uniquely theirs. If they can learn to project that sense of control to a new, related experience, they take a big step in establishing a sense of self.

# With Our Bodies

## GOALS

- To provide opportunities for children to develop body and spatial awareness by becoming aware of their physical selves in the environment
- To promote development of fine and gross motor skills
- To encourage tactile and kinesthetic awareness
- To assist in the development of laterality and directionality
- To provide opportunities for participation and success, thereby enhancing self-concept

UNIT 1

## Body Image and Awareness

"Body awareness" primarily refers to the process through which a child comprehends that he or she is a separate entity from other persons and objects. Early in this process, children learn body parts—to locate them accurately on themselves and identify them on others. Children also must learn what the body parts can do. Once they can do this, the next step is to integrate this knowledge into a cognitive sense of their bodies.

A child who has become aware of the body and its changing abilities and limitations, is better able to interact with other people and objects. Through reaching out, touching, and exploring, the child experiences new sensations and continues to develop a self-image. Bodily movement and sensory stimulation are key components in this process. A focus of intervention should be to make sure a disability does not jeopardize this development.

The following explorations enhance awareness of the body. Music, painting, and other arts contribute greatly to the enjoyment and value of these explorations. Feel free to use your imagination in implementing these ideas; as you'll see, many are followed by suggested variations. You'll probably think of many more.

**Talking body parts.** Talking about what each body part can do helps children learn functions and movements of the parts. For example:

- My eyes can (open, shut, blink, cry, wink)
- My hands can (crayon, hold, paint, squeeze, touch, "scrunch")
- My mouth can (cry, laugh, sing, eat, drink)

**Variation:** Have the children sing the "Body Song" while doing the motions.

## Body Song

I kick with my (feet, feet feet,) I see with my (eyes eyes eyes,) I hear with my (ears, ears ears.) I eat with my (teeth teeth teeth,) I kiss with my (mouth mouth mouth) I smell with my (nose nose nose,) I clap with my (hands hands hands,) and I wig-gle my (toes toes toes.)

**Part by part.** Isolating different parts of the body focuses children on how their bodies work. Play some music and have the children lie on the floor and move their legs, feet, arms, and fingers to the music.

## Variations

- Do "stop and go" activities, having the children stop and start movements as you stop and start music.

- Change the tempo or volume of the music.

- Have the children move around the room like birds or other animals (like worms wiggling or ducks waddling, for example).

- A more strenuous activity is to pretend to chase a mouse, hide from Mr. McGregor, or seek out Cookie Monster.

- If the children are spread out, tell them to come back to "home base" while rolling like a ball, roaring like a lion, or being a little puppy dog coming home for supper.

**Musical tag.** Have the children move around the floor while the music is playing. When the music stops, they must touch another person's head or leg as instructed.

**Touch the rope.** Make a circle on the floor with a long rope. You also need an instrument (like a drum or chime) or something that makes a pleasant sound. Have the children lie near the rope. Pick a body part and tell the children to touch the rope with that part every time you make the sound.

**Variation:** Let the children name the body part they must touch to the rope.

**Elbow dancing.** Have the children move their elbows in a dance to highly rhythmic music. Let them suggest other parts of the body they can dance with: for example, the chin, tongue, bottom, or belly button.

**Be a ball!** Suggest that the children lie on the floor and roll up into a ball. Tell them that each time you ring a bell, they can unroll one part of their body—a finger, arm, and so on—until they are all "unfolded."

**"Getting Ready" song.** This song enhances awareness of body parts. It is particularly good for younger children who may be language delayed.

**Note:** An asterisk (*) marks songs especially suitable for younger children or children whose language is delayed.

**Variation:** Have the children brush their teeth or wash or touch various parts of the body.

**Video recordings.** Video tapes show children how their bodies perform and how their movements and gestures look. Take care that the camera encourages (rather than discourages) activity; don't portray the child in an unflattering way. Make simple recordings of play, outings, or special events. Playing back the video provides a great opportunity for verbalization (and fun!).

**Variations**

- Using a video camera hooked up to a TV monitor, play "get in the picture." Use a zoom lens to focus in on something distant from the camera but accessible to everyone. As the children see the object on the television monitor, have them locate the object in the room and touch it (with their hands, or nose, or feet, or other body part).

- Play "stay in the picture." Station the monitor so that the children can see themselves on it. Slowly pan the camera back and forth and up and down while keeping it focused on the play area. Have the children try to stay in the picture frame by moving as they watch themselves on the monitor.

- Periodically close the camera aperture so that the monitor goes dark. At this point, everyone stops moving until you open the aperture and they can see themselves again.

**Handprints and footprints.** Children can explore footprints and wheelchair tracks in mud, sand, or snow. Individual and group prints can be examined, as well as tracks made by animals and birds. Start finger-painting play by making prints of hands and fingers.

**Variations**

- Have the children use their fingers to make patterns that look like tracks, making their fingers "walk," "jump," and "run" on the paper.

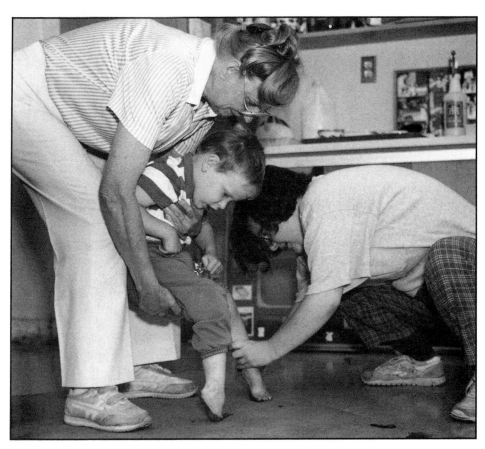

*Feet painting is messy—but fun!*

- Show the children how they can use two fingers to simulate wheelchair tracks.

- "Feet painting" is particularly good for children with impaired upper extremities. The paint should be quite thick to give the print a well-defined edge. (Using more tempera or adding glue to the mixture can achieve the desired thickness.) Have a pan of warm soapy water ready: washing feet is part of the fun.

Put mural paper down on the floor and let children who walk make prints, either at random or in a specified pattern. One possible theme is to make a rainbow. Children who are unable to walk can be held above the paper by two people, who then place the children's feet in the appropriate places.

You can also tape mural paper to the wall and have the children lie on the floor. Children with cerebral palsy can make footprints this way. If a child hesitates to get his or her feet wet, suggest putting hands in the paint instead.

## UNIT 2    Gross Motor Activities

Gross motor movement involves the balance, coordination, and large muscle activity necessary for efficient rolling, crawling, walking, jumping, and other physical activities. Offer plenty of opportunities for gross motor play. Activities should be child-centered and movement-oriented. Take advantage of children's desires to explore, experience, and discover their world.

Many children with physical disabilities have poor body control, use up a great deal of energy trying to control their movements, and have problems with balance and coordination. They may have difficulties using both sides of their bodies simultaneously, independently, or in alternation. Developing motor skills and achieving motor milestones profoundly affect all areas of a child's advancement, not just body movement. The body gives expression to our mind and spirit, allowing us to bring our thoughts to the world—to communicate. Here are suggested ways to explore gross motor awareness.

## EXPLORATIONS

**Swaying arms.** Have children follow with their arms the rise and fall of a melody played by one instrument (such as a flute or recorder). Waving a sheer scarf to the melody creates a nice visual effect.

**Balloon play.** Play some upbeat music and throw a balloon into the air. Have the children try to keep the balloon in the air any way they can.

**Ribbon wands.** Put a colorful ribbon or scarf on a light wand or stick. Give the children similar sticks and have them move their sticks to the music. Use short streamers for children in wheelchairs, or they will have difficulty. For children who cannot hold the wand, attach it to a mitten or elastic band that can be slipped over the child's hand.

**Hand puppets.** Put large paper napkins over the children's hands, securing them at the wrist with large elastic bands. Use crayons or markers to make faces (perhaps ghost faces, or sad or happy faces) on each puppet. Play music that goes along with the faces while the children make their hand puppets dance.

**Variation:** Dress up like a big ghost and have the children make their ghost puppets play with you or fight you off. This stimulates a lot of arm movement.

**Snowball fight!** Children love to pretend to make and throw snowballs to the sound of a piano glissando (rapid notes up or down the keyboard). As each child takes a turn throwing, the "target" pretends to be hit in the face and to brush off the snow.

**Making waves.** Put sheer saris or other thin, silky, colorful material over the children's heads. Let them move their arms, heads, and upper bodies to the music. The group can pretend to be a huge monster, a billowy cloud in the sky, or a large ocean wave.

**Shake a leg.** Tie small containers (such as film or pill containers) to bicyclists' pant clips. Fill the containers about a third full with rice or beans, then put the clips on the children's legs. These leg rattles promote experimentation with shaking and rolling.

**"Fish Song."** Let the children sing the "Fish Song" while they wave a large blue sheet with pictures of fish sewn or drawn on it.

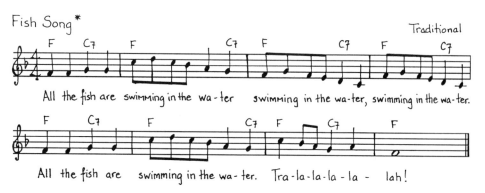

Fish Song*  
Traditional

All the fish are swimming in the wa-ter  swimming in the wa-ter, swimming in the wa-ter.

All the fish are swimming in the wa-ter. Tra-la-la-la-la-lah!

**Variations**

- The children pretend to become fish swimming, floating, and rolling in the water. As the "fish" swim around, they get caught (put the sheet over them). Very loud chords on the piano (or from a recording) signal that the fish are caught. They must struggle to free themselves; when they succeed and swim away, the music decreases in volume.

- Read *Swimmy* by Leo Lionni (Panther Press, 1963). This story can be mimed to a recording (such as Hap Palmer's "Seagulls").

**Be an animal!** Have the children lie on the floor and move to music, imitating animals: slithering snakes, slow-poke turtles, galloping horses, angry lions, lumbering crocodiles, or tiny inchworms.

**Variations**

- Play lyrical music and encourage the children to pretend they are birds soaring in the sky. Possibilities include looking for twigs for nests, and searching and scratching for food.

- Tell the children that pigs love to roll around in the mud. Suggest they try being piggies who want to cool off in a mud bath.

**Move to the music.** Play a medley of music with different rhythms and tempos. Have the children move to the music as it changes. Make sure you tailor this activity to a given child's abilities; not all movements are possible for those with limited mobility. The many possible movements also vary with the children's positions:

- *If lying on the floor:* Try rolling, crawling, kicking, bicycling.

- *If sitting:* Try shaking hands, waving arms, stretching arms up and out, moving arms around.

- *If standing:* Try walking forward, backward, sideways, like a baby, or like a very old person; taking small steps and large steps; skipping; jumping.

**Roly poly.** Have the children take turns pushing a roly-poly clown doll to make it move from side to side. Suggest that they can be roly-polys too—tell them to sway their bodies from side to side whenever you play a chime.

*"Put your hand up and give it a shake."*

**Giants and pixies.** Tell the children that heavy chords or drumming is "giant music." Lighter music, perhaps bells or flutes, is "pixie music."

Play giant music and have the children go around the room, stretching "as tall as giants." Children in wheelchairs can do this with big pushes on their wheels. As they move, the children chant "fee fie foe *fum*" until the music changes. When the pixie music begins, the children must be very quiet and take little steps, perhaps on tip-toe. Children in wheelchairs can do this with small pushes on their wheels.

**Leaf crunch.** It's great fun for children to help gather autumn leaves into a big pile, lie on top of the pile, and roll around in it.

**Variation:** Bring bushels of leaves into the classroom or playroom and put them in a big plastic swimming pool or sand table. Children love to make "crunchy" music to rhythmic music. Taping the sounds enhances the experience by letting children revisit it.

| UNIT 3 | # Fine Motor Activities |

Children with fine motor problems have difficulty getting their eyes, hands, and thoughts to work together. They may lack the strength or control for activities requiring fine motor coordination, such as tying, sorting, buttoning, and cutting. They may not be able to grasp or use a fork or crayon.

*Just messing around with a glue stick.*

Grasping, manipulating, and releasing are difficult for children whose hands are severely involved because of cerebral palsy. These skills, however, are fundamental to lifelong independence, and it is critical that children develop them. A child who can grasp with both hands can use this ability to aid mobility when pulling up from a lying to a sitting or standing position. This skill is also useful in pushing a chair or walker or in using furniture for support while moving.

Fine motor control is important to writing and drawing, which begin with the control of certain hand and arm muscles, as well as with the visual awareness of scribbles and marks made with fingers, crayons, chalk, and paint. Every experience in making marks adds to the child's store of information. This store, combined with coordination and control of small hand and finger muscles, eventually culminates in the meaningful markings we call writing and drawing.

Here are some suggestions for exploring fine motor skills:

**Finger plays.** Young children love finger plays, which are simple poems or ditties accompanied by hand movements that help to tell the story. Finger play is much more than a diversion; it demands refined movement and coordination of the small muscles of the fingers and hand. Some suggested plays follow.

## Ladybug

*by Fran Herman*

| Rhyme | *Action* |
| --- | --- |
| The ladybug went crawling, Crawling, crawling, The ladybug went crawling Up my thumb. Oh what fun, it's on my thumb, I'll have to say The number 1 . . . 1. | *(Pointer finger goes along fingers of opposite hand stopping at the thumb.)* <br><br><br><br><br><br> *(Hold up one finger.)* |
| The little ant went walking Walking, walking, The little ant went walking, On my shoe. Oh dear, what should I do? I think I'll have to count, To number 2 . . . 1, 2. | *(Finger walk on shoes.)* <br><br><br><br> *(Hold up two fingers.)* |
| The little bug went jumping The little bug went jumping, On my knee Oh gee, what do I see? I think I'll have to count, To number 3 . . . 1, 2, 3. | *(Jump fingers all over body.)* <br> *(Touch knee.)* <br><br><br> *(Hold up three fingers.)* |
| The little snake went wiggling, Wiggling, wiggling, The little snake went wiggling, On the floor. Go on, open the door. I think you'll have to count To number 4 . . . 1, 2, 3, 4. Now . . . SHUT IT! | *(Wiggle palm all over with fingers closed.)* <br><br><br> *(Touch floor.)* <br> *(Open pretend door.)* <br> *(Hold up hand and show four fingers.)* <br><br> *(Make a loud clap.)* |

## Open and Shut

*Traditional*

| Rhyme | Action |
| --- | --- |

Open, shut them.      *(Open hand, then make a fist.)*
Open, shut them.
Give a little clap.
Open, shut them.
Open, shut them.
Put them in your lap.

Creep them, creep them    *(Have fingers start to walk up*
Creep them, creep them    *the body to the chin.)*
Right up to your chin.
Open up your little mouth   *(Open mouth.)*
But do not let them in.     *(Hide both hands behind back.)*

## Ten Little Fingers

*Traditional*

I have ten little fingers,
And they all belong to me.   *(Hold up hands, with fingers spread.)*
I can do things with them,
Would you like to see?

I can shut them up tight.   *(Make a fist.)*
I can open them wide.    *(Open hands.)*
I can clap them together.   *(Clap hands.)*
I can make them hide.    *(Hide hands behind back.)*

I can make them jump high.  *(Reach up.)*
I can make them fall low.   *(Let hands fall.)*
I can clap them together.   *(Clap.)*
And sit just so.      *(Fold hands in lap.)*

## Knock with Two Hands

*Traditional*

I can knock with two hands.  *(Knock, knock, knock.)*
I can sock with two hands.  *(Sock, sock, sock.)*
I can tap with two hands.   *(Tap, tap, tap.)*
I can clap with two hands.  *(Clap, clap, clap.)*

## Brother Hands

*Traditional*

This little hand is a good little hand. *(Hold up right hand.)*
This little hand is its brother.   *(Hold up left hand.)*
Together they wash and wash and wash. *(Wash hands.)*
One hand washes the other!

Fuzzy Caterpillar

**Note:** To make fuzzy caterpillars, cut the fingers off old woolen gloves and glue or sew two eyes on each finger. Put the caterpillars on the children's index fingers. Play to the following song, sung to the tune of "Twinkle, Twinkle, Little Star."

| Rhyme | Action |
|---|---|
| One day Arabella Miller Found a fuzzy caterpillar. | (*Show caterpillar to all.*) |
| First it crawled upon her mother, | (*Crawl up the outside of one arm.*) |
| Then upon her baby brother. | (*Turn arm around. Crawl down the inside of the same arm.*) |
| All said "Arabella Miller, | (*Point index finger.*) |
| Put away that caterpillar!" | (*Hide caterpillar behind back.*) |

## EXPLORATIONS

**Eyedropper painting.** Squeezing eyedroppers is a good way to develop small muscle coordination. Fill several small jars with water. Drop a different food coloring in each jar. Provide a small eyedropper for each color. Show the children how to pick up water with the eyedropper and squirt it onto a piece of paper, cloth, or newsprint. Once the children catch on to using eyedroppers, they'll enjoy seeing how the squirted colors change as they mix.

**Making shapes.** Show the children how to fold. (Aluminum foil and tissue paper are excellent folding materials.) The children need to see you first fold, then press down on the fold. As material is folded over and over, the children will become aware of its changing shape and size. This shows them that one shape can be changed into another.

**Making colored paper.** Lovely designs can be made with folded, dyed tissue paper. Have the children fold the tissue paper into smaller shapes. The corners of the shapes can then be dipped into dyes or food coloring. If you use absorbent tissue paper, the children can create pretty designs. Keep the sheets folded until dried. They can then be unfolded and taped to a windowpane, where sunlight will give them varying intensities of color. The sheets can also be used as gift wrap.

**Art in the bathtub.** Art materials for the bath can both delight youngsters and contribute to fine motor development. Scribble Stix® by Coleco are bright crayon-like art materials that can be scribbled on the tiles or side of the tub, then washed off. This mild nontoxic soap will not stain the tiles or children.

Another nontoxic material, Funny Color Foam® from Creative Aerosol Corporation, makes foamy molded shapes that children can remold in the tub, poking them, squishing them through their fingers, or breaking them up into little shapes.

**Finger houses.** Very young children enjoy making a "house" by holding their thumbs and index fingers together in a circle. Use a small mouse figure or finger puppet or a tiny plastic one as you sing:

Little mouse, little mouse,
Come inside my little house. (*Mouse goes through fingers, to the child's delight.*)

**Mural painting.** Tape a big piece of mural paper on the floor or table. Have children paint the whole paper in one color. When the paint is dry, have the children make handprints in contrasting colors all over the paper and put fingerprints around the border. The finished piece makes a great bulletin board.

**Grasp and release movements.** The following activities may help younger children who have difficulty grasping and releasing.

- Give each child a jelly bean (or a bigger item, if a child lacks fine grasp). As you recite the following poem, the children try to throw their items into a large container whenever you say "throw":

    Jelly bean, jelly bean,
    In your hand,
    Will you *throw* it
    Into the can?

- Have the children pass an object from one hand to the other to the beat of the drum. Then have each child pass the object to their neighbor on each drumbeat. Adjust the tempo to match the children's ability to release the object.

- Transferring objects from one hand to the other may be difficult. Use a small soft object at first to allow a good grasp. As grasp improves, you can use cardboard cutouts (of eggs, hearts, or fish, for example).

    In a similar but more sophisticated game, children pass the object to a friend of their choice. This involves choosing where to pass the object, as well as getting the object in the hand closest to that person.

- Have the children pretend to hold snowflakes in their hands, then release them on a musical signal (such as a glissando or chime) or when they chant "falling" in this rhyme:

    See the snowflakes twirling round,
    Now they're *falling* down to the ground.

**UNIT 4**

# Spatial and Kinesthetic Awareness

It is important that children learn to recognize how much space their bodies occupy, to locate objects in space, and to develop fundamental movement abilities. Visual mechanisms provide continual input that, if properly integrated, allows consideration of a number of objects quickly and simultaneously.

Gradually, children learn to judge distances, spaces, sizes, and shapes in their immediate surroundings. This perception of space helps develop the precise visual discrimination skills important to activities such as appreciating detail in pictures, solving puzzles, detecting differences among shapes and letters, and, eventually, reading.

## EXPLORATIONS

**Circles and wheels.** Show circles and wheels to the children. Ask them to explore the room for any circles or wheels they can find. Suggest that they may also find round things on people's clothing.

Ask the children if they can turn circles with their bodies to music. Although some may be quite disabled, they can be very innovative as they turn on the floor to create, for example, a "bum dance," a "knee dance," or a "tummy twirl."

**Variations**

Explain the two basic kinds of shapes: round and straight.

- Circles are round, flat shapes. Some round shapes feel round all over like a ball or balloon. Ask the children if they can make their bodies be round like a ball. Can their round body roll like a ball on the floor?

- Now show a ruler or pencil. Ask the children to make a straight line with their bodies. Can they move while they are straight as a pencil? Ask them to point out straight lines in the room.

**Body language.** This is a good problem-solving activity for five- and six-year-olds who know the alphabet. Ask them to make letters or numbers with their bodies, while either lying on the floor or standing. (Good letters or numbers to make are I, J, T, O, U, Y, F, C, H, 1, 2, 3, 7, 9.) Working in pairs makes this activity easier for some children and lets a child who is standing work with a child in a wheelchair.

**"Me tracing."** This exercise uses drawing and painting skills on a large scale and also familiarizes children with their own body image. Have children choose partners (or pair them up yourself). Let each take a turn tracing their partner's shape while the partner lies very still on a large piece of craft paper. Once the body shape is traced, each child can fill in details or decorate it (perhaps disguise it!) using various media.

**Variation:** Before tracing, double the craft paper. Cut the tracing out, leaving wide margins for stapling, so the shape can be stuffed with shredded newspaper. To add to the fun, the image can be "dressed up" with some of the child's clothing and a large photograph glued on for the face.

**Tiny eggs, big eggs.** Have the children lie on the floor. Make sure they are not touching anyone. Tell them they are inside tiny eggs and must become as small as possible. When they hear you tap a drum, they tap with one hand or foot to try to break through the egg. Once they break through, they stretch to become as big as they can. To emphasize spatial relationships, have one child "hatch" while the others watch to see the difference between being "small" and "big."

**From seeds to trees.** Being a seed and growing into a flower or tree is very appealing to young children. Talking about how plants need sunlight and water is essential for children to understand this theme of growth. The "Seed Song" takes children through the process of being a tiny seed and growing bigger.

**Variation:** Ask the children what kind of flower, tree, or plant they want to be. (Some answers we've heard: "peanut butter tree," "button tree," "teddy bear tree.")

**Obstacle courses.** Challenging and fun for children of all ages, obstacle courses use many muscles in different ways and enhance kinesthetic and proprioceptive awareness. Children are usually eager to try to conquer the course.

Make a course with large objects such as cushions, hassocks, chairs, tables, and boxes. Make sure children have to go around, under, and through things. Suggest the children crawl through the course without touching any part of it.

## Seed Song*

Caroline Fynney

See the lit-tle seed in the ground, in the ground, in the ground.

See the lit-tle seed in the ground. Someday it's gon-na grow up. And it's

gon - na be a flo - wer, a flo - wer, a flo - wer. It's

gon - na be a flo - wer sway-ing in the wind. Go

side to side, side to side, side to side and stop! Go

side to side, side to side, side to side and stop!

You can also use tape to make lines on the floor that the children must stay within while keeping their balance. Children who have visual or perceptual difficulties may need ropes for extra guidance.

**UNIT 5**

# Tactile Discrimination

Tactile discrimination is the ability to identify and categorize objects by touch and feel. As with visual and auditory perception, tactile discrimination is developed by experiencing objects in the environment. Tactile awareness and discrimination are important to development, particularly the development of body awareness.

Try to provide many experiences involving touching or feeling for children whose disabilities restrict or impair movement and sensation. Remember that texture, size, shape, weight, temperature, and pressure can all be felt by receptors in the skin. Any or all of these attributes can be valuable in exercises to enhance tactile discrimination and children's awareness of their surroundings.

## EXPLORATIONS

**"Guk."** This frothy substance, a mixture of water, detergent or soap flakes, and tempera paints, is easy to make and fun to handle; the children call it "guk." Making and playing with "guk" enhances both tactile and visual senses, providing a kinesthetic experience and stimulating awareness of color.

(Soap flakes are better than detergent because they retain their foam and color longer.) First beat soap flakes and water until frothy. Then add the tempera for color. The result will be a lovely pastel shade.

Have the children sit around a low table. Plop some "guk" in front of each child. (Use oilcloth or a piece of plastic if the table does not have a waterproof finish.) Youngsters in wheelchairs with lap trays can use the trays instead of the table.

*Finger-painting with guk.*

### Variations

- Play music and have the children make patterns with "guk" to the music. Brahms' "Lullaby" encourages a swaying motion, and marches emphasize straight lines. Waltz music goes well with circle-making. Show circles to the children and then have them make circles, first in the air, then in "guk" on the table.

- Instead of "guk," use a soft gelatin dessert, chocolate pudding, or whipped cream with food coloring for outdoor fun on a warm day. Finish with the children being washed off (or, if they're wearing bathing suits, being dunked in a wading pool).

**Search the bag.** Collect materials with distinct textures (such as scraps of sandpaper, foil, fake fur, plastic, screen, foam, or sponge). Describe the objects and handle them with the children. Let each child choose one item and drop it in the bag. Shake the bag. Each child then takes a turn reaching into the bag to find the object she or he chose. (Help with verbal hints if the child has difficulties.)

**Making hands.** Trace the outline of a hand on heavy paper or fabric. Cut out the tracing and have each child glue "things to touch" on the hand. Put the child's name on the decorated hand and display it where it can be touched and added to.

**Variation:** For younger children, a textured quilt or tablecloth is a good introduction to tactile awareness. Take a sheet or large piece of material. Sew pieces of textured material to the sheet. (You can also use fabric glue.) If a child has allergies, avoid wool. When the child is lying on or playing with the cloth, describe what the textures feel like and what they are called.

**Feelie box.** Collect various objects that can be identified by touch, such as a key, comb, button, spoon, pencil, ball, and coin. Let the children see the objects, then put them one at a time into a cardboard "feelie" box with two holes on one side. Have the children take turns putting their arms through the holes in the box and, without seeing the object, trying to identify it. Give clues if needed.

**Taste tests.** The mouth's nine thousand taste buds can distinguish four qualities: sweet, sour, salty, and bitter. At snack time, give the children several drinks or foods to taste. First ask them to name the foods by their tastes. Then have each child wear a blindfold and try to identify a food by taste *and* touch. (Watch out for food allergies, especially to peanut butter, milk, eggs, and chocolate.)

**Smell tests.** Smell is our most primitive sense. Talk with the children about noses and what they do. Have the children breathe in and out through their noses. Assemble a group of jars containing substances with distinctive aromas, such as lemon, onion, flowers, cinnamon, soap, peppermint, coffee, baby powder, wood shavings, and perfume. See whether the children recognize the odors, and whether they like or dislike them. Talk about where each substance comes from (lemons grow on trees, onions grow in the ground, and so forth).

**Variations**

- Have children sprinkle herbs and spices on paper covered with wet glue. After the glue dries, the children can use their paper to learn to identify the odors.

- Rub hand lotion on the children. This stimulates touch as well as smell.

- Put dabs of cleansing cream on the children's noses. Have them remove it with tissues, cotton balls, or soft leaves. A mirror adds to this scent study.

**Hunt with your hands.** Blindfold the children. Ask them to explore the room for objects you've put on the floor. Use familiar things, such as:

- Things they eat with

- Things they color with (such as crayons)

- "Squishy" things (such as beanbags)

- Things they sleep with (such as pillows)

**Variations**

- Without blindfolds, have children explore the room for something smooth or rough, hard or soft, warm or cold.

- Reverse the preceding exercise and have the children describe what they are touching. (For example, "The rug is woolly/soft/fuzzy.")

**Feelix the feelie snake.** To make Feelix, sew together six-inch segments of material with varying textures (such as silk, wool, burlap, corduroy, nubby loops, and fake fur). Fill each segment with a different material (such as dried beans, marbles, pine cones, foam plastic peanuts, paper, cellophane, and cotton balls). Have children explore each of Feelix's segments by touching, then by holding it and rubbing it on their cheeks. Encourage the children to squeeze the segment and talk about how it feels.

**Cutting up.** Using scissors is a good opportunity for tactile-kinesthetic matching and duplication exercises. Cut fringes, curves, straight lines, and forms from paper, cloth, soft cardboard, fruit skins, and leafy vegetables such as cabbages or lettuce leaves.

**Testing the waters.** This activity helps children learn about temperature differentiation. Line up four bowls containing water of various temperatures (first cold, then cool, then warm, then hot). Make sure the "hot" is not too hot for the children to touch. Let the children put their hands in each bowl in

*This spiral will become a pumpkin vine in a Halloween project.*

sequence and describe how the water feels. The children might then be able to name other objects or substances that have similar temperatures.

**Variation:** Blindfold the children then have them dunk their elbows in each bowl and describe the temperature.

**UNIT 6** — # Laterality and Directionality

*Laterality* refers to awareness of the two sides of one's body and the preferential use of one side or the other. A child must learn to distinguish between the right and left sides of the body and to control both sides, individually and cooperatively. Laterality also includes the ability to relate physically to an object in space.

*Directionality* refers to knowing right from left, up from down, and forward from backward, and having the ability to use this knowledge. Lack of this skill may cause one or more of the following problems: difficulty in orienting puzzle pieces, reversal errors in copying shapes and letters, and left/right confusion in reading and writing.

Some children have trouble moving across the midline of the body and are confused when their hand crosses to the other side of their body. Similar problems can show up with visual stimuli that require the eye to track across midline. The resultant confusion interferes with the child's interactions with his or her environment.

## EXPLORATIONS

**Mirror, mirror.** Whenever children identify their own body parts in a mirror, they learn about themselves. Have a child stand or sit before a mirror. The other children or an adult suggest various parts of the body for the child to touch. The child then sees himself or herself reaching down to touch the knee, across to touch the belly button, and so on. This experience gives children a picture of how their bodies look in different positions.

**Variations**

- Invite two children to look in the mirror at the same time. Ask them to make a funny face or do something silly. Children love to see the different ways their faces can look.

- Suggest that two children play "copy cat": with both children side by side in front of a mirror, one child makes a motion. The other child must see and imitate the motion (if the first child raises her right arm, the copy cat raises his right arm). The game encourages children to tell right from left to avoid right/left reversals. This is an excellent exercise for developing visual perception.

**Magic feather.** Use a stiff, bright feather. Tell the children it's your "magic feather," which gives wonderful tickles. One by one, have the children close their eyes and, at the sound of a chime, tickle the child whose eyes are closed with the feather. Then ask the child to touch the spot you just tickled. To emphasize crossing the midline, touch the side opposite the dominant hand.

**Beanbag toss.** Put a big plastic hoop on the floor and give each child a beanbag. When they hear a bell ring, the children must put the beanbags wherever you indicate: *inside, outside, near,* or *on top of* the hoop.

**Touch here, touch there.** Have children cross their midline to this chant:

> Put your hand on your ear,
> Now touch your other ear.

Adapt the chant to have them touch each eye, knee, foot, and so on.

For children who are learning right from left, try this chant, repeating it for various body parts:

> Put your left hand on the floor,
> Now count from one to four,
> 1, 2, 3, 4.

**Right Day, Left Day.** For "Right Day," put a colored ribbon or elastic band on each child's right hand. (You can also stamp the hand.) During that day, have the children do various tasks with their right hands. You can put on music and have the children touch their right shoe, knee, eye, elbow, and so on, to the beat. They can color only on the right side of the paper until given other directions, and dance to the right or using motions with the right side of the body. For "Left Day," enjoy the same activities with emphasis on the left side.

**Songs for left and right.** "Looby Loo" or "Hokey Pokey" are ideal for helping children learn the right and left sides of the body.

**Musical sticks.** This activity can help develop the ability to cross midline. Get light sticks (such as rhythm sticks) for you and the children. Have the children try to touch their sticks to yours to music with a definite beat (the Mexican dance "La Raspa" is a good example).

At first, hold your stick to each child's dominant side. When the children can touch your stick on this side without difficulty, move your stick to the midline, and then to the other side. The children will begin to work to the music's rhythm, avoiding random movements.

**Close and far.** Younger children love this directional chant:

> Move close to me everybody,
> Close to me today,
> Now everybody
> Go far, far away.

**Put the bear on the chair.** Have the children get into a circle, with one child sitting in the middle and holding a teddy bear beside a small chair. As the group sings to the tune of "Put Your Finger in the Air," the child puts the bear wherever indicated:

> Put the bear on the chair, on the chair,
> Put the bear on the chair, on the chair,
> Put the bear on the chair, and now comb its hair,
> Put the bear on the chair, on the chair.

You can adapt the song for other directions and locations:

> Put the bear (beside/beneath/behind) the chair . . . .

**Follow the bread-crumb trail.** Tell the story of *Hansel and Gretel,* emphasizing the part about the trail of bread crumbs through the woods. Suggest the children make a journey following crumbs, cereal, pieces of paper, or beads. Make a trail for them, leaving a surprise or snack to be discovered at the end.

### Variations

- Have one group make a trail for another to follow.
- Make outdoor trails, using chalk on pavement or a large flour-filled shaker on unpaved areas.
- Make a trail on paper using markers, seeds, or string glued to the paper. Have the children "walk" along it or trace it with their fingers.

**Pointing song.** This song can help youngsters become aware of directions, their surroundings, and other people.

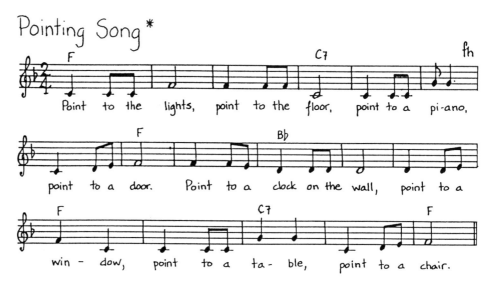

Pointing Song *

Point to the lights, point to the floor, point to a pi-ano, point to a door. Point to a clock on the wall, point to a win - dow, point to a ta - ble, point to a chair.

You can adapt the song to focus on other objects, people, or aspects of the children's surroundings:

- Point to the trees, sun, sky (the outdoors).
- Point to your teacher (people).
- Point to somebody wearing yellow (colors).
- Point to somebody wearing earrings (how people are dressed).
- Point to yourself, point to a friend (you/me).

# With Our Ears

## GOALS

- To promote awareness of sounds in the environment
- To encourage the ability to receive and differentiate auditory stimuli
- To reinforce the ability to retain and recall general auditory information
- To emphasize the development of good habit patterns of auditory attention

**UNIT 1**

## Auditory Awareness

Listening is a *learned* skill. Many children acquire it automatically; others must nurture it. Skills important to listening include receiving, differentiating, and responding to auditory stimuli. Some children may have trouble determining where a sound comes from because their poor auditory discrimination makes it hard to integrate information.

From the beginning, emphasize hearing and reacting to all types of sounds. Make the most of children's natural affinities for mimicry and for rhythm, in speech, in the wind, in the ocean's waves, in a bird's song. Music, of course, is an invaluable and greatly enjoyed experience. Children are full of music, as we find when we provide opportunities to have fun with it. As children experience music and sounds of all types, they develop their auditory awareness.

*Listening is a learned skill.*

## EXPLORATIONS

**Spoon music.** Put small and large spoons around the edges of the room. Have the children roll or crawl (or carry them if necessary) to the spoons. Ask, "Have you got your spoons?" When they all say yes, say, "Now tap on the floor with the big spoon. Now tap on the floor with the little spoon."

You can create a whole session around searching for the various sounds the children can discover in the room once they are made aware of the spoons' different timbres.

**Variation:** "Take the big spoon and tap on the wall" (or on the table, or on the door). Let the children discover the room's sound scape, then play some music and encourage tapping to it.

**What's that sound?** Have children listen to distinctive sounds from different sources:

- *Rubbing* two pieces of coarse sandpaper
- *Blowing* empty bottles
- *Tapping* a wastebasket with a ruler
- *Shaking* tin cans partially filled with nuts

The children must be quiet in order to listen to the sounds. After they listen, ask them how they want to move to each of the sounds. Invite them to experiment with these movements.

### Variations

- Form two groups. Children in one group make the sounds, while the other children move to it in a "sound dance." Ask one child to be the conductor who points to each sound-maker as a signal to make the music.

- Have the children experiment with various sounds made by different types of paper and plastic, such as cellophane, foil, newsprint, paper bags, or plastic garbage bags. Have them make a sound symphony with these materials. (As always, supervise children closely when using plastic materials that could cause suffocation.)

**Listening walks.** Take a walk and bring sounds to the children's attention: birds and crickets chirping, car sounds, and so on. If you are in the country, have them listen carefully for animal sounds: a frog croaking, a brook running, or leaves rustling. Encourage the children to identify all the sounds they hear. They might also have fun trying to imitate the sounds.

### Variations

- On cold days, you can take "listening walks" indoors. Perhaps you could listen for a person hammering, a tap dripping, or a typewriter tapping. You can also audiotape the walk, which can be fun and educational when you replay the tape to identify the sounds.

- Turn a rainy day into a special experience by taking a walk outside. If there is no heavy thunder and lightning, children enjoy feeling the rain against their cheeks and may try to catch the raindrops in their hands. Some may even try sticking out their tongues to feel what happens. Alert them to rainy-day sounds: splashing made by cars, and rain hitting the ground, trees, and houses. If the children have boots on, they might also enjoy splashing in puddles and listening to the noise.

**Rising and falling.** Play some music that rises in pitch. Have the children build an imaginary sand castle, piling it higher and higher as the music builds. Tell them to reach up and put a flag at the top of their castle. Then play discordant music; tell the children that now the castle is falling, and have them dramatize this by tumbling to the ground.

**Variation:** To the beat of music, have the children "stretch to the sky" with both arms. When the music changes, they relax "like a bowl full of jelly."

**Mystery music.** Have several people each make a sound on an instrument held behind their backs. Ask the children to identify the person making the sound. At first, the sounds should be distinctively different (for example, a rattle, chime, and tambourine). As the children's auditory discrimination increases, use instruments which sound more alike.

**Colors and sounds.** Give children paper shapes in three colors (such as red triangles, yellow circles, and green rectangles). Show them instruments that match the shapes (such as a triangle for the paper triangle, a drum for the circle, and a wood block or chime bar for the rectangle). As you play one instrument behind your back, tell the children to show the shape that goes with the sound. Very young children find this game particularly appealing.

**Jangling jars.** Cover small jars with masking tape or paper to hide their contents. Fill the jars with small objects (such as beans, pennies, rice, pebbles, or nuts), filling two jars with each type of object. Have the children shake the jars to find the matching sounds.

**Listening games.** You can play listening games virtually anytime, anywhere. Make sure the children can't see you, and do the following:

- Slap your arm, stamp your foot, snap your fingers, or tap your foot. Then ask, "What part of my body did I use to make that sound?"

- Ask, "Point to where the tapping is."

- Using a stick, shoe, or piece of metal, ask, "What did I tap with?"

- Tear paper, bang a door, bounce a ball, walk, play a piano scale, or open a drawer. Ask, "What made that sound?"

- Adults take turns talking behind a screen. Ask, "Guess who is speaking."

- Have adults take turns singing out of sight. Later, try having a child sing, too. Ask, "Guess who is singing."

**Guess who?** Choose one child to be "it" and sit on a chair blindfolded. The other children take turns going up to knock on the chair or a nearby drum. "Who is knocking at my door?" the blindfolded child asks. "It's me!" the knocker answers. Then the blindfolded child tries to guess who "me" is. If the child guesses correctly, then the knocker becomes "it."

---

**UNIT 2**

# Auditory Acuity and Concentration

Helping children become perceptive listeners is extremely important in developing communication skills. Children must learn auditory attention skills to be able to follow a conversation or the development of an idea, or understand what is being asked of them.

Some children with neurological disabilities have a short attention span and are easily distracted by extraneous sounds and by movements or sights in the room. For these children, it is best to have a quiet corner for play and other activities. Start off lessons with a structured exercise to help keep the children focused. If the children become distracted, change to a slightly different exercise to recapture their attention.

### EXPLORATIONS

**Pictures and songs.** Draw lines on a piece of tagboard to divide it into four to six squares. In each square, draw a simple picture representing a familiar song. For example:

- A star for "Twinkle, Twinkle, Little Star"

- A sun for "You Are My Sunshine"

- A birthday cake for "Happy Birthday"
- A happy face for "If You're Happy and You Know It"

Hold up the card and allow a child to point to a picture to select a song for the group to sing.

**Variation:** After everyone has had a turn selecting a song, sing the song first, then have the child point to the corresponding picture. Playing (not singing) the tune makes this activity more challenging.

**Music bingo.** The preceding activity can lead to "music bingo," which promotes auditory and visual discrimination and concentration. For this game, make several bingo cards containing age-appropriate symbols for familiar children's songs, such as "Baa, Baa, Black Sheep," "Old MacDonald Had a Farm," and "The Wheels on the Bus." With young children, put no more than six to nine squares on each card. Laminate the cards for children who drool.

Each child should have a card and a pile of lima beans or poker chips. As a song is sung or played, the child tries to find and cover the symbol representing the song. The children may need help recognizing when one of them has "bingo." Place a ruler over the row or column that has been covered. If the ruler touches all the markers, the child has "bingo." (A small prize or treat for the winners adds to the fun.)

**Variation:** Make bingo cards with specific themes. For example, select songs and symbols relating to a specific holiday or season.

*A music bingo board.*

**Magic word.** Choose a "magic word" in a story to be told or read to your group. Make sure the word occurs frequently in the story. Give the children a certain motion or sound to make every time the magic word is read. For example, in *Harry the Dirty Dog* (by Gene Zion, Harper and Row, 1956) "Harry" occurs frequently. In this example, you could tell the children to sway their bodies like a dog wagging its tail or say "bow-wow" every time you read the magic word "Harry."

**Follow the colored stick.** Have the children follow a colored stick or wand with their voices. As it goes up, their chanting or singing increases in volume; as it comes down, they make their voices softer.

**Variations**

- All of the children chant or sing until the colored stick touches them; one by one, they stop singing as the wand touches them. Then reverse the game: the children stay silent until you touch them.

- Wave your finger in the air. The children focus on your finger and yell "Ouch!" when it touches the "hot" piano. Children adore this game and try very hard to keep their eyes focused on the finger as it moves from side to side, in circles, or up and down before touching a key. For variety, you can wave a drumstick though the air, eventually striking the drum.

**Sitting-down dance.** Play some highly rhythmic music and lead the children in a sitting-down dance. Keep your movements simple and your pace moderate so the children will be able to mirror your movements. This dance activity is appropriate for even the most physically challenged children.

**Pop up!** Have the children lie still with their eyes closed. Start counting to 10 while you beat a drum, beating harder as you count higher. At a surprise number, any number before 10, make a big Boom!—the signal for all the children to pop up and wriggle around.

**Popcorn game.** Have the children sit in chairs. Play some quiet music. At various points, "strike" a triangle or other instrument to cue the children to "pop" or move a part of their bodies. Changing tempos adds to the fun.

**Cat and mouse.** Have one child pretend to be a sleeping cat. The other children are mice who creep up and tickle the cat when you play the "tickle music" (a quiet sound, such as that from a music box). When you play loud music, the cat wakes up and chases the mice.

**Flashlight music.** Have the children sing, beat drums, or ring bells when you turn on a flashlight and stop when you turn it off. Try this first with the room lights on, then dimmed.

**Bing-bong music.** You can get different pitches by using bongo drums of various sizes or by filling glasses of the same size with different levels of water. Play two of the drums or glasses. Have the children tell you which drum or glass has the lower or higher pitch.

**Hide from the bear.** Have the children pretend they are picking berries in the woods. Suddenly, a bear comes out of a cave and starts growling. The children know the bear doesn't see very well but can hear very well. So they must freeze wherever they are until the bear goes back into the cave. The bear will catch any child who moves or makes a noise. That child then becomes a bear and is taken back to the cave. Children love this game and will try very hard to concentrate and be quiet.

**Beanbag pass.** Have the children sit in a circle. Play some recorded music or a drum and have the children pass a beanbag around the circle to the right. When you play different music, for example on a chime or triangle, the children must start passing the beanbag in the opposite direction. Children must concentrate closely to keep the beanbag going in the right direction, particularly if you change the music frequently.

**Variation:** The children move clockwise in a circle until a chime tells them to reverse direction. This dance is more challenging if you add commands—such as, "When you hear the chime, clap your hands (or stamp your feet/stick out your tongue/stretch up high) and go in the opposite direction." At first, suggest just one motion before the change in direction. When the children become more adept, you can ask them to do more than one motion.

**"Listening song."** Sing the following song, adding verses as concentration develops. If children cannot move to touch the appropriate body parts, have them point, or have an adult help them achieve as much as possible.

© 1988 by Jimani Publications.

**Variation:** Adapt the lyrics to encourage interaction. For example:

- Put your hands on yourself, put your hands on somebody else.

- Put your hands on somebody's head, put your hands on your own head.

- Put your hands on a friend (or a teacher, and so forth).

---

**UNIT 3** | Auditory Memory and Sequencing

Children should be made aware that what they hear is important. They need to learn several skills in this regard: (1) to pay attention to instructions so they can carry them out correctly, (2) to identify the location and sequence of sounds, and (3) to retain and use auditory information in both short-term and long-term memory. Some children can readily summon up what they have heard. Others remember visual stimuli better, and still others have poor powers of recollection in all modalities. For all these children, memory may be strengthened through a variety of auditory experiences.

## EXPLORATIONS

**Echo clapping.** This game can recapture children's attention as well as aid listening. Clap a simple rhythm, then have the children repeat it. Gradually increase the pattern's length and complexity.

**Variation:** Have the children echo a sound you make (with your voice, by clapping, by slapping your thighs, and so on). First let the children see you make the sounds, then make the sounds behind their backs or while their eyes are closed.

**Which came first?** Make two sounds, while the children have their eyes closed or you stand behind them (for example, walking and then scraping a chair across the floor). Have them try to remember the order of the sounds. As they progress, add more sounds (such as snapping your fingers, tapping a table, coughing, or tapping a glass with a spoon).

**Variation:** Ask the children to close their eyes. Then bounce a ball on the floor and count the bounces. Add sounds (for example, bounce the ball, then tap a glass with a spoon) as the children progress.

**Tick, tock.** Have the children clap to the slow beat of a metronome. Show them that the metronome beats faster as the weight is moved lower. Have them clap in time with various speeds.

**Variations**

- Let children take turns moving the metronome weight.

- If you have a keyboard with a built-in rhythm section, let the children press the buttons for the various rhythms and turn the knobs controlling speed and volume. Ask them to describe the beat they heard: Is it fast or slow? Is it getting louder or softer?

**Zoo sounds.** This game encourages children to evoke, by voice or motion, an animal sound you've assigned them. Get ready to tell a story about a trip to the zoo, but first give each child an animal sound. Tell the children to express their sound (by voice or motion) when you talk about their animal in the story. Repeat the story, but before you introduce each animal, ask the children, "which animal comes next?" Encourage them to recall the order in which the animals appeared.

**Animal hunt.** Tape sounds of animals and birds and hide the tape recorder somewhere in the classroom. Hide pictures or stuffed toys of the animals or birds making the sounds in various locations around the room. As you play the tape, have the children hunt for each animal or bird they hear.

**Variations**

- Show the pictures (or stuffed toys) to the children and ask them to make the corresponding animal sounds.

- With the children's help, make a tape of a variety of environmental sounds. Then play the sounds back later and ask the children to identify them. Possible sounds include:

| | |
|---|---|
| running water | a bouncing ball |
| pennies being dropped into a jar | rustling plastic bags |
| paper being torn | jingling keys |

A story board for Goldilocks and the Three Bears.

**Up, down.** As you play music, have the children close their eyes and raise and lower their arms as the volume increases and decreases.

**Where's that cow?** Have one blindfolded child sit in the middle of the room. The remaining children sit scattered around the room. On a signal from you, one of these children starts to moo. The blindfolded child must point in the direction of the sound. You can also use other animal sounds or "hello."

**Variation:** With older children who can sit in a darkened room, have one child sit blindfolded in the middle of the room holding a flashlight. The other children each make a sound as you wander the room and touch them. The child with the flashlight must point it in the direction of the sound.

**Musical stories.** This exercise, which is best for older children, prompts them to incorporate sound effects to communicate or enhance a story. Using a familiar story (such as *The Three Bears*) or a story the children make up, the children are each assigned a character in the story. They sing their lines in voices that help to portray the character. In *The Three Bears,* for example, the designated characters could sing or chant, "Who's been eating my porridge?" in high-pitched, medium-pitched, and low-pitched voices. The remaining children guess whether Papa Bear, Mama Bear, or Baby Bear is speaking. (You might want to precede this story with experiences of hearing and identifying different pitches on a piano.)

Suggest that the children choose instruments that help tell the story. With *The Three Bears,* they might pick a big drum for Papa Bear, a chime for Mama Bear, a small tambourine for Baby Bear, and a triangle for Goldilocks. Give four children these instruments to play, and then tell the story. Each time a character is mentioned, the appropriate child plays the corresponding instrument. The children will have to listen carefully to the story in order to express the events musically. For example, when the bears go for a walk, the children might choose a measured beat to portray them treading through the woods. A skipping rhythm might represent Goldilocks skipping down the path, and a fast tap-tap-tap might represent Baby Bear jumping up and down and scampering around.

Challenge the children to devise sounds and figure out the combination of instruments and other sound effects they need. *The Three Bears* presents opportunities for many sounds other than instrumental sounds. Examples include Goldilocks snoring in her sleep, eating porridge, rocking in the chairs, crashing, jumping up in fright, and running away.

**Variation:** After the children become adept at staging the sounds while an adult reads or tells the story, use visual aids to "tell" the story, eliminating the need for words. Let the children discover much of this for themselves. Once they find ways of exploring with sound, they will be ready to tackle other stories, poems, and rhymes.

**THEME THREE**

# With Our Eyes

## GOALS

- To develop an awareness of shape, color, tone, line, and form, both as found in the environment and in various art media
- To provide a visual means of communicating ideas, preferences, feelings, and energies
- To use (manipulate and control) art materials
- To develop observational skills, satisfy curiosity, and make discoveries
- To provide opportunities to improve control and coordination of the upper extremities

Visual experiences can have many aspects; all are important. The units that follow encourage development of visual awareness; awareness of color; and discrimination of shapes, textures, and visual forms.

The following suggestions and information will be helpful when undertaking explorations in any of the units concerning development of visual skills.

## Encouraging Words

Our reactions to any creative work should emphasize the process the children are involved in and our pleasure in their involvement, rather than emphasizing the end product. If we ask, "What is this you have painted?" we suggest that we are interested only in those elements in the painting that resemble objects in the real world. Using visual skills creatively requires making choices, solving problems, and generating ideas. Encourage children by emphasizing their efforts and process:

- "Hey, I like the way you used the big brush."
- "Sure looks like you had fun doing this."
- "Can you tell me a story about your drawing?"
- "Do you like your painting?"
- "Oh, I like the colors you used."

Public display also shows that a child's work is valued. Rotate display pieces so that each child's work is shown. However, while sincere approval helps to instill confidence, be cautious about praising efforts the child is not yet ready to exploit. Premature endorsement can inhibit a child's inclination to experiment and explore.

## Subject Matter

*The addition of popcorn turns a simple cut-and-paste project into a tactile experience.*

*Drawing becomes more integrated as the child nears school age.*

Ideally, children should use their own themes and subject matter. If a child needs inspiration, make suggestions based on his or her experiences. These suggestions allow room for individual choices and imagination.

Early creative efforts will be self-centered with subjects based on personal experiences. These children will tend to describe their artwork in terms of themselves:

- "Me and my house."
- "I play on the playground."
- "I have a dog."

In time, the child's subject matter expands to include others with the child—things "we" do and places "we" are. Children whose subject matter is more developed might describe their subject as:

- "Playing with my friends."
- "We saw a parade."
- "Our trip to the zoo."

With all children, one likes to see a progression toward the fluent use of symbols. Using symbols or schemata in expressive media can have a positive impact on school readiness skills. The need to recognize and use symbols is more important than ever with the ever-increasing daily barrage of symbols of all kinds from the print and electronic media.

## Getting Ready for the Arts—Some Practical Tips

Position children appropriately. Put their feet on the floor, and make sure the table surface is large enough to support the forearm (from elbow to wrist). For children with severe involvement, consultation with their occupational or physical therapist regarding the most effective positioning is strongly recommended. You may have to adjust the heights and angles of working surfaces; a small easel tray or podium may also be required.

Paper—what you use and how you use it—is an important part of minimizing distractions in the activity area. Provide paper of various sizes, shapes, and colors. You may have to tape drawing paper to the table.

Give children with diminished fine motor control large sheets of paper, gradually reducing the size as their control and confidence increase. Children with muscular weakness or restricted joint movement may need to work on a smaller scale.

For children whose disabilities preclude independent drawing, the following may be helpful:

- Drawing toys, such as Etch a Sketch® (from Ohio Art Company), which draws thin lines on a screen controlled by a horizontal and a vertical control knob, or Magna Doodle® (from Ideal), which draws lines and shapes on a screen using magnetic markers. The latter can be particularly good for a child with poor hand control.

- Putting carbon paper under a sheet of paper. This reproduces "secret" drawings done with a fingernail or "magic wand" (any hard object).

### Getting Ready to Paint

The arrangements suggested for drawing also apply here. Painting can, and will, be a bit messy. There's almost certain to be some spillage and mess; don't overreact to it. Excessive concern diverts attention from painting, inhibits expression, and suggests clumsiness or inadequacy. Let the children know that messiness is part of creative activity and is accepted.

To minimize spills, make sure each child has:

- Room to work without interfering with a neighbor
- Uncluttered work space
- Only materials needed for immediate use
- Paints set in low containers (preferably in a holder) to guard against tipping

### Computers Can Help

Computers offer extraordinary assistance with communication and other basic skills for children with special needs. A great range of drawing and painting programs are available. Most can be set up in a simple configuration to make line drawings using a mouse, joy stick, or the arrow keys on the keyboard. Children with poor fine motor function can benefit from adapted keyboards and template devices.

Nonreading children can use many drawing and painting programs because the menu options are depicted with simple symbols rather than text. The child can select a stylus for drawing, a rectangle or circle as a shape to work with, or a pattern-fill symbol to decorate an existing drawing. The child can move the selected image to any location on the screen, make it bigger or smaller, and use the "eraser" function to make changes. Drawings can be saved on the computer for future play and printed out if you have a printer (appearance, including the possibility of color, depends on the type of printer available).

*Computers are opening up all kinds of new opportunities for children with disabilities.*

**UNIT 1**

# Visual Awareness

The visual arts can provide an alternative means of self-expression for children whose disabilities restrict or distort efforts to communicate. Visual activities are also readily accessible: mobility is not a prerequisite for participation, nor are special facilities required.

It's important to note that visual awareness is more than a passive reception of stimuli—it's an active process. This process of visual response and interaction is better described by the action word *visualizing*. When young children enjoy a visual-arts activity, they are exercising, without conscious effort, their sense of directionality and spatial organization, their eye-hand coordination, and their ability to use and interpret graphic symbols.

## EXPLORATIONS

**Painting with candles.** Allow the children to draw on paper with wax candles. They then use brushes or sponges to coat the paper with water-thinned tempera. Only the unwaxed part of the paper absorbs the paint, creating mysterious images which will fascinate the children.

**Finger-painting, with a flair.** Finger-painting doesn't demand the dexterity required to use drawing instruments. You can also make it an especially interesting tactile experience, particularly for children with low vision, by adding elements such as sand, sawdust, salt, soap flakes (whipped into the paint), or glycerine to the paint. (Adding anise seeds to black paint makes a wonderful scent.)

**Printing.** Printing—making an impression of an object on paper or another surface—encourages an appreciation of texture. Printing can be done simply, right on a table. First, let the children finger-paint. After they wash and dry their hands, have the children put a sheet of absorbent paper (such as newsprint, bond, or construction paper) over the damp painting. Rub the back of the paper all over (make sure hands are clean and dry!), then lift it off slowly. (If the children are using textured paints, they'll get better results working directly on coated finger-painting paper.)

**Sponge-printing parade.** Making a "parade" of sponge-printed shapes exercises grasping skills and sequencing of images. Sponge pieces cut into interesting shapes are dipped into thinned tempera and pressed onto a long strip of paper (damaged or discounted wallpaper is an inexpensive source for this).

To introduce the idea of a parade, let the children march around the room to drumbeats or march music. Then talk about what a parade is before they print their parade on paper.

**Variations**

- "Mesh dabs" work like sponges, but are easier for young children to hold. Fill a plastic mesh bag (such as onions are sold in) with pieces of foam, fiber, or fabric scraps and tie securely.

- Many objects can be used for printing—household gadgets, spools, blocks, even balloons. Look around the room and outside to discover new shapes. The most ordinary objects can make the most wonderful prints.

**Seeing a pattern.** Follow up on the idea of a parade by examining patterns. Point out and explain the organization and repetition that creates patterns. Have the children draw their own patterns on paper cut in the shape of a mitten, scarf, snake, or sock.

**Variation:** Have the children decorate their pattern drawings by pasting on seeds, cereal pieces, beads, or shapes cut from construction paper.

**Fold-over paintings.** These activities introduce children to mirror images and many stimulating shapes. Fold a piece of paper, then thickly apply or drop paint on one side of the fold. Fold the other side over the paint and press gently. Unfolding the paper reveals a symmetrical painting.

**Variation:** Before folding the paper, fold a long string in half and put it in the paint, with the ends extending beyond the paper toward the child. When pulled out, the string makes the paint spread wider.

**Eyedropper painting.** Use food coloring or thinned tempera applied with eyedroppers as an alternative means of painting. Children are rewarded with a dramatic splotch of color for carrying out a sequence of manipulations—squeezing, filling, moving, and emptying the eyedropper.

## Variations

- Color can also be applied with feathers, cotton swabs, shaving brushes, or evergreen boughs.

- Squeeze bottles filled with thickened paint let young children make drip pictures.

*Texture painting with lilacs.*

*Salad spinner art.*

**Salad spinner art.** Children with minimal motor control can create pleasing images with salad spinners, which are relatively inexpensive plastic utensils for drying salad greens.

Cut a heavy piece of paper to fit in the bottom of the spinner. Let the children choose the colors for their picture and dribble or spoon them onto the paper on the bottom of the spinner. Put the lid on and spin. The paint disperses radially in dramatic color bursts that can be used to make greeting cards, mobiles, or collages.

**No fuss, no mess.** Children can enjoy the sensory experience of painting almost everywhere, and without paint.

- Provide water and brushes for water painting on exterior walls or the pavement.

- Let children use brushes or fingers on misted or frost-covered windows. (Make sure first that skin won't stick to the frost.)

- Mirrors and windows can be painted with glass wax.

- Let children wax a glass door that is not in use. They can then sit on opposite sides of the door and have drawing "conversations."

**Splatter painting.** Use an old picture frame to make a splatter-painting frame, or construct one from 1" x 2" lumber. The frame should be approximately 8" x 10". Cut plastic window screen the same size and staple it to the frame.

Put a piece of paper on the table and have children lay flowers, leaves, grasses, and twigs on the paper and objects. (Other materials or objects can also be used.) Put the frame over the paper. Have one child rub a toothbrush dipped in tempera paint across the screen while a partner holds the frame still. After the paint dries, lift the flowers and other material off the paper, revealing an interesting silhouette.

**Variation:** For an entirely different effect, brush liquid starch on the paper and scrape colored chalk across the screen.

**UNIT 2**    # Awareness of Color

Color is a direct visual sensation that children often appreciate and respond to even if their visual processing is impaired. Children can express emotional and aesthetic color preferences without achieving a high level of intellectual or conceptual sophistication. Choosing and using color can yield almost immediate satisfaction and pleasure.

All too often, we bombard children with prescriptive, corrective learning experiences. Color play gives us a clear opportunity to recognize and support children's inventive and intuitive powers. We can then build on those powers in other areas where we seek independence and original effort.

Children with limited vision should hear frequent references to colors and their associated qualities to help them establish a conceptual foundation for color. You can help these children learn to distinguish colored media by always arranging them consistently in the same order in front of the child. Select and arrange the colors in ways that create the highest possible contrast. The primary colors (red, yellow, and blue) are easier to distinguish than are the adjacent secondary colors (for example, orange versus red, or green versus blue). Children with perceptual problems may see light or pastel colors more easily if they are on a dark background material. Fluorescent colors on black or dark backgrounds are also easier to see because of the high contrast.

## EXPLORATIONS

**Finger-painting.** Enhance this tactile experience by thickening the children's favorite tempera paints with cornstarch. Give each child a different color of paint. Have the children pair up, then dip their index fingers in their own paint. The children rub, tickle, or "duel with" their partner's paint-covered fingers until the paint mixes to create a new color.

Repeat the game to mix more colors. The children can wash their hands, then start over with a new partner. Or they can continually exchange partners (without washing their hands) until they have all achieved a uniform muddy brown.

### Learning Colors

You can teach colors using the experiences that follow. Introduce one color at a time—beginning with the primary colors—and emphasize it until the children recognize it consistently. The examples given here emphasize yellow, but they work equally well with other colors.

**Color days.** Declare "Yellow Day." Bring in a big yellow bag filled with yellow things. One by one, the children close their eyes and take something out of the bag. As the child reveals the "prize," have the group make up a song or chant about it. Extend this exploration to the other senses:

- Holding a ball of yellow wool against the skin
- Smelling a lemon
- Tasting a grapefruit
- Peeling a banana

**Pointing song.** Have children sing the "Pointing Song" (see page 68) while they point to something yellow in the room.

**Colored block chant.** Set up a tray with one yellow block and two blocks in other colors. Give each child a turn to pick out the yellow block. Then recite this chant, using the child's name:

> [Linda] found the yellow block,
>
> She saw it sitting on the tray.
>
> Now she knows the color yellow,
>
> That's what we all learned today!

**What color is today?** Put a yellow rubber band (or woven bracelet) around each child's wrist or paint a yellow design on each hand with makeup or a nontoxic washable marker. This helps the children remember the color all day long!

**Rainy-day song.** Have children chant while they take turns holding a small yellow parasol, or wearing a yellow raincoat or rain hat:

> I don't care if the rain comes down,
>
> If the rain comes down,
>
> If the rain comes down.
>
> I don't care if the rain comes down,
>
> 'Cause I've got my yellow umbrella (*raincoat / rain hat*).

**Colorful clothing song.** For "Red Day" sing "Mary Wore Her Red Dress." Have a picture of Mary with a red dress, shoes, hat, and gloves, and sing about each item.

## Mary Wore Her Red Dress*

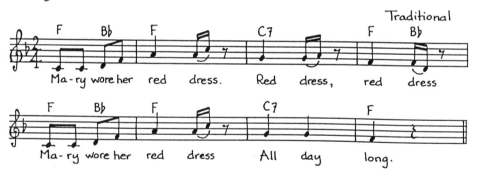

For a "Blue Day" use the same song, "Mary Wore Her Red Dress," this time substituting the phrase "Jason wore a blue suit."

For a "Green Day," sing the "Green Hat" song:

## Green Hat*

*A rainbow puppet.*

**Rainbow day.** Once the children recognize several colors, have a "Rainbow Day." Rainbows have strong appeal. You can create them with prisms or by spraying water in the sunshine. Have the children examine the bright colors comprising the rainbow.

**Rainbow puppet.** Cut some paper plates (unwaxed) into thirds, and glue or tape the pieces to tongue depressors or craft sticks. Then draw or paint a face on the plate. Children can create their own puppets by gluing strips of ribbon or construction paper in rainbow colors to the curved edge of the plate. When the puppets are finished, have a dance to the "Wish upon a Rainbow" song as the sun comes from behind a cloud or as you dim and then brighten the room lights.

Wish upon a Rainbow

See the rain-bow in the sky, Look at it way up so high.
Such pretty co-lours I can see I'll make a wish for you and me.
I see orange and pink and yel-low Blue and green and vi-o-let too.
I love to see a pret-ty rain-bow Now make a wish for me and you!

*© 1990 by Jimani Publications.*

**Rainbow drawings.** Put a rubber band around a manageable number of crayons or colored pencils. Have the children try using the cluster of crayons or pencils to make "rainbow drawings."

*A handful of pencils creates a rainbow.*

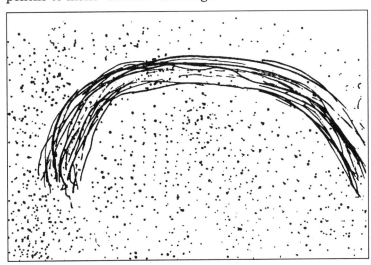

**Bubble colors.** Blow bubbles toward a light, naming the colors that can be seen. Add food coloring to the bubble mixture and catch the bubbles on a piece of white paper; as the bubbles burst, they'll leave a colored residue.

**Kaleidoscopes.** Have the children name the colors they see when they look through a kaleidoscope. Paint a kaleidoscope image.

**Colorful coolers.** Make sugar-free drinks from powdered drink mixes in several colors (flavors). Let children combine the liquids to make their own drink, in their own color. Make gelatin snacks the same way.

**Colored ice melts.** These are easy to make and they intrigue children. Fill small plastic containers or ice-cube trays with water and add food coloring. The next day, look at the patterns the coloring has made in the ice (it may freeze evenly or coagulate in pockets).

Empty the colored ice into a container of water. (The dark ice will make the water murky, so add darker-colored ice at the end.) Watch how the ice melts and gives off layers of color. Feel and watch the shape of the melting ice and talk about what is happening. Children will enjoy touching and pushing the ice around, and seeing whether it sinks.

**Variation:** For a completely different visual effect, let colored ice cubes melt on a dish of cornstarch.

## UNIT 3 — Shape, Texture, and Visual Form Discrimination

Too often, children with disabilities feel controlled by objects. Play with shapes, textures, and sculpture can provide a pleasant reversal: an opportunity for them to control events and materials in their environment. Present children with play material and encourage them to delve into it, letting them discover independently as much as possible. Be ready with words of encouragement when motivation wanes or frustration threatens to overwhelm them. Initially, let children manipulate materials directly, without the complication and distraction of tools. This direct work allows a better tactile sense of the material.

*The delight of discovering clay!*

### EXPLORATIONS

**Free forms.** Potter's clay, modeling clay, moist sand, snow, plaster, and papier-mâché immediately attract most children. Let them follow their own ideas: making balls, rolling "worms," shaping "things." Don't press for realism in the children's creations. Instead, encourage them to transform the material as their imagination suggests.

**Everyday fun.** Children's natural love for playing with objects can lead to all sorts of fun. Provide the children with a selection of objects, and observe and encourage their manipulations: stacking, sorting, nesting, gathering, sweeping, spinning, burying, tidying, piling, scattering, tipping, and arranging in lines, circles, or other patterns. Free-flowing materials can encourage packing, dumping, holding, filling, emptying, and so on.

These everyday activities exercise a wide range of manual, cognitive, and perceptual abilities, and there is no dividing line between these activities and what we call sculptural play in the expressive arts. The associated vocabulary is also useful both in sculptural play and in daily functioning.

**Making just about anything.** Potter's clay, modeling clay, and modeling paste compounds (for example, Plasticine® modeling paste) are excellent sculptural play media. They can be used alone or with blocks, animals, and many other toys. Sticks, straws, containers, lids, tubes, or wooden dowels can also add to modeling fun. Before beginning, children should know whether their creations will be preserved.

**Making an impression.** Help the children find some textured surfaces or objects. Have them press a ball of modeling clay or modeling paste (the latter is more impressionable when warm) on the textured surface, thus making an impression on the modeling material. After collecting a number of impressions, ask the children whether they can tell which object made each impression.

*Collage making allows children to make choices of color, size, and placement of shapes on the page.*

**Match game.** Assemble various textured materials, with two samples of each texture (but not necessarily the identical objects). Mix the materials up, then have the children pair them up by texture.

**Collages.** Explain that a *collage* is a design made by putting together different things. Provide a wide variety of materials, such as fabric scraps, pipe cleaners, beads, bottle caps, feathers, eggshells, and seeds. Have the children select objects and glue them onto cardboard or heavy paper.

**Can you find the ball?** Put a variety of solid geometric forms—such as balls, square blocks, cones, and tubes—in a bag or box. Show the children an example of the shape you want them to find, then have a child reach into the bag or box to find it by feel.

**Mobiles.** To construct a mobile, begin with wire that is easy to bend and holds its shape. (Telephone wire is plastic-coated and is relatively easy to obtain.) To prevent scratches, put masking tape over the wire ends. Each child takes a piece of wire and decorates it with beads. Pieces of paper with holes punched in them also are easy to slide on, and create a pretty effect. The wire can be bent various ways and other segments added. Hang the mobiles from the ceiling, where they will twist with the passing breeze.

**Weaving.** Children who have good manual dexterity may be intrigued by weaving different colored shoelaces through a plastic basket of the sort strawberries are sold in.

**Loom Weaving.** Lean a loom against the wall or put it on the floor. (A large, sturdy picture frame makes a good loom.) Wrap a continuous length of string or wool closely spaced about 20 times vertically around the loom. Have children take turns weaving paper strips, pipe cleaners, ribbons, or twigs in and out of the string to form the weft.

**Plaster of Paris fun.** Mix plaster of Paris with warm water. (Make sure no plaster goes down the drain.) Let the children manipulate the creamy texture on tables covered with plastic. When the plaster begins to thicken, you can add tempera powders to give the mix a pleasing pastel color. Put the plaster in a small plastic bag and seal with tape or wire. Have children press the bag against an object or form, such as a rock or the face of a big doll. When the plaster has hardened, remove it from the bag. The children will have made a free-form sculpture.

**Casting call.** Children who are physically challenged often have to spend time in orthopedic casts. Children can become less fearful of the casting procedure if they first make casts of their toys (doll faces, arms, or legs) or their own body parts in a creative context.

The plaster-impregnated cloth used to make orthopedic casts is easy to handle. The cloth makes a shell when strips are dipped in warm water and laid on a contoured surface. Three layers of strips should provide sufficient strength. The plaster hardens almost as quickly as it can be applied. It will come off in one piece if it does not curve around the back of the object being cast. Casts may be decorated with markers or paints, although prolonged exposure to the moisture in glues or paints will soften the plaster.

**Magic balloon.** Wrap glue-soaked yarn or string around a balloon. When the glue dries, pop the balloon.

**Variation:** Make a creature out of twisted balloons. Cover the balloons with strips of newspaper dipped in papier-mâché, leaving an opening near the top. When the papier-mâché has hardened, allow the children to decorate by gluing on scraps of tissue paper and other materials to create a homemade piñata. Pop the balloons and fill the interior with candies or other treats. Hang the piñata from the ceiling and allow the children to swing at it with a walking stick or light baseball bat. When the piñata breaks, a mad scramble for the contents ensues. To make breaking the piñata more challenging, drape a long rope over a hook in the ceiling, with one end attached to the piñata. By pulling on the other end of the rope, you can raise and lower the piñata as the children swing. The children may also be blindfolded.

**THEME FOUR**

# With Our Mouths

## GOALS

- To explore a wide range of expression through vocalization and verbalization
- To experiment with making sounds using one's mouth and breath
- To reinforce language development and communication skills

**UNIT 1**

## Mouth Sounds

From birth, babies use their voices to cry, to babble, and to gradually form word approximations such as "mama" and "dada." It is not until they enter their second year, however, that children begin to speak words with any definite intention. By imitation, trial and error, and with encouragement from significant persons around them, children begin to make themselves understood.

Imitation and experimentation are critical exercises in children's constant efforts to learn to communicate. Trying to imitate a sound produced by an instrument or voice helps children explore what their mouths can do—both in terms of speech sounds and in terms of other vocal sounds they can use to express themselves. As with any area, experimentation encourages children to learn and expand their vocal capabilities.

As always, feedback and participation are invaluable, especially because the ultimate goal is to communicate *with* others. Mirror and imitation activities are included here to encourage the simple game that is the beginning of communication: "I imitate you, you imitate me."

### EXPLORATIONS

**Mouth talk.** Show the children several unrelated pictures including one of a mouth. Have them each touch the mouth picture. Ask what we do with our mouths. Have the children experiment with mouth sounds and movements—kissing, smacking lips, blowing, smiling, making sounds such as "shh," "tsk, tsk," "hiss." Use a mirror to help the children see how their mouth moves.

**Lipsticky.** Put lipstick on the children and have them make mouth print pictures on paper. Children adore this.

**Chew, chew.** At snack time suggest the children experiment with chewing quickly, then slowly. Try different foods and drinks and talk about how they feel in the mouth. (Soft? Hard? Mushy? Crunchy?) **Note:** If some children have feeding difficulties, be sure to consult with a speech-language pathologist or occupational therapist regarding which food textures and chewing movements are safe for specific children.

**What sounds can you make?** Invite the children to experiment with their voices (humming, whispering, puffing, coughing, grunting, squealing). Have them try to imitate sounds (birds, animals, the wind, ghosts, fire engines, clocks, popcorn popping, bacon sizzling).

**Voice play.** Have children sing a steady "ee" sound to a tune consisting of three to five musical notes played on chimes or a piano. Then try "oo," "ah," and "oh" sounds. Other possible sounds to put to music:

- tra-la-la
- boo-hoo-hoo
- ding-a-ling-a-ling-a-ling
- na-na-na-na-na
- ticky-tocky, ticky-tocky
- choo-choo, choo-choo

**Chant, chant.** Try chanting familiar and fun names and phrases:

- Names of children in the class (Mary Ann, Peter, Leah)
- Actions (knock, knock)
- Descriptive sounds (pitter-patter; ding-dong; crash, bang; slurp-slurp)
- Greetings and farewells (yoo hoo; how do you do; see you later, alligator; see you soon, baboon)
- Things to eat (hot dogs; meat and potatoes; popcorn and peanuts; soup, soup, we love soup!)

**Variation:** Combining clapping and chanting in a rhythmic pattern challenges the child to concentrate on two things simultaneously. This can be made more complex as the children gain proficiency.

**How do you sound when you're happy?** Have the children explore the kinds of sounds they make when they are crying, happy, angry, sleepy, eating. Suggest they try being voices for dolls and toys.

**Scat singing.** Play a simple melody or chords and have the children sing nonsense words that you make up together. For example:

- Oogemi-oogemi-woogemi-woo
- Scoobi-doobi-doobi-doo
- Tinky-tinky-slinky-poo
- Higgledy-piggledy-figgledy-boom

---

**UNIT 2**

# Blowing

To produce voice, a steady stream of outgoing air from the lungs must be coordinated with the movements of the voice box and mouth. Many children whose breathing and speech musculature have not developed normally will have difficulty with these essential ingredients of speech. They need encouragement to learn to control the outgoing air and to make sounds.

A word of caution should be given about the activities in this unit. Although many of them are time-honored practices, there is mounting research evidence that practicing nonspeech activities, such as blowing, does not improve children's speech very much. Children can have a lot of fun with the following blowing activities, but you may not see a direct improvement in their speech unless you have them make sounds or words at the same time.

Being relaxed and properly positioned are both critical to controlling outgoing air. Music can help relax children and may be especially helpful to children with cerebral palsy, who often become more tense and have more trouble with coordination when making an effort.

A piano or Suzuki Omnichord® electronic musical instrument (a harp-like touch-sensitive instrument; see Appendix A) can be useful for the blowing activities that follow. Each time a child blows, the act can be accentuated by a piano glissando (rapid slide up or down the keys) or a strum on the Suzuki Omnichord®.

## EXPLORATIONS

**Flutter play.** Hold up a silk square and have the children try to make it move by blowing on it.

**Feathers.** Lightly hold a peacock feather so it will wave as a child blows on it.

**Magic candle.** Light a magic candle (relights by itself). Have children blow it out each time it relights. To add a sound component, have the children pretend they are ghosts in a haunted mansion. Have them make spooky, scary sounds as they make the candle flicker.

**Cotton balls.** Put a "snowball" (cotton ball) on your hand and have the children blow it off. They can use their voices to imitate the sound of wind blowing.

**Tiny table tennis.** Put a table-tennis ball on a small tray and position the child across the tray from you. Play "table tennis" with the child by blowing the ball back and forth. The child who is adept at this can play this game across a table or try to blow the ball through a simple maze on the tabletop.

**Dandelion puff, puff.** Children love to blow on dandelion puffs and watch the seeds float into the air.

**Bubble up.** Have children blow bubbles with straws in soapy water. Add food coloring and see whether it colors the bubbles. (**Note:** Many children naturally tend to suck on straws, so be sure they do not swallow the soapy water.)

**"The Three Little Pigs."** This familiar story provides many excellent opportunities to blow. Draw the straw house on a big paper napkin or towel. Hold it up in front of a child, who "huffs and puffs" it down as you play loud sounds. Do the same for the house of sticks. Build the brick house out of blocks so it can't be blown down. Have the children pretend to be the wolf and roar in a loud voice. "Huff and puff" before blowing the house down.

**Wind bag.** Have a "Wind Day," during which you make a "wind bag" holding all the wind instruments you can find (such as reed horns, kazoos, melodicas, slide whistles, harmonicas, recorders, bird-call whistles, and wind chimes made of metal, wood, plastic, or pottery). Take the instruments out one by one and let the children experiment with them. The children will delight in blowing on the instruments and discovering the various sounds.

For a special touch on "Wind Day," create a "wind environment." Put a child's tent up in the room or drape sheets over chairs to make a "cave." Hang several wind chimes where the children can play them by touch as well as by blowing. This all takes time, but enhances the activity.

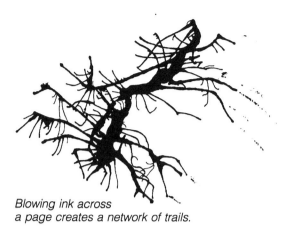

*Blowing ink across
a page creates a network of trails.*

**Jet bubbles.** Use an eyedropper to drop colored nontoxic paint (thinned with water) on a relatively nonabsorbent (shiny, coated) paper. The children then blow through straws to "chase" the bubbles across the page and mix them together (leaving thin spidery trails).

UNIT 3 # Language Development

Language—whether spoken, signed, pointed to on a symbol board, or synthesized—is a vital tool if children are to achieve their fullest potential. Children naturally learn prelanguage skills, such as vocalization, attention, concentration, listening, and following directions, through expressive activities. Together, these skills form the foundation for learning conventional methods of communication.

Seeing, feeling, hearing, thinking, moving, and, eventually, speaking are closely interwoven in early childhood. As children are exposed to various modes of expression, they begin to acquire vocabulary to help them explore and explain what they see, feel, hear, think, and do. We enrich all of these activities by emphasizing any one of them.

Fluency of speech comes from regular verbal stimulation, plus numerous opportunities and experiences. The arts foster language learning because they sustain and strengthen imagination. Imagination is the salt and pepper on the meat-and-potato events of children's daily lives, adding enjoyment and realism to experiences with language.

## EXPLORATIONS

**Can you say it this way?** Encourage children to say words expressively. For example, have them try to say "hello," "goodbye," "ouch" or "baboon":

- Quickly, or slowly

- Sadly, softly, loudly, or in a funny way

- As though they have peanut butter in their mouths

- As though they have a tummyache

**Variation:** Have the children sing a simple song, such as "Twinkle, Twinkle, Little Star," in the ways listed above.

**What happens if . . .** Soliciting predictions encourages verbal expression and logical thinking. Try these three steps:

- Ask what would happen in a given situation. ("What happens if I drop this cork into this bowl of water?")

- Demonstrate the situation. (Drop the cork into the water.)
- Have the children tell you what happened. ("The cork gets wet/floats/ stays on top.")

Other possibilities:

- Drop a stone in water.
- Put red coloring in a bowl of water.
- Drop salt in a bowl.
- Put a snowball in the sun.
- Put a snowball in a freezer.

**Giving instructions.** To develop skills in giving precise instructions, gather a jar of peanut butter, a jar of jelly, a knife, fork, spoon, and a loaf of bread. Tell the children you're going to make a peanut butter and jelly sandwich, and they must help by telling you what to do. Then, do exactly as they say. If they say, "Put the peanut butter on the bread," put the jar of peanut butter on the loaf of bread. The children will giggle, but their directions will soon become more precise. Chanting or singing all of this reinforces the importance of clear expression.

**Tell me about your present.** Have each child mime opening a special secret present. Then everyone tries to guess what the present is, asking questions about its size, color, the noises it makes, and so forth. When the group finds out what the present is, a simple song, chant, or poem can be made up about it. For example:

Johnny wants a jack-in-the-box,
So he can watch it pop.
He'll wind it up, then close the lid.
And then he will say, "Pop!"

**Whose voice is that?** Children love to hear recordings of their own voices. An adult can "interview" the children about their pets, things they like to eat, favorite colors, or things they like to do, guiding and drawing out children who may be hesitant. Children will have great fun listening to themselves afterwards.

**Can you sound like a balloon?** Blow up balloons one at a time, then let them go (without tying the opening). They make funny noises and wild turns as the air escapes. Have the children make sounds or use words that evoke the balloon losing air.

**Variation:** Play appropriate music and have the children do a "balloon dance," pretending to be balloons being blown up. Change the music to something that suggests deflation and have the children pretend they are balloons losing air, with all the accompanying sounds.

**What do you say when . . . ?** To help children become aware of the social graces, frequently ask them questions such as:

- "What do you say to someone who just came into the room?"
- "What do you say when you leave to go home?"
- "What do you say when someone gives you a toy?"
- "What do you say when you want something from someone?"

Some children speak languages other than English (or use sign language); take time to learn how they say these social phrases in their language. Children can try saying "hello," "good-bye," and "thank you" in these other languages.

**Musical plays.** Music can be a catalyst to children answering questions about what they do and like. A musical play—acting out and talking about daily activities, all to music—is especially helpful for younger children with communication difficulties.

*Music is a great context for encouraging communication.*

For example, to improvised music, have the children pretend they are getting up in the morning, stretching, yawning, washing, and getting dressed for school. They can then proceed to breakfast, telling what they like to eat. Talk about putting sugar and milk on cereal, eating eggs, making toast, all to improvised music.

Then the children can become bus drivers headed for nursery school. Children like to pretend to drive: they can mime taking the key out of their pockets, putting the key in the ignition, turning it, pressing their foot on the gas pedal, and driving away!

"Red light, green light" can be played during the "drive." Have ready round circles of red and green paper glued to sticks. Explain that the red light means the buses and the music must stop, and the green light means for both to "go." Have the children take turns being the police officer who changes the lights. Children who are practicing their speech can say "stop" and "go" as they hold up the lights.

When the buses reach school, the children become students and pretend to go into their classroom. (Children usually switch from one role to another easily.) They can talk about getting their coats off and put away, and mime the various activities they do in school.

This scenario is just one example; many of the simple daily routines in children's lives can be explored in a similar manner. You can also do any of this without music, although music is a great inspiration and enhancement. The essential thing is to allow each child an opportunity to express his or her thoughts and experiences.

**A friendly ghost.** Make a picture of a friendly looking ghost. Tell the children that the ghost likes to scare people away by saying "Boo," but gets upset because the ghost has no friends. Tell the children, "The ghost wants to know if you like to scare people away."

Have a discussion with the children about the ghost's characteristics:

- Is the ghost a boy or a girl?
- What is the ghost's name?
- How is the ghost dressed?
- How does the ghost scare people?
- What does the ghost want to know?
- What would you say if you met the ghost today?

**Telephone talk.** Have conversations with the children on toy telephones, helping them learn appropriate greetings. Keep conversations to familiar topics about family, school events, holidays, and pets. Frequent repetition of such activities gradually helps the child's fluency of speech.

**What's that we see?** Playing with a flashlight brightens dull moments on a rainy day and can also sharpen a child's memory and vocabulary. Demonstrate how a flashlight is switched on and off. When the children feel comfortable, tell them you are going to close the curtains and turn off the lights so they can see the flashlight shining on different objects in the room. Have the children take turns naming the objects lit up by the flashlight. (This activity can be made more challenging by lighting only part of an object.)

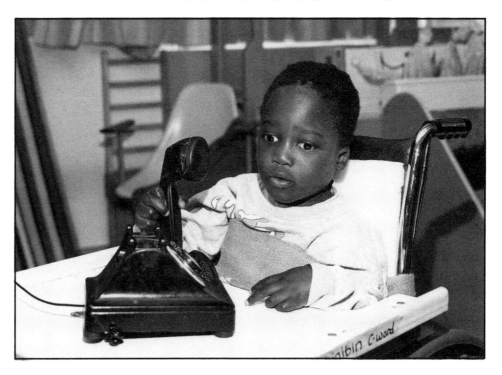

*I'm gonna call Mom.*

**Variation:** Reverse the procedure to challenge a child's visual memory. Have the children look around the room before the lights are turned off. Have one of the children shine the flashlight on an object you name. Begin with big pieces of furniture, going to smaller items as the exercise progresses.

**Tell a story.** Make up five cards with clear, sequential pictures (for example, a garden story with simple illustrations of a person planting, hoeing, watering, harvesting, and eating vegetables). Begin the story by describing the first two pictures, then hold the other cards up one at a time and have the children describe what is happening. Afterwards, mix up the cards; have the children rearrange them in sequence and tell a story, using the cards as prompts.

## UNIT 4   Songs

Songs can be an integral part of a child's world and a primary vehicle for a child's communication. Child development specialists are now beginning to recognize just how important music is in a child's life. Children have their own "child culture" in which songs and music games are an important aspect of communication and contact with others. This culture begins in infancy, when lullabies are a sign to children that they are safe and bound for sleep. Young children's early experience with songs sung by loving parents intensifies and stabilizes their emotional connection to the parents, even when children seek independence.

Older babies discover the delight of creating their own songs from babbled sounds. Later, young children may try out a short phrase, singing it over and over while playing and making it a sort of signature song. The song may be rambling and lack traditional musical organization, but it focuses on the meaningful things in children's lives. It's also fun: children sing because they enjoy it. Adults can acknowledge children's signature songs by singing along, thus showing the song is worthwhile.

### Choosing Songs

Selecting songs for preschoolers is especially important because speech and song are so closely related. A child whose disability affects sight, hearing, coordination of speech musculature, or opportunities to explore may be slow in learning to communicate. Therefore, every effort must be made to select songs that stimulate and reinforce efforts to produce speech.

Folk songs are particularly suited to young children because they are very simple, usually focus on a single theme, and have a narrow vocal range. They also have a predictable musical structure, which makes children feel comfortable.

Many children with disabilities sing with very low voices, so it's best to start with songs in a three- to five-note range around middle C. Movement and word repetition are assets. To engage children's interest, words should be simple and the ideas expressed understandable and relevant.

## Introducing a Song

It's important to grab children's interest when you introduce a song:

- First, sing or play the song at its normal speed. Let the children feel the rhythm with their bodies, moving freely.

- Next, have them sing "la" to the melody.

- Finally, say or sing the words slowly, enunciating carefully before having the children repeat them.

Make sure you don't lose eye contact: the children should focus on you as you sing and give instructions. Children will mirror your expressions, so use your face and gestures freely.

Don't labor with rote drill to learn the lyrics. The words will sink in as the song is repeated. What is important is that the child feels comfortable singing in an uncritical atmosphere.

## Songs Children Like

Songs become meaningful when based on things familiar to children, and if the children can contribute ideas to the lyrics. The songs we suggest here are short, have easy lyrics and musical phrasing, and reflect children's experiences. Each has been found effective, encouraging fun and imaginative thinking.

**Note:** An asterisk (*) marks songs especially suitable for younger children or children whose language is delayed.

## EXPLORATIONS

**Greeting and goodbye songs.** These songs lend structure to a lesson. Children should be encouraged to greet people in appropriate ways. Some children may not be able to speak, but they may be able to wave, smile, or nod. For them, making and maintaining eye contact is not only a social grace, but may also be essential to communication and interaction.

Greeting Song

Hel-lo. Hel-lo, and how are you to-day? Hel-lo, Hel-lo and what do you have to say? Can you wave your hand to say that you're feeling fine to-day? Can you smile and shake my hand? Will you be my friend?

## Hey, Do You Have Something To Say?

Anne Bindernagel

Hey, do you have some-thing to say? Some-thing that you want to share to-day? Hey, do you have some-thing to say? Some-thing you want to share to-day?

"Somebody's Knocking At Your Door" is a delightful traditional spiritual that lends itself very well to learning greetings, particularly with children who have little or no speech. Choose a child who, with an adult, leaves the room and knocks on the door at the appropriate time in the song. When the song is finished, have the group say, "Come on in" any way they can. The child comes into the room and shakes hands with everyone, saying or gesturing, "Hello" and "How are you?" The other children may answer, "Fine" or "It's good to see you." Children will play this game for a long time with enthusiasm and concentration.

## Somebody's Knocking At Your Door

Old Spiritual

Somebody's Knocking at your door. Somebody's knocking at your door. Oh, (Child's name) sit there and list-en Somebody's knocking at your door.

## Goodbye Song

Good - bye. I'll see you a-gain. Wave good-bye. I'll see you a-gain, good-bye, good-bye, good-bye, good-bye. I'll see you soon a-gain, a-gain. I'll see you soon a-gain. Good-bye Kev-in. Good-bye A - my. Good-bye A-man-da. Good-bye Paul. Good-bye Heath-er. Good-bye Jes-se. Good-bye Ma-ry. Good-bye to all.

**Lullabies.** Many young children do not go to bed willingly; there are too many interesting things to do, and lying in bed can be a lonely and sometimes frightening experience. A lullaby can be a soothing ending to the day, and children often sing them to their dolls and toy animals. Teaching lullabies to children may diffuse some of their anxieties about bedtime.

## Lullaby

Go to sleep my lit-tle one lit-tle one, As I sing to you.

Go to sleep my lit-tle one lit-tle one, sleep the whole night through.

**Songs that reflect feelings.** Songs about feelings can help children recognize their emotions and learn that their moods are part of being alive and that it's acceptable, even good, to express feelings. As just one example, we sang the "Sad Song" with 5-year-old David, who was homesick. Putting his loneliness into words helped him talk about missing his family.

A simple song can help children become aware of the little things in life that make them happy, be it going to the zoo, visiting someone, or shopping with the family.

The next song gives children a chance to sing about wanting to show affection. It has been used with success by many young children in our center.

Truck

Jim Newton

Truck, truck, If I had a truck, Oh Truck, truck, If I had a truck, Oh If I had a truck, I'd fill it up with love and come a-long and dump on you. The big-gest truck in town, I'd put my arms a-round and May-be you would squeeze too. We al-ways need a friend so why do we pre-tend, Now come a-long and don't be shy. Love to love and hug to hug a friend, a friend so true. A friend to friend like you.

The children we work with asked for a song about Father's Day, and learned this one for the occasion. (Other people—mothers, sisters, teachers, and so on—can be substituted in this song.)

## Daddies Are Special

\* substitute: Mommies, Sisters, Brothers, Friends, Teacher etc.

**Songs about the world around us.** Kids love to correct things—it demonstrates their knowledge about the world. Combine this with nonsense verse, and you have a surefire hit! (Again, you can use other people in the song.)

## Cleanin' the House

2. Today my Papa's cleanin' the house,
   Cleanin' for a lion,
   Cleanin' for a mouse,
   Cleanin' for a turtle,
   Cleanin' for a cat,
   "And that," says my Papa, "is that."
   Does he iron the fridge? "No."
   Does he wash the dishes? "Yes."
   Does he polish the bed? "No."
   Does he vacuum the rug? "Yes."

3. Today my kid is cleanin' the house . . .

A song to help very young children learn about animals can be coupled with identifying animals using pictures, miniatures, or toys.

### Farm Song*

One day I went to the farm. And I saw an an-i-mal there. And the an-i-mal said moo moo moo. Now what do you think it was?
(Answer is spoken)

© 1988 by Jimani Publications.

2. One day I went to the farm,
   And I saw an animal there,
   And the animal said, "Oink, oink, oink."
   Now what do you think it was?

**Songs that work out problems.** This folk tune may help dispel fears of the barber's scissors.

### Johnny Get Your Hair Cut*

Traditional

John-ny get your hair cut, hair cut hair cut.

John-ny get your hair cut, just like this.

**Variations**

- Have children sing the song as you pretend to cut a wig on a foam plastic form with a face painted on it.

- Have each child pretend to cut the wig. Have children (and you!) take turns pretending to give each other haircuts.

- Explain that scissors work by opening and closing. Ask the children what parts of their bodies they can open and close. As each child discovers a body part to open and close, have the group imitate this movement while playing or humming the song. Similarly, have children do open-and-shut movements to an umbrella opening and closing.

**Songs that involve movement.** Motions suggested by the words of a song help children become aware of their bodies and the capabilities of each part. This song combines music, movement, and language marvelously.

*Shake My Sillies Out* *

Music by Raffi
Words by Bert & Bonnie Simpson

Got-ta shake, shake, shake my sil-lies out. Shake, shake, shake my sil-lies out. Shake, shake, shake my sil-lies out. And wig-gle my wag-gles a-way.

© 1985 by Homeland Publishing from *The Second Raffi Songbook. Reprinted by permission.*

Children love to hear their own names in a song; it adds to their feelings of belonging. Don't be afraid to experiment with this song.

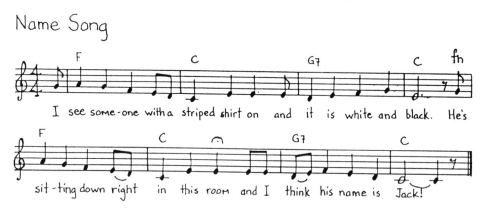

*Name Song*

I see some-one with a striped shirt on and it is white and black. He's sit-ting down right in this room and I think his name is Jack!

© 1988 by Jimani Publications.

2. Someone is wearing two pink shoes,
   And they are both the same,
   She's sitting down right in this room,
   And Alissia is her name.

3. I see someone with a great big smile,
   He's looking happy today,
   He's dressed in blue and his name is Lou,
   So let's all sing hoo-ray!

**Rhyming songs.** Rhyming involves many verbal communication skills. Some young children can make up simple rhymes; for those who can't, this becomes just a funny song.

## You Can't Love a Duck

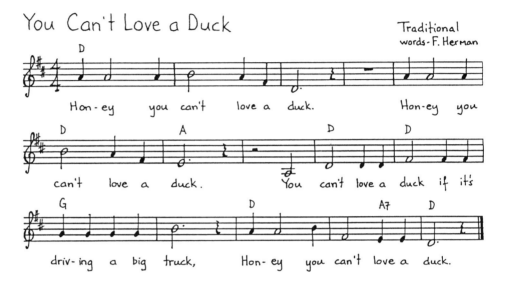

2. Can't love a *fox* if it's wearing purple *socks* . . .

3. Can't love a *cat* if it's wearing a *hat* . . .

4. Can't love a *dog* if it's sitting on a *frog* . . .

5. Can't love *Milly* cause she'll think you're pretty *silly*.

Don't be afraid of boring children by repeating songs many times. Young children love the familiar and never seem to tire of a delicious word, sound, or song. A sense of security and confidence comes with knowing a song and its movement patterns.

**Songs to play with.** These next four songs appeal to young children's desire to "be" and "do" everything.

## The Elephant Song

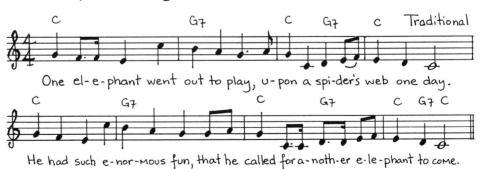

Make a huge spider web on an old sheet with a black marker, cutting out the shape of the web. Children can crawl or wheel onto the sheet when asked to play. You can also put a smaller web made from construction paper on a table, and have each child put a paper elephant on the web when called.

## Beat the Drum *

Rebecca Loveszy

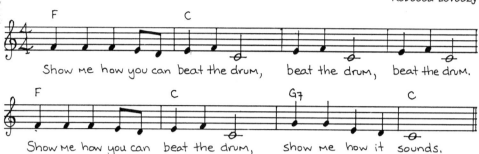

Show me how you can beat the drum, beat the drum, beat the drum.

Show me how you can beat the drum, show me how it sounds.

© 1990 by Jimani Publications.

Children around the circle take turns beating the drum any way they like. For children who are severely involved, you may have to hold a large flat drum close to them so they can drum.

## Sally go Round the Sun. *

Traditional

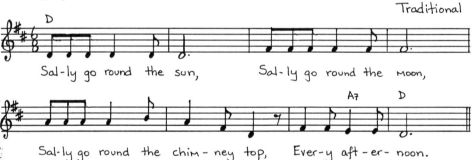

Sal-ly go round the sun, Sal-ly go round the moon,

Sal-ly go round the chim-ney top, Ever-y aft-er-noon.

Make a large card with three pictures on it: the sun, a moon, and a chimneytop with smoke coming out of it. For the very young child, pointing to each picture as it is mentioned encourages attention.

## Show Me the Sun *

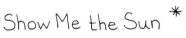

The sun is shin-ing in the sky Show me the sun show me the sun. The

sun is shin-ing way up high, Oh show me the sun to — day.

© 1990 by Jimani Publications.

Have the children look at pictures of circles and suns. Tell them they can make circles with their arms to depict the sun whenever the lyrics suggest it.

**Nonsense songs.** Children love silly songs or words, and will repeat them frequently. Such songs often spring out of an incident or an occasion; a very hot day inspired this next song.

WHEW! Song

It is so darn hot, (whew!) It is so darn hot (whew!) I'd like to be a po-lar bear a-

- sit-ting on some ice. I think that would be nice 'cause it's so darn hot! YEAH!

A discussion about foods we like and don't like produced these two songs.

Yummy Yum *

Yum-my Yum-my Yum Yum-my Yum-my Yum I love jel-ly and

pea-nut but-ter sand-wich-es. Yum-my Yum-my Yum Yummy Yummy Yum

That's what I want for my lunch.

When the children started naming food they didn't like to eat, one little boy said, "Bugs." The resulting song caused much giggling.

Yucky Song *

Oh I don't like to eat little bugs, to eat little bugs, to eat little bugs.

No one can make me eat little bugs 'cause they're yucky, yucky, yucky, yucky, yuk!

We made up this funny food song together after one boy painted a picture of his dinosaur, saying he was taking the dinosaur to lunch.

### Dinosaur Song

I took my di-no-saur out for lunch Be-cause we felt We wanted to munch

Munch munch here Munch munch there We munch on po-ta-to chips e-very where

Chorus:
Oh! po-ta-to chips Po-ta-to chips. How we love our po-ta-to chips

Munch munch crunch crunch, that's all I want for lunch. Yeh!

2. I took my elephant out for a walk,
   And on the way we had a long talk.
   Talk, talk here,
   Talk, talk there,
   We kept on talking everywhere.

Chorus:
   Oh, lots of peanuts, lots of peanuts,
   Oh, how we love lots of peanuts.
   Munch, munch,
   Crunch, crunch,
   Yeah! That's all we want for lunch.

3. I took my octopus out for a swim,
   He liked it so much, he started to grin.
   Two arms here, two arms there,
   He seemed to have two arms everywhere.

Chorus:
   Oh, herring fish, herring fish,
   Oh, how we love to eat herring fish.
   Slurp, slurp,
   Burp, burp,
   We love herrings with chocolate syrup!

Our last silly food song came about when an orange fell off the table onto the floor. This is what we imagined happened to it.

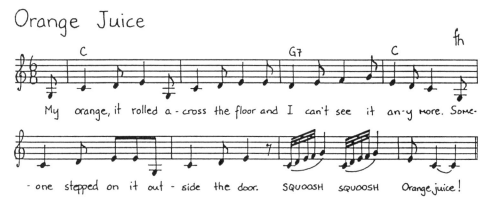

My orange, it rolled a-cross the floor and I can't see it an-y more. Some-one stepped on it out-side the door. SQUOOSH SQUOOSH Orange juice!

*Nonspeaking children enjoy sing-alongs, too.*

**THEME FIVE**

# With Our Feelings and Imagination

### GOALS

- To encourage fantasizing and improvisation through play, puppets, mime, movement, and stories
- To contribute to a sense of well-being through participation in play
- To promote a healthy self-concept and expression of feelings
- To increase the richness and appeal of stories
- To foster kinesthetic awareness of oneself in space and time

*Play is one way this child makes sense out of her world.*

**UNIT 1**  # Self-Concept and Feelings

*Self-concept* refers to an awareness of one's personal characteristics, to a sense of worth—or worthlessness. It is how we see ourselves and how we think others see us. It represents the feelings of "I'm good" or "I'm bad," "I can" or "I can't" that we all have within us.

Children learn self-concept from the people around them. This learning starts in infancy, when babies need "strokes"—being cuddled, rocked, talked to—as much as they need food, water, and protection. The quality and frequency of the strokes we give children are important. If children feel loved and wanted, they begin to know they are valued. As they grow and explore, each encounter and attempt to cope contributes to self-concept.

Children with disabilities may encounter many areas in which they cannot cope successfully due to lack of muscle strength, coordination, or other impairments. Their confidence can suffer, their learning falter, and their sense of self-worth plummet. These children need strong, positive responses to their every initiative, no matter how fragile. This support will encourage them to respond to challenges and foster their feeling of self-worth.

### EXPLORATIONS

**"Feelings" song.** It takes a lifetime to learn how to handle personal feelings. Some children do not recognize their feelings; they don't understand what feelings are, and they may have limited ability to communicate them. The following song points out that everyone has feelings, and that it is good to express them.

Feelings — Paulo

Chorus:
Feel-ings, feel-ings, tell me what you feel I will lis-ten 'cause I care. I'm your friend so will you share your feel-ings feel-ings. Tell me what you feel——.

Verse:
Are you hap-py or are you sad? Are you an-gry or are you glad? If you are, well, I want to know. It's im-por-tant to let your feel-ings show!

*How do you look when
you're happy?*

2. Are you bashful or are you shy?
   Are you hurt or do you want to cry?
   If you are, well, I want to know.
   It's important to let your feelings show.

**Note:** In the first verse, "show" can be substituted for "tell me" for children using alternative communication devices.

**Naming feelings.** The first step in dealing with feelings is knowing how to name them. When a child shows an emotion, take a moment to label the feeling. "Ramón, you look angry right now. Your face has a big frown on it. Maybe you'd feel better if you say that you're angry."

If words are not sufficient, it's a good idea to have an "angry corner" in the classroom, where the child can cool off, where he or she knows it's safe to be quiet or to shout or cry or kick or punch a pillow. When the child is calm, try to discover what caused the situation. Talk with the child, affirming that he or she is still okay with you. If possible, change the circumstances that may have triggered the upset.

You can also work on naming feelings in a music session. Have two drums side by side, the "angry drum" and the "happy drum." Have the children take turns beating the drums while verbalizing their likes and dislikes. At first children may copy each other, but this will disappear after a few sessions.

**Faces and feelings.** Discuss with the children what makes them happy, sad, afraid, angry, and frustrated. Draw simple faces to illustrate the feelings. Play music that the children can match to the pictures. Have the children use their faces and bodies to act out ways people express their emotions.

**Tell me about you.** Ask the children:

- What did you like best about today?

- What new thing did you learn today?

- What was the weather like today?

- What do you most want to do tomorrow?

**Baby memories.** Ask the children what they did when they were babies. Ask them what human and animal babies are like. Children love to imitate babies, and wonderful music sessions can be built around this interest. They enjoy kicking their feet, sucking their thumbs, crying, gurgling, cooing, and so forth. Much of the activity will depend on the cues the children give you. All of it can be done to music. At the end, sing:

Hug Your Baby*

Nancy Minden

Hug your BA-BY. Hug your BA-BY. Hug your BA-BY Now —

Hug your BA-BY. Hug your BA-BY. Hug your BA-BY Now —

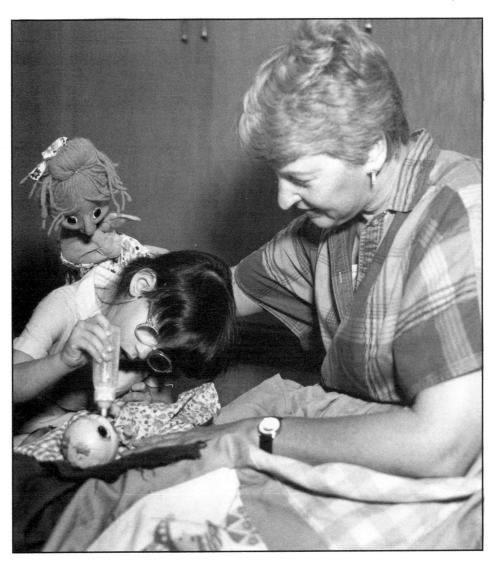

*Looking after Baby Suzy.*

**Variation:** Have the children sing "Hug Your Baby" while hugging and rocking a doll, stuffed animal, or pretend baby.

**What *I'd* like to do.** Have each child tell the group what he or she would like to do more than anything else. Then everyone tries to find ways to briefly act out or dramatize what has been described.

**Variation:** Have children say what they would like to be, such as what animal they would like to be and so forth.

**"Can do" box.** This kind of activity lets children reflect on some of their more positive points. Get a large card-file box. Make sure the alphabetic letters on the dividers are large, capital letters.

Say each child's name as you print it on the chalkboard. Have the child come and look in the box for the first letter of his or her name. Print the child's name on a card and ask the child to tell you one thing she or he "can do." (The child may say something like, "Paint a picture" or "Tie my shoe" or "Get out of my wheelchair without help.") Print on the card exactly what the child says. Put the card in the box for next time. Repeat this activity from time to time, reading the child's accomplishments before eliciting a new thing the child can do. The child will enjoy hearing the card read and gain confidence.

**What's special today?** Mesh activities as closely as possible with children's social awareness: select or adapt poems, stories, and songs to reflect seasonal changes, special holidays, and birthdays. Include art to enhance all of these projects.

**What did my neighbor do?** After drawing, painting, or sculpting activities in which the children produce individual (not group) creations, ask the children to look around at what their friends have done. Hold up the creations one piece at a time and have the group discuss them. This recognizes and affirms children's efforts while sensitizing children to variations in style and content.

**Who is this baby?** Have each child bring in one of their baby pictures, and suggest they not show it to anybody. Put all the baby pictures up on the wall and have the children guess who's who. This can provide a great deal of pleasure, and others in the school can also be brought in on the guessing game.

**Guess who.** Describe a child in the room by clues such as hair color, eye color, clothing, and abilities. Say or sing your clues until the children guess who the "secret star" is.

**You are *wanted*.** This game works well with very young children. Make "Wanted" and "Reward" posters for each child to post on the door to your room. You can make posters that will delight the children by enlarging their photographs on a copying machine and embellishing the resulting poster with mustaches, hats, and so forth. Write three or four lines on each poster about the child. The following posters were seen in one "crime-ridden" classroom:

**Wanted: Sandy**

For shaking hands,

Sitting up straight,

Eating cookies,

Being a good friend.


**Wanted: Kaitlin**

For smiling too much,

Laughing at jokes,

Listening to songs by Raffi,

Shaking her sillies out.


**Wanted: Jonathan**

For saying everyone's name,

Eating all his lunch,

Making his friends feel better,

For winking at the teacher.

**Caution: Dangerous**

**Reward! Reward! Reward!**

**Name book.** Suggest that each child make a "name book." Have the children put in their drawings and stories (dictated), as well as things they like or don't like, what they can do, and what they are learning to do.

**Just plain talking, and listening.** Conversations with children help them learn to talk about what is on their minds. Children become better communicators with practice. If they lack opportunities for expression or are criticized when they do talk, they become hesitant to speak.

Being a good listener promotes talking. Plan a daily "listening time"; children will soon look forward to these special moments. Dialogues should improve and grow as the children become more articulate and better able to form opinions about events in their lives.

This song can be used to initiate children's discussions about things they think about or do each day.

© 1986 by Nancy Minden. Reprinted by permission.

(Spoken)
What did you do today?
What's your favorite game to play?
Can you count to five today?


(Repeat song)


(Spoken)
What did you eat for lunch today?
Can you make your shoulders go hunch?
Can you make your knuckles go crunch?


(Repeat song)

## UNIT 2  Play and Dramatic Play

Play is the young child's improvisational drama. This drama is serious business—it is essential to children's sense of well-being, and it is an important means by which children learn about themselves and their world. It can also enhance listening and conversational skills, and add enjoyment to children's experiences with language.

Dramatic play can also serve a special function for children with disabilities. These children spend much of each day conforming to rules, be they "social rules" (time to eat; time to go to the bathroom) or "treatment rules" (put your foot down this way; sit in a good position; take your medication). "Let's pretend" games let these children make up their own rules and decide on words and actions that are meaningful to them.

A few simple props add to dramatic play. Old clothes, for example; young children love to dramatize situations while "dressing up" and can be very inventive with a few old clothes. An old scarf and pocketbook, combined with a child's imagination, can be the stuff of which kings, queens, moon monsters, and fairies are made. Try creating a play corner with a box of old hats, scarves, clothes, and sheer curtains to provide many opportunities for children to experiment. Large mirrors on a nearby wall let children appreciate their explorations with costumes, facial expressions, and body movements.

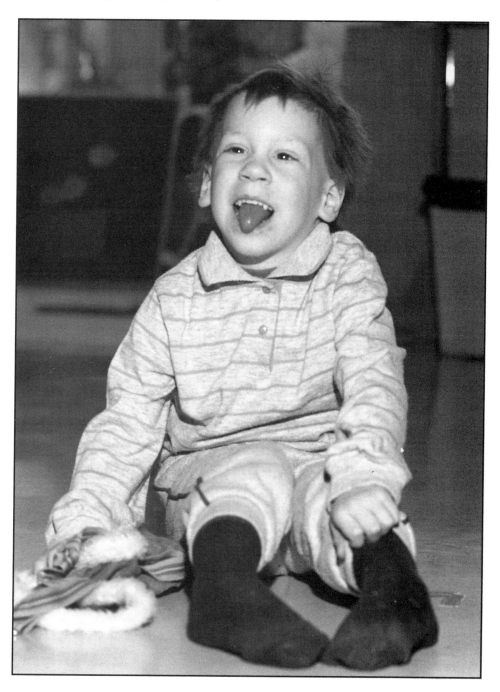

*Playtime is my favorite time of day!*

Make sure that young children are allowed to act out their experiences for themselves, and not just be involved in preparing shows for audiences. Growth of the children's feelings, thoughts, and social interactions should always be the focal point. Dramatic play that is free and spontaneous seems to let children explore a wide range of interpersonal contacts. Children do not need to be taught dramatic play; they need only to be allowed to experience it in a free and stimulating environment. In such unstructured situations, children can vent a wide range of fears, facts, fantasies, and ideas, thus preparing themselves to move on and explore new and exciting explorations.

## EXPLORATIONS

**Note:** This unit presents a few specific themes. Additional thematic material can be found in many of the explorations in Part III.

**Rainy-day dance.** Many young children are afraid of thunder, strong winds, and heavy rain. Acting out a storm by becoming thunder, wind, or rain in a Rainy-Day Dance can relieve some of their fears. Talk with the children about how thunder and lightning looks, sounds, and feels. Explain that lightening comes first, followed by claps of thunder. Then flicker the lights off and on and have the children make thunder sounds immediately afterwards on percussive instruments. They can also add voice sounds for the wind and finger drumming for rain.

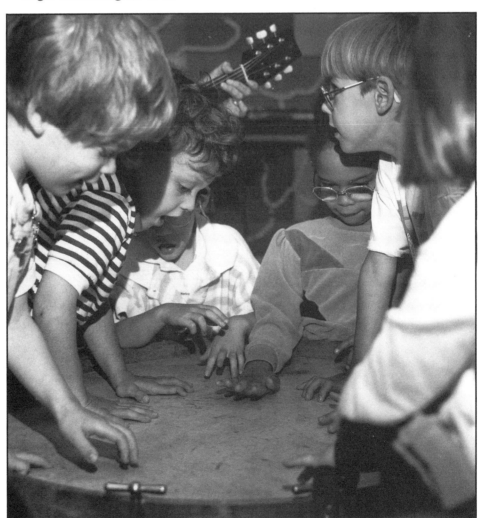

*Listen to the raindrops— made with many fingers on the drum.*

## Raindrops *

List-en to the rain drops. List-en to the rain drops Falling all a- round.

Listen to the rain drops Listen to the rain drops Falling to the ground.

### Variations

- Older youngsters might enjoy making a tape of storm sounds. They can experiment with blowing into the tape machine, crunching paper, cellophane, and garbage bags near the microphone, or rubbing the head of the microphone against corrugated cardboard. They can make sounds that are quite realistic and will be delighted with the possibilities.

- After the sound-making part of the Rainy Day Dance, divide the group in two. Have one group express in movement the elements they have been exploring, while the others provide the sound accompaniment. Then, reverse the groups.

- The next day, suggest that the children depict their ideas of some aspect of the Rainy Day Dance on paper using pastels, crayons, or paints.

**Fantasy shelter.** This activity stimulates role playing and dramatic scenarios that can evolve in response to the children's imagination. Look at and talk about pictures of shelters: a house, tent, tepee, igloo, castle, shack, and so on. Suggest that it might be fun to create a fantasy shelter, and that everyone can help.

You can provide materials appropriate for the project (such as cardboard, fabric, branches, plastic sheeting, string, and tape). The finished shelter can be decorated, perhaps by those who have not been able to actively participate in the "construction."

**What would you do if . . .** Have the children pretend they are taking a walk outside. As they walk along, they see a kitten with a hurt paw lying on the grass. Ask the children to show with their bodies, faces, and words what they would do with the kitten. Music can be used to enhance the play.

**Variation:** Ask what the children would do if they saw—

- A police officer riding a big horse

- A big fire in a house

- A baby crying in its carriage

- A beautiful butterfly sitting on a flower

- A hat flying in the wind

*The young child recreates and integrates many experiences through fantasy and dramatic play.*

**Clown time.** Talk about clowns, noting that some clowns do funny things to make people laugh, while other clowns look unhappy and walk in a slow, sad way. Ask the children to try to do funny things with their faces, hands, and bodies. Then ask them to become sad clowns with big handkerchiefs for crying into.

**Mime time.** Mime can tell a story. Even young children enjoy simple pretend situations if they are about familiar things. For children with little or no speech, mime provides a creative outlet. Have the children mime:

- Painting a picture

- Eating an ice-cream cone

- Swimming

- Bouncing a ball

- Throwing a snowball

- Washing face and hands, and brushing teeth

- Playing a drum or a piano or a guitar

- Picking apples off a tree

- Patting a puppy

**UNIT 3**  Story Play

As attention spans increase and children become more comfortable with their expressive abilities, a story becomes a creative group experience. At this stage, stories can be read or told to the group and then dramatized to music. This process can involve each child as an active participant who contributes to the story through voice, movement, or both. Dramatization both reinforces the young child's understanding of the experience depicted by the story and develops imagination and spontaneity.

Throughout the story, improvise music to:

- Heighten awareness and responsiveness

- Help the children visualize characters

- Act as a catalyst for miming

- Enhance auditory and language skills

- Reinforce the idea that reading and books are fun

When you choose stories to dramatize to music, match the story with specific goals for the session. For example, if you want to emphasize motor activities, choose a book like Gene Zion's *Harry the Dirty Dog* (Harper and Row 1956), which offers many opportunities for rolling, crawling, and standing tall. To emphasize verbalization, consider *The Little Red Hen,* which suggests many exercises growing out of its "I won't" and "I will" statements.

Many stories contain the repetitive segments that young children like because they enjoy echoing actions and sounds. Because storytelling to music is direct communication, you can adjust the storyline and the text to the child's experiences and language abilities. It is important to keep the story line simple and direct because we are dealing with a variety of auditory and visual responses, as well as with motor and language skills.

A good example is *Singing David* by Sekiya Miyoshi (Methuen, 1971), which is presented in the explorations. This story lets you emphasize emotional responses through gesture and voice. It also has very appealing childlike illustrations that enhance the story line and dramatic effect.

### EXPLORATIONS

**Singing David.**

*David lived in a country far away. One day, his father gave him a little lamb to look after. The lamb cried all the time.*

- Play "Baa, Baa, Black Sheep" in a major key, with the children singing just the word "Baa." Then repeat it in a minor key. Ask them whether it sounds the same or different.

- Next, try to sing the "Baa Song" as though you are crying.

*David thought his lamb was hungry so he took it where the sweet grass grew. But the lamb cried.*

- Repeat the "Baa Song."

*He thought his lamb might be thirsty, so he brought it to the water. But the lamb cried.*

- Repeat the "Baa Song."

*David was troubled; he didn't know what to do. Then a cloud in the sky with pretty colors whispered: "Sing, David, sing!"*

- The reader says, "Sing, David, sing," at first in a whisper, then louder and louder. Children repeat this.

*So David began to sing this song.*

- Children sing "La, la, la" to the tune of "David's Song."

## David's Song *

*Then the birds wanted to sing, too.*

- Ask, "What sound do you think the birds would make?" (Use whatever syllable the children make.) Children sing "David's Song" as they think the birds would.

*Next, the flowers wanted to sing.*

- Ask the children for the flowers' sound. Children sing "David's Song" as the flowers would.

*Later, the stars came out, and they also wanted to help.*

- Children sing "David's Song" as the stars would.

*Now everyone was singing. The lamb, hearing the wonderful singing, lifts its head, looks about, and smiles.*

- Children mime this and sing the "Baa Song" in a major key.

*Soon David's father gave him other lambs to look after. If one of them cries, David sings his song to them.*

- End by singing "David's Song" again.

***The Very Busy Spider.*** This Eric Carle book (Philomel Books, 1984) is an interesting story with lively illustrations about a spider spinning her web. She is visited throughout the day by animals who ask her whether she wants to ride, play, run, and so forth. She ignores them and continues spinning, catches a fly, and finally falls asleep after her hard work.

Young children enjoy making various animal sounds while singing the "Animal Song" and have fun spinning their hands to simulate the spider during the "Spinning Song."

## Animal Song

Baa, Baa, Said the sheep. Will you come and play with me?

Baa, Baa, Said the sheep but the spi-der went on spin-ning

2. "Woof, woof" said the dog,
"Will you chase a cat with me?"
"Woof, woof" said the dog,
But the spider went on spinning.

## Spinning Song

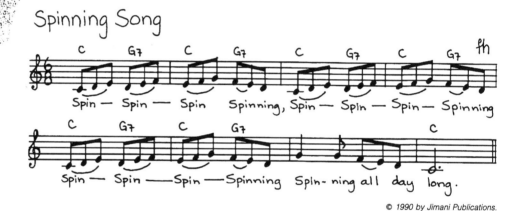

Spin — Spin — Spin Spinning, Spin — Spin — Spin — Spinning

Spin — Spin ——Spin —Spinning Spin-ning all day long.

**UNIT 4** | # Puppet Play

### GOALS

- To promote practice in communication skills
- To afford inarticulate children an alternative learning experience
- To enhance a positive self-concept
- To provide acceptable avenues for releasing emotions

Puppet play is a land of magic for children, a chance for make-believe and self-expression. It also helps children learn to communicate: as soon as children pick up a puppet, they want to make it talk and make sounds, to bring it to life. Children will experiment with puppets without inhibitions, using various pitches and character voices in giving their puppets voice. Language development naturally follows when the puppets—and thus the children—interact with others.

For children with disabilities, puppet play holds unlimited possibilities for both teaching and therapy. Puppet play can be adapted to each child's needs, taking into account individual strengths and limitations.

Today's children are increasingly exposed to puppets and their possibilities. They see puppets on television and in libraries, schools, and theaters, and some children have puppets at home. But puppets will never be predictable. Puppets become different things to everyone who uses them, and there is no end to the kinds of puppets that can be made and used—from finger puppets and handkerchief ghosts, to quirky creatures made from wooden spoons, cardboard tubing, old socks, and tongue depressors.

Encourage puppet play, without adults, by setting aside a corner where children can interact with puppets. Providing a variety of puppets here can create opportunities for children to engage in spontaneous dramatic play with one other. Remember that the children are participants, not performers, in this play: the creative process, not the product, is what's important.

## EXPLORATIONS

**Simple hand puppets.** Simple hand puppets are often the most enjoyable for very young children, especially if they are soft and cuddly. Children find it easier to get involved with these puppets because they are simple to use (and perhaps because the children have to make more use of their bodies than when holding a puppet on a stick). They are easy to make: take some old socks or mittens and have the children embellish them by gluing on facial features of animals, persons, or creatures.

**Fun on a stick.** For a younger child, cut out one of the child's drawings and have the child glue it to a tongue depressor or craft stick. (Tracing a hand makes an interesting drawing that the child can then turn into a puppet.)

**Spoon puppets.** Let the children paint a wooden spoon with white tempera. After it dries, the children can use markers to draw facial features on one or both sides of the spoon. Fabric, ribbons, tissue paper, or foil can be wrapped around the handle.

More adept children may draw different features on reverse sides of the spoon (a doll's face that is awake on one side and asleep on the other; a girl on one side and a boy the other; a monster and a fairy; and so on).

**The easiest puppet.** Here's the easiest puppet to make: Put a facial tissue or piece of cloth over the child's thumb or hand and secure it to the wrist or finger with a rubber band. With crayons or markers, draw eyes and a mouth.

**Fingertip puppets.** Children have puppets literally at their fingertips. Simply by adding color with markers, a finger can become a mouth, a goose, a rabbit, or a green crocodile.

Adding a face to a thumbnail delights many small children. "Talking thumbs" is another impromptu way to stimulate conversation between children.

**Storytelling.** Telling stories through puppets adds to the excitement of puppet play and is visually enriching. The puppets are not used as they are in a puppet show, but rather to enhance the story line.

In Richard Scarry's *I Am a Rabbit* (Golden Books, Western Press, 1963), a bunny puppet can portray the rabbit in the story. The children can get involved in the motions of picking and smelling flowers, trying to catch butterflies, and watching leaves fall to the ground. Similarly, a small blue train can

*A hand puppet made from a tissue or napkin.*

be used for Watty Piper's *The Little Engine That Could* (Platt and Munk Publishers, 1961). You can have the train puppet slowly chug its way up one side of a big pillow as the children provide a chorus of "I think I can, I think I can. . . ." Most children's stories can be enriched by using a puppet, creating a three-dimensional sensory experience incorporating visual and auditory elements with action.

When you use puppets, keep these tips in mind:

- Have the puppet appear to speak directly to the children. The adult will indeed be speaking, but the children will watch the puppet as though it is relating to them.

- Keep the action and voice lively enough to hold the children's interest. Move the puppet horizontally as well as up and down, and make sure your voice is as expressive and varied as possible.

- Make an appealing "signature puppet." (A signature puppet is one that is used frequently for transitions and classroom management, for example to greet children, tell them to clean up, announce events, and so on.) Give this puppet a personality quirk to which the children can relate. Perhaps the puppet sings wildly off-key, says "Hello, hello" in a funny voice, or falls asleep in the middle of a sentence. It might trip and fall flat on its nose, or sneeze a lot and need a huge handkerchief. Whatever characteristic you devise will pay off with the children looking on the puppet as an endearing friend.

*A foam wiggle worm.*

**"Wiggle worm" puppets.** These small puppets made from wire and foam can help younger children see how measurements are made. A four- to six-inch puppet can be easily made by gluing a piece of wire to each end of a narrow piece of foam. Painted and decorated with eyes (glued or marked on), it becomes a "wiggle worm." As you measure a child's arm or leg by putting the two wires together, then apart (like an inchworm), you can say, "Here we go up the leg, one wiggle worm, two wiggle worms, three wiggle worms, four. Goodness gracious, your leg is four wiggle worms long." Soon children will want to use the wiggle worm to measure each other.

*A puppet apron.*

**Puppet aprons.** A puppet apron—a sort of mobile home for puppets—is easy to make. Cut an old brightly colored skirt down the back. Attach ties to go around the waist. Sew on pockets of various shapes, sizes, and fabrics, and you have an intriguing prop in which to hide puppets when not in use. The children will sit with great anticipation as one child puts a hand in a pocket to find out which puppet is hiding there. The child can then have a talk with the puppet until it's the next child's turn.

**Talking through puppets.** Children will often speak through or to a puppet when unable to speak as themselves. An upset child, for example, may "talk out" concerns to an empathetic puppet.

It is essential that the puppet directly face and talk with the child, while the adult working the puppet sits back and is as unobtrusive as possible, thus eliminating communication barriers. The child will ignore the adult and focus on the puppet, often revealing worries and concerns.

The adult must become a skilled and sensitive listener who can gently question the child to elicit an exploration of feelings, worries, and concerns. The adult/puppet should be open and aware, repeating and reflecting back the child's concerns, putting them into words the child will understand. Soon the puppet will be seen as a friend and the child will seek it out when troubled.

*Children are often able to verbalize feelings to puppets that they do not express in other contexts.*

**Note:** Know your limits when dealing with the child's emotions. Do not attempt psychotherapy without formal training. It is one thing for the child to talk about feelings through puppet play; it is a very different thing to try to treat the child. What is important is to pass on the information derived from the play session to the appropriate people, be they parents or therapists working with the child.

**UNIT 5**    Dance Play

### GOALS

- To promote nonverbal communication
- To foster individual creativity and achievement of movement skills
- To increase body awareness
- To develop children's abilities to reflect on and interpret elements in their world

Moving the body to sounds starts in infancy. Babies and young children constantly hear sounds and music: a radio or television, a doorbell buzzing, a telephone ringing, or a family member singing. Children often respond to these sounds with body movement, and these early responses give children their first knowledge of music. From the earliest stages of development, children strive to gain control over self (their body, feelings, and ideas) and environment. Recognizing these strivings is the start of working with creative movement.

Young children should be given opportunities to move to music with complete freedom. It is also helpful to plan experiences that will help children learn to use their bodies more expressively and to explore space by moving individual body parts in various positions. These explorations can be accompanied by a drum, piano, or tone block. For children with disabilities, opportunities to respond to music heighten physical awareness, spark vitality and energy, and help shed inhibitions. Movement experiences also encourage children to test their limitations and discover their strengths.

## EXPLORATIONS

**Circle dance.** Sit with the children in a circle. To music with a definite beat, start to make a single repetitive motion with your hands or body. Make sure the pattern is within the imitation capabilities of the group. Keep changing the motion to keep the children's concentration.

**Magic words.** Tell the children that you want to play a special game called "magic words." If the magic word is "stretch," they are to stretch any way they like every time you say it. Ask them to show you all the ways they can stretch. (Other magic words can be "spin," "crawl," "jump," or "make a shape.")

Start the game by telling a short story in which the magic word appears several times. For children in wheelchairs, adapt this activity to each child's physical abilities.

**Winding up, winding down.** Show the children wind-up toys, how they are wound up and wind down. Explain that a wind-up toy does one action over and over until it runs down. Suggest that the children can pretend to be wind-up toys. Put on some appropriate music ("The Syncopated Clock" by Leroy Anderson is excellent for this dance) and pretend to wind up all the "toys." The children do their toy dance until the music slows down, then stops. (To slow and gradually stop a record, put your hand on it gently.)

**Zoo dances.** Use these dances before or after a trip to the zoo. Show pictures of lions and ask the children to describe how the lions look to them. Tell the children that lions are called "kings of the jungle" and that they roar loudly, walk proudly, and are always looking for food when they aren't sleeping. To a slow, loud drumbeat, have the children do whatever they think is a lion dance. Similarly, they can become elephants, giraffes, or monkeys.

For each animal, suggest a characteristic the children can use in their dance movements. (For example, monkeys swing from trees, make funny faces, scratch themselves, or eat bananas; giraffes stretch their necks to eat the top leaves from the trees; snakes slither along the ground and dart their tongues out.) Encourage the children to make sounds to accompany their portrayals.

**Drum talk.** You'll need a drum for this exercise in auditory concentration and movement. Tell the children your drum can talk and will tell them how to move. Tell them they must listen to the drum carefully because you will not say anything during the dance. Explain that you will change the drumbeats and they are to follow how the drum tells them to move.

Beat a very rapid light tempo on the drum and have them respond to it. Then improvise with changing the tempo and volume of the drumbeats as the children follow along with dancing. Children can become quite intrigued by this nonverbal effort.

**Bridge dance.** Read the *Three Billy Goats Gruff,* then show or draw pictures of bridges. Explain that bridges go over water or rocky land, helping people cross from one side to another. Ask the children how they can make a bridge with their bodies. Children in wheelchairs can join hands with someone who is standing or sitting. Have the children dance out the different ways the three goats crossed the bridge—the small and timid goat, the bigger and more confident goat, and the biggest, strongest goat. Making a bridge with a big cushion or padded mats adds to this activity.

**Variations**

- Follow the bridge exercise with a trolls' dance using *St. John's Night on the Bare Mountain,* by Mussorgsky. Before the children begin, ask them to describe the trolls, including how they think the trolls look, sound, and move.

- Show pictures of tunnels and explain that they go under bridges or through mountains. Drape material over two chairs and let the children go through the tunnel. Ask the children to make tunnels with their bodies. They can explore this concept individually or by holding hands. At the end of the session, have the children line up and move as a train through the chair tunnel.

**Wiggle dance.** This dance helps children gain an awareness of body control and of the concept of stillness versus movement. To very upbeat music, have the children wiggle as many parts of their bodies as they can at one time. Then, stop the music to let them relax. When you begin again, have the children start with moving only one part (such as an arm or finger), adding other body parts as the music progresses. The children can try leaving out a body part when they seem ready for this (omitting a body part from the dance is harder than adding one).

**Rumpus dance.** Read Maurice Sendak's *Where the Wild Things Are* (Harper and Row, 1963), emphasizing the word "rumpus." To drumming, have the children do a wild rumpus dance until you say, "Stop."

The story also offers a contrasting mood; when Max leaves the Wild Things, they are very sad. Have the children do a dance that conveys sadness and loneliness.

**Listening dance.** This activity encourages children to become aware of changes in tempo and volume. Play some music and ask the children how they would show that the music is getting louder, then softer.

**Dancing to stories.** Creative movement based on situations and characters from familiar stories can stimulate children's imaginations. Don't tell the children how to move; they can move to express how they feel when listening to the music and to depict an event or character. Here are some possibilities:

- How Red Riding Hood walked through the woods
- The wolf's dance after falling into the pot of boiling water in *The Three Little Pigs*

- The Giving Tree and how it always gave to the little boy, in Shel Silverstein's book, *The Giving Tree* (Harper and Row, 1964)
- How angry the giant in *Jack and the Beanstalk* was with Jack
- Jack chopping down the beanstalk in a big hurry
- Cinderella dancing with the prince and running away at the stroke of midnight
- The gingerbread boy as he danced around telling everyone how fast he could run and how smart he was

**Snow dance.** Have the children pretend they are snowmen and snow ladies out for a walk. (The music and dance must be slow to suggest clumsiness.) As the sun comes out, the snow people slowly begin to melt, starting with their heads, then their shoulders, arms, trunks, and legs. Finally, the snow people melt into big puddles on the ground.

## Wheelchair Dancing

The dance activities we've just described can be carried out by children with mild to moderate disabilities. Some children, however, have extensive physical and communication needs and will need special considerations. Once you've tried wheelchair movements, you'll find that there are many possibilities for your group. Don't assume that these children get nothing out of dancing; many will enjoy the stimulation and exhilaration of movement, whether they are independently mobile in their chairs or need to be pushed. Socialization is another important aspect of these activities that should not be overlooked.

If there are enough classroom aides that each one can push one wheelchair during dance activities, it is best if the aide faces the child while dancing. Facing the child establishes and maintains eye contact. In this position, the aide can pull the chair forward, sway it from side to side, and turn it around. For folk dancing and square dancing, the chair can be pushed, rather than pulled, because the child needs to face others in the circle or square.

**Elimination dances.** Children enjoy elimination dances, particularly if humor is added:

- Everyone wearing purple socks with pink polka dots must get off the floor
- Anyone with a ring in their nose must get off the floor
- Anyone who is a hundred years old must get off the floor

Eventually, you can add realistic items. ("Anyone wearing a yellow shirt . . .") Children matching these descriptions are out.

**Hat dance.** For this elimination dance, put a funny hat on a child. As the music plays, the hat is passed from child to child. This continues until the music stops; the child wearing the hat is out.

**Parachute dance.** In this colorful activity, all of the children try to hold a silk parachute while making it go up and down. While it is raised, one child moves underneath it, changing places with another in the circle.

**Variation:** The popcorn dance is a modification of the parachute dance. Put several white paper cups or crunched-up pieces of paper or foil on top of the parachute before lifting and lowering it quickly to rhythmic music, simulating popping popcorn. Great fun!

**Paper dancing.** Each child chooses a piece of colored tissue paper. (Tissue paper is easy to tear and makes "crunchy" sounds.) To the rhythm of music, the children swing the tissue up and down, in and out, and all around. As the music continues, everyone tears up their paper into pieces to make a large mural in the center of the circle.

Smear a large cardboard form with glue and call for children whose paper is a certain color to come to the center. (For example, first the children with green paper, who decide where the green paper should be glued; then children with blue paper, and so forth.) Gluing all the paper completes a Dance Mural.

**Little bird dance.** This dance is an all-time favorite with children. It can be done to Thomas Randall's well-known recording, "Dance Little Bird" (Mustard Recording, M-141), also known as "The Chicken Dance."

The song has two themes. We show a dance for each theme.

First, make a circle. Before you start the dancing, show the children how to make "beak" motions, with their thumbs and fingers, and "wing flap" motions, with their elbows out and forearms facing in. The "beak" and "wing flap" motions are used in Theme 1 (the first few bars of the record).

### Theme 1

- Go forward for three phrases. On the fourth, "beak."

- Return home (go back) for three phrases. On the fourth, "wing flap." (Some children need help with this.)

- Repeat this series twice.

### Theme 2

- Push the child clockwise in place once. Then push counterclockwise until Theme 1 reappears.

This completes the sequence, which is repeated several times. Towards the end of the recording, the tempo gets slower, then faster. Move in toward the center, then out again, following the tempo.

**Square dances.** Very simple square dances are feasible for children in wheelchairs. Square dances are a good choice if you don't have enough aides to push all the wheelchairs, because only half the children are in motion at any one time. Divide the children into groups of four, and have each group form a square. Number the dancers in the square from 1 to 4. Should space be limited, dancers may be doubled or tripled up. To a recording of relatively slow square dance music, make up your own simple calls, such as these:

- "1 and 2 go into the center and make a little bow." (Encourage children to nod their heads.)

    "1 and 2 go home now, yes, go home now." (Return to places.)

Repeat calls for children 3 and 4.

- "1 and 2 cross over and turn around just so." (Cross over to opposite side, turn, and stay.)

Repeat call for children 3 and 4.

- "1 and 2 cross over because back home you must go."

Repeat call for children 3 and 4.

- "Now 1, turn around, turn around, I say."

Repeat call for children 2, 3, and 4.

- "Now everyone into the circle and shout a big hoo-ray!" (If the record allows, each group can go into the center, one at a time.)

    "Now our dance is finished—and we'll all go away!"

# Special Ways with Special Days

*It's Christmas Eve at Jimmy and Mary's house. Guests are coming soon, and Mom and Dad hope the two children will greet the guests by saying "Merry Christmas!" along with the rest of the family.*

*Jimmy, four, and Mary, two, are both hard of hearing, so their parents repeat "Merry Christmas! . . . Merry Christmas!" to make the words clear.*

*But Jimmy looks mad. He won't say it. Finally he clenches his fists and yells, "Not Mary Christmas . . . say Jimmy Christmas, Jimmy Christmas!"*

Children love special days and holidays; everyone else likes those days too, and we can put that mutual interest to good use. Special days are celebrated by a wider community than children's usual groups, and so there is an integrative or mainstreaming effect when children celebrate in concert with that larger community. Special days also tend to bring out good feelings, encouraging participation by children who may be unsure of their social skills.

It is helpful for children to see what's ahead. Post a large monthly calendar and mark special days with a symbol that represents the occasion. You can use a cake with candles, for example, for a birthday, a pumpkin for Halloween, a heart for Valentine's Day.

Preparation is very important. Keep in mind that these highly anticipated days can have quite an impact on children, who are often intense about special days. Some children may also lack focus or fear involvement because of their expectations of failure. Reassure children that nothing beyond their capabilities will be required of them. Talk about and repeat plans for the day; this will support those who might be hesitant or fearful.

You don't have to wait for the traditional days: you can make them. Almost any theme can be used, such as:

- Book Day—Visit a library, make a picture book

- Red Day—Wear red clothing, eat red food, go for a "red walk" to look for red things

- Money Day—Visit a bank, go shopping, make a piggy bank

131

- Home Day—Look at pictures of different homes (see the "Different Peoples, Different Homes" exploration in the "Native Celebrations" unit), read stories about houses, talk about animal, bird, and insect homes, make a bird house

- Family Day—Make a book about the family

There's also Me Day, Food Day, Fast Day/Slow Day, Face Day, Foot Day—the possibilities are almost endless.

Part III highlights explorations for the seasons and some of the more popular holidays and theme days. Incorporating these interests will help children appreciate commonly celebrated holidays and experience a sense of community. As with all explorations in this book, the children's functional levels will determine which activities you choose and how you present them.

Try also to tailor events to reflect ethnic and local interests. As the ethnic makeup of North America continues to diversify, cultural sensitivity is becoming an increasingly important issue. The majority of recent immigrants come from cultures other than the Judeo-Christian culture we have often taken for granted. Be prepared for some of these children to have limited familiarity with our "traditional" holidays or to have different traditions surrounding events such as birthdays. Invite the children and their families to share their special days and traditions with the class, and use your imagination and creativity to build opportunities for creative expression around these events.

*Jim with a budding artist.*

# The Seasons

Young children may not easily comprehend the concept of changing seasons. However, they can be exposed to the many and delightful signs of the seasons, and eventually will understand what these signs mean.

Children who need help with the sequence of seasons may enjoy two books: *Spring Is Here,* by Taro Gomi (an Owen Morgan book from Fitzhenry and Whiteside, 1989), and *I Am a Rabbit,* by Richard Scarry (Golden Press, 1963). The Gomi book is a charming story for very young children with lovely illustrations and three or four words per page. The Scarry book describes, with little text, the many delightful things the Rabbit Nicholas can see and do in the various seasons of the year.

For children who live in climates with defined growing seasons, a year-round and very visual activity that helps them become aware of the seasons is to make large cards depicting the sequence of tree growth:

- Spring—a tree with tiny leaves and blossoms
- Summer—a tree with full green leaves
- Fall—a colorful tree with leaves on the ground
- Winter—a bare tree surrounded by snow

Describe how the tree changes from season to season. Mix the cards, then ask the children to put them into sequence, telling a tree story as they do so.

**UNIT 1**

# Spring

Spring is a wonderful time to take children for a walk, listening to the new sounds, looking at the new sights, and enjoying the wonders of the season.

Growth, coming to life, transformation, and rebirth are themes central to our aspirations for children with disabilities. The quickening spirit we all feel in the spring will, we hope, lead children to visualize growth and transformation in art activities that involve nature in a special way. Observing and sensing spring exposes children to nature's creative power. With reassurance, the children will respond by finding the creative powers within themselves.

## EXPLORATIONS

**Pussy willows.** The pussy willow comes out before even the earliest flowers. Children are intrigued by its texture and will enjoy making a pussy-willow picture. This can be a drawing and gluing activity. Have them draw a curved line across the paper with a dark crayon. They can then paste on puffed wheat, puffed rice, or cotton balls. Singing "Pussy Willow" makes a nice ending.

Pussy Willow Song *

Traditional

I have a little pussy, Her coat is silver grey. She lives down in the meadow Not very far away. She'll always be a pussy, She'll never be a cat, 'Cause she's a pussy willow, Now what do you think of that?

Meow meow meow meow Meow meow meow scat!

**Old and new.** Talk about things that are old and new in the children's immediate environment. Determine which is newest and oldest in terms of people (baby, child, adult, grandparent) or things. On an outing, have them identify various objects as being new or old.

**Spring babies.** Talk about spring as a time for newborns. Invite a mother or dad to bring their newborn baby for a visit. Take a field trip to a zoo, animal shelter, or farm to see newborn animals. Talk about the extra care and attention a newborn needs.

Getting a young pet for the children to observe and care for stimulates discussion, but avoid bringing a pet into the room if any of the children are allergic. Fish may be safer; try to buy a pregnant female. The children will be enchanted with the tiny fish fry (babies). It is best to keep the fry in a special unit in the fish tank so that they won't be eaten by the larger fish.

**Special seeds.** Sprout a variety of seeds (such as radishes, beans, alfalfa, or grass) on layers of paper towels kept continually moist. The children will be intrigued when the seeds sprout stems and leaves (usually within a few days).

They'll also enjoy similar preparations of bulbs for a springtime burst of blooms. Bulbs are easy to maintain and will reinforce the child's concept of growth. The bulb work can be followed by planting a few seeds in soil-filled plastic margarine tubs. Put the tubs on a sunny windowsill and keep them moist. The children can eventually take the plants home—a special treat.

**Seed skins.** Show how seeds are protected by having the children examine shells on nuts; skins on apples; peels on bananas; husks on corn; rinds on oranges; and pods on peas, beans, or milkweed. Discuss how hair and skin protect people.

**Spring walk.** Have the children tape all the sounds they hear on a spring walk. Afterwards, have everyone listen to the tape and try to identify the sounds.

**Buzzing bees.** Talk about how bees fly from flower to flower gathering nectar from the blossoms. In a music session, have the children pretend they are bees buzzing around. At a signal (a chime, for example), the music stops and they pretend they are sitting on a flower—until the music begins again.

**Seed dance.** Tell the children that the plants they see outside come from little seeds, and that seeds need water and sunshine to grow. Suggest they do a seed dance in which they pretend they are small seeds in the ground. As the children portraying seeds all curl up, have one child pretend to take a watering can and water each plant. Another child plays the sun and dances around everyone, warming them. Play a tambourine or a recording of music, softly at first, as each child puts up a hand and slowly begins to grow. The sound increases as the children rise up to become flowers. The dance can be expanded by adding other roles, such as butterflies or birds.

**Spring air.** Talk about ways we can "see" air. Use straws to blow bubbles in water or in a detergent-and-water solution, and watch the breeze carry away the bubbles. Mix one part liquid dish detergent to six parts water for a good bubble solution. **(Note:** Many young children automatically try to suck on straws. Supervise closely to make sure no one drinks the detergent mixture.)

### Variations

- Fly a kite or paper airplane, make a pinwheel spin, or watch a flag or windsock wave in the wind.

- Drop maple seed keys from as high as possible and watch them spin to the ground.

- Watch clouds wafting in the sky. Then, make a cloud picture with blue construction paper, white paint, chalk, crayons, cotton balls, and glue.

- Have the children play wind sounds by humming through tissue paper folded over a comb. To get this effect, they must be able to make some sound. Making sounds may not be possible for some children with cerebral palsy who do not have control of their speech musculature. An alternative would be to make thunder sounds on a large drum or by hitting a cymbal with a muted beater. As the "storm" passes, the winds diminish, and the birds begin to sing (whistles).

**Bee tracking.** Using a drawing like the one shown, the children can follow a trail of dots to a bee flying to a colored flower. Each child holds a toy bee and moves it from left to right along the horizontal dot path to the flower. This can be repeated until the child follows the line with ease.

*Follow the dots to lead the bee to the flower.*

**Tree decorations.** Cut some blossoms and leaves from tissue paper. Then have the children paste the cutouts to a tree trunk made from construction paper. Explain that many flowering trees bear fruit later in the season. Have the children make a second tree with fruit on it.

**"I love the green grass."** This poem lends itself to various things children like about the seasons. Other verses may grow out of things the children mention.

### I Love the Green Grass

*by Fran Herman*

I love the green grass,
I love the birdies,
I love the flowers,
I love the great big trees.
I love the big sun
When it shines the whole day through,
'Cause that's when I can go
And play with you.

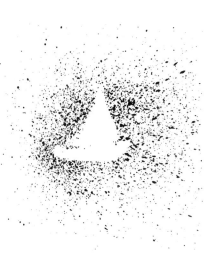

---

**UNIT 2**

# Summer

Children can see the many and splendid changes of summer: the full green of the trees, the vast array of garden flowers and vegetables, the insects and birds. They can also perceive the effects of the sun and rain—or the lack thereof—challenging their powers of observation and differentiation.

## EXPLORATIONS

**It's hot!** Talk about how summer days are long, about shadows, and about how plants and animals use the sun or protect themselves from its heat. Mime the various ways we protect ourselves from the sun: wearing a hat or sunglasses, putting on sunscreen, drinking lots of water, swimming or paddling. To music, have the children continue their play by pretending to swim at the beach, roll or throw beach balls, and look for seashells.

**Sand and water.** The fascination of sand makes it a year-round mainstay of any creative environment, especially when water is nearby to add to sand's many different possibilities. A beach is the best place to indulge in these open-ended, easily manipulated media; however, sand and water tables and sandboxes are often more accessible, especially for those with mobility problems. For an individual child's indoor sand play, cat-litter boxes are ideal. Fill with fine-grained sand that has been sterilized and is free of debris (sift if necessary).

For young children, plastic sand pails, cups, and shovels are often the first tools they use in play. As they discover the tactile differences between dry and wet, warm and cool, packed and loose sand, they also discover the perceptual skills needed for pouring, filling, and emptying and the spatial relationships between shallow and deep, smooth and bumpy, thick and thin.

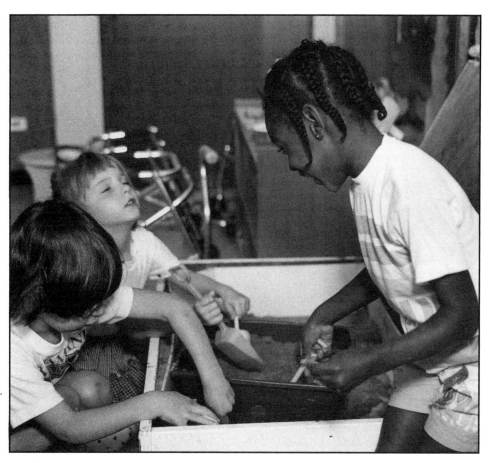

*Sand play holds much fascination for youngsters. Wet or dry, sand has endless possibilities.*

"Sand combs" are among the many tools children enjoy using to make intriguing designs in sand. You can make these combs by cutting plastic lids in half and then cutting tines on the flat edge. The tines can be widely spaced, shaped like waves, or cut in a zigzag pattern.

**Sandpainting.** Activities based on this traditional Native American religious practice can promote fine motor skills for all children. Color sterilized sand with natural dyes, then let the sand dry. (Aquarium sand is an alternative that provides coarser but more brilliantly colored materials.) Use a number of colors, making separate piles for each color.

One section of a piece of cardboard is then covered with glue, either in a design or at random. Sprinkle one color of sand over the cardboard, then tilt the cardboard to remove the excess sand. Repeat with the other colors of sand until the picture is completed.

**Variations**

- Add tiny shells to the sand painting to make a three-dimensional collage.

- Cover a section of cardboard with sprinkled sand; when dry, paint it with tempera paints.

**Water play.** Children love water, and experimentation with it can further many skills. Pouring is a good example: learning to pour juice or milk can be a significant step towards the independence that is the ultimate goal of all education.

In living centers, sink activities provide experiences for washing dishes and doll clothes as well as for pouring from one vessel to another. Many children enjoy using funnels, plastic tubing, small plastic bottles and cups, sprinklers, and ladles, either in small tubs or larger water tables. Children also enjoy squeezing sponges and playing with objects that float, such as table-tennis balls and other plastic forms.

These activities relax and intrigue children. Let them play without adult intervention.

**Birdbaths.** Set out a shallow basin of water and watch birds bathe in it. The basin can also be used for sailing boats made of paper, scrap wood, walnut shells, or plastic foam (cut, for example, from packaging). Blow through a straw to propel the boats.

Observing floating and sinking is a good opportunity to talk about *heavy* and *light*. Have the children collect a variety of objects and see whether they float or sink (straws, flowers, balls, corks, and confetti are good examples).

**Sidewalk art.** Have the children make chalk designs on the sidewalk. On a warm day, have them paint a hot sidewalk with large brushes or sponges dipped in water to discover the evaporating power of the sun.

**Catch the sun.** Have the children sit inside in sunlight and use unbreakable mirrored surfaces to redirect the sun's rays to shaded areas of the room. To structure or broaden the activity, designate "targets" or suggest that the mirrored lights chase each other or play tag.

**Prisms.** Show the children how prisms can break light into a spectrum. Sunlight shining through a fine spray from a hose or sprinkler also creates a rainbow. Have the children chase the rainbow and discover how it moves as

*Children love playing with water—splashing it, pouring it, and swirling it around.*

the spray moves. Using water-soluble markers on wet paper, have the children make their version of a rainbow. Don't insist on a precise arc of colors of the spectrum; instead, encourage close observation and discussion of the feelings the children have about rainbows.

**Magic glasses.** Using tinted cellophane, acetates, or theatrical gels, have the children hold the tinted screens in front of their eyes and choose a favorite color. Talk about how they would like to live in a violet, red, or green world.

**Faraway looks.** Provide binoculars and magnifying glasses for the children to examine their surroundings from a different perspective.

**Path tracing.** On paper, draw a road connecting a house on the left to a school on the right. Have the child "drive" a miniature toy car or bus from the house to the school. The road can be several inches wide at first, and narrower in subsequent tracings. Encourage the child to stay within the lines so as not to "drive off the road." This is a particularly good exercise for children with visual-motor problems.

## UNIT 3    Autumn

There are many signs of autumn that children can notice and recognize. In many parts of the country, sudden chills and warmer clothing tell us that winter is just around the corner. Nature's colors change, pumpkins ripen in the fields, grapes become lush and heavy, birds fly south, and the sun sets earlier each evening. Talking about the indicators of autumn where you live will help children understand seasons and their signs.

### EXPLORATIONS

**Feelie box.** For tactile discrimination, put leaves and differently textured objects into a "feelie box." Ask the children to find the leaves.

**Leaf collage.** Have the children gather fallen leaves to make a leaf collage.

**Variation:** Suggest that the children glue a leaf to a piece of paper. They can think of the leaf as the body, drawing arms, legs, and a head to turn the picture into a leaf person.

**Leaf cookies.** Have the children make sugar cookies in the shape of leaves. Many leaf-shaped cookie cutters are commercially available. Yellow, orange, and red frosting with sprinkles provide a fall look. (Food coloring can also be added to the batter.)

**Wind song.** Make paper leaves in various fall colors. Sing this song with the children, having each listen for the color of his or her leaf to be released on cue.

Wind Song *

The wind is blow – ing Woo-oo-oo Woo! Woo-oo-oo Woo! Woo-oo-oo Woo! The wind is blow – ing Woo-oo-oo Woo, It makes the leaves fall down.

© *1990 by Jimani Publications.*

**Leaf dance.** Show the children fresh green leaves as well as dead brown ones. Have them smell and feel the difference; the green ones smell fresh and feel firm, while the old ones crumble when crunched. Ask the children to make up dances describing how the green leaves and old leaves make them feel.

**Variation:** Divide the group in half to do an autumn dance. One group can be the wind, making wind noises as they twirl and sweep along the floor. The second group can be leaves drifting in the wind, falling gently to the ground.

**Tree pictures.** Have children tear or crush leaves they find on the ground and glue them to a drawing of a tree trunk.

**Leaf dominoes.** Make domino cards using leaves that are different in shape and color. (You will want to collect several of each type of leaf.) Play proceeds as in traditional dominoes: each child places a card on the table such that matching leaves are adjoining.

*Leaf domino cards.*

**Seed collages.** Seeds and nuts are great collage materials because they are easily glued to a paper surface.

**Flying milkweed seeds.** Set free some milkweed seeds; it's an ideal way to show clearly a breeze's direction and strength.

**Counting and comparing.** Chestnuts, pine cones, acorns, or whatever is available locally can be used in games of "how many?" "same and different," "few and many," "which one doesn't belong?" and "which is smallest, which is largest?"

**Sponge painting.** Cut sponges into irregular shapes that easily fit the grasp of a small hand. Tape a large sheet of paper to a table or put it on the floor for easy access. Spread a shallow layer of tempera paint on a small tray. Children can dip their sponges into the paint, and then press the sponge repeatedly on paper. If autumn colors are chosen, the paper will soon resemble leaf-covered ground (or a multicolored treetop, if cut to that shape).

*A leaf rubbing.*

**Leaf rubbings.** The image of a leaf can be created with a rubbing technique. Put the leaf or leaves (veined side up) on a table or hard surface. Tape a sheet of bond paper over the leaf. Using a thick dark-colored crayon, rub across the area covering the leaves. This rubbing transfers the leaf textures to the paper. Have the children find other surfaces on which rubbings can be made.

**Figure-ground discrimination.** Have the child find and color a leaf hidden in a picture that has many busy elements.

**Pressed leaves.** Children love to preserve pretty leaves and can do so by pressing them between two sheets of wax paper. It is important to have the waxed sides facing the leaves. Put newspapers underneath and above the wax papers, and have an adult press them together with a warm iron. The resulting leaf collage can be trimmed and hung from a light fixture or in a window.

**UNIT 4**

# Winter

Wintry transformations attract children's interest as the sun drops on the southern horizon, the hours of daylight dwindle, and the temperature drops. Children will be fascinated by many of winter's changes. If relevant to your area, you can observe and talk about natural adaptations for protection from cold, such as migration, hibernation, heavy winter coats, or camouflage. You can also focus on changes that occur in the children's homes and communities, particularly with respect to individual habits and activities. Knowing that everyone must adapt to circumstances is important for children whose disabilities require them to undergo many adaptive regimes.

**Note:** In colder climates, make sure that children who have reduced sensation in their limbs or circulation problems are well protected from the cold. To ensure safety, check with the child's family or therapist when planning a winter outing.

## EXPLORATIONS

**Snow makers.** Whip soap flakes or powder with a little water to make "snow." The mixture should be fairly stiff to maintain peaks. Have the children feel, squeeze, and mold it into shapes. Show them pictures of igloos, explaining how they are made. Give children paper bowls and suggest they be inverted and covered to create igloos (these will become hard when they dry).

**Snow murals.** Making a snow mural can extend into a weeklong project. Draw a line across the entire mural paper, with the upper part designated as sky and the bottom part as ground. The children may paint the sky and ground; trees with bare branches can then be added, by the children if they are able and by an adult if not. The ground can then be covered with white packing material and the sky with cotton balls or dabs of white paint to signify falling snow. Other embellishments may be added as interest grows.

**Winter picture.** Provide white chalk or paint and a choice of colored construction paper for making an individual winter picture. For a snowlike effect, whip soap flakes plus a small amount of liquid starch and white tempera in a blender until frothy. Children can brush or daub this mixture on their paintings.

**Figure-ground discrimination.** Have children find a snow figure in a picture with many visual distractions.

**Cold!** Bring some snow or an ice cube into the group. Ask the children about other things that are cold. Have them mime touching something cold, being cold, shoveling snow, and snow melting.

**Variation:** To chords on an instrument or beats of a drum, have children pretend they are picking up a handful of snow and packing it three times to form a ball. Then, to a piano glissando (a slide up or down the keys), have them pretend to throw the ball. Children adore this mime. They can "throw" the snow at adults as well as each other. A child "hit" by a snowball must then pretend to wipe it off his or her face. This can be followed by mimes of drinking a cup of hot chocolate.

**Ice crystals.** Have the children make a crayon picture on dark blue paper. The picture can then be painted all over with a solution of equal parts Epsom salts and water. As the paper dries, "ice crystals" will appear, transforming the art.

**Making ice.** Children love ice as much as they do water. Have the children soak string or fabric in water, drape the objects over a coat hanger, and put them outside on a freezing day or in the freezer. The frozen shapes can be handled by the children; warming will make them pliable once again.

**Feed the birds.** Children who require almost continual care from others relish an opportunity to take care of others (in this case, birds).

A simple feeder can be created from large pine cones. Collect cones and dry them in the oven to open them up. Tie string to the cones so they can be hung outside a window. Have the children spread peanut butter into open areas of the cones. Spread birdseed in a tray and have the children roll the cones in the seeds, embedding them in the peanut butter. **(Note:** Many young children are severely allergic to peanut butter.)

As birds come to the feeder, have the children observe them closely. Help them try to identify the birds, matching them to illustrations in a bird-identification book.

**Frosty window fun.** Frosty windows can be a marvelous visual tableau that children can look at, touch, and add their own markings to. If children don't discover this on their own, point out the effect of breath condensing on a cold window. Children will soon explore this new drawing medium.

**Variation:** Glass wax can make a thin opaque coating—and an enticing drawing surface—on windows or mirrors.

**Tracking!** Talk about animal and vehicle tracks and look for some in the snow, sand, or mud. Help identify any tracks that are discovered.

**Variation:** Have one child make a trail for the others to follow. Point out that one can make paths in geometric shapes (such as a circle, triangle, or square).

Connect the dots to string the mittens together so one doesn't get lost.

**Connect the dots.** Connect-the-dot activities help eye-hand coordination and visual attending skills. Have the children trace around a variety of winter objects such as a pair of winter mittens. Suggest that the children connect the dots to make a string between the mittens that will prevent one from being lost. Use simple outlines for lower functioning children and more complex ones for children who are more adept.

**Snowflake dance.** To music, let the children pretend to be snowflakes falling softly to the ground. If the music is lyrical and quiet, the children will create snowflakes that gently twirl and drift. A change of music can suggest a strong wind that causes the "snowflakes" to dart about with slashing actions.

**Making angels.** Children can leave an angel-like imprint by lying on their backs in snow, spreading their arms and legs, and then bringing them together. If children cannot do this, they may simply lie on their backs in the snow to leave an impression of their bodies. This activity helps familiarize children with their body image and dramatically illustrates the spatial imprint of gross motor movements.

***The Snowy Day.*** Read this Ezra Jack Keats story (Viking Press, 1962) to the children and suggest they mime parts of the story. Improvised music will be a great asset, although the story alone will capture the youngsters' imaginations. Elements to mime include:

- Peter wakes up on a wintry day to see snow everywhere outside.

- He puts on his winter clothing and goes out to play.

- He makes tracks in the snow by turning his toes in and out and by dragging his feet.

- He hits a tree with a stick to make the snow fall down.

- He makes angels and a snowman in the snow.

- At last, he comes into the house for a hot bath.

- Next morning, he looks outside; the snow is still there.

- He phones his friend, and they both go out to play.

**Snow song.** This song can be added to *The Snowy Day* mime or sung by itself:

Snowy Day

I want to play out in the snow, That's where I really want to go, The snow is white, The snow is bright, It came down softly in the night.

# Special Days

# Halloween

Halloween is a unique time: it is an opportunity to tolerate, and even encourage, children's efforts to scare others (and be scared themselves). During Halloween celebrations, it is essential to protect children who may already have difficulty handling fears in everyday circumstances. These fears may be eased if the children have chances to "play" with surprises. A good idea is to "practice" a few times with darkness, masks, and makeup before the day itself.

Emphasize fun, surprises, and treats, not scares. Remember, as well, to avoid extremes in supervised Halloween activities. As children mature and develop some sophistication, they can begin to interpret a "frightful" experience as stimulating drama rather than reality.

## EXPLORATIONS

**Paper jack-o'-lanterns.** Younger children can paste pre-cut black construction paper features onto a paper pumpkin. Older or more adept youngsters can cut as well as paste.

**Sprinkled pumpkins.** Children outline a paper pumpkin with glue and sprinkle orange-colored grits or rice on the picture.

**Variation:** Make pumpkin Halloween cookies topped with soft frosting. Let the children sprinkle them with candy sprinkles.

**Pumpkin patches.** Children enjoy making pumpkin patches, either on a large mural or all around the room. Make vines by cutting large spirals of green construction paper to run around the edges of the room or around the edge of a large table. Next the children cut out large leaves and pumpkins of various sizes for the patch. Leaves may be sponge painted (demonstrate how to dab, rather than smear, the paint on the leaves).

If a black light is available, outline the pumpkins and leaves with fluorescent markers or chalk to create a delightfully "spooky" atmosphere for a Halloween party.

**Variation:** Pumpkins for the patch can also be three dimensional. Take paper bags and stuff them with torn-up newspapers. Twist shut the end of the stuffed bag to make a stem. An adult can help secure

*Making a vine for the pumpkin patch.*

it with a rubber band, tape, or string. The pumpkin and stem are painted and features can be glued on or painted.

**Finger tracings.** Finger trace a black cat looking for a witch or a pumpkin. Have the cat move from left to right until it finds the pumpkin.

**Halloween mimes.** Halloween lends itself to a number of mimes:

- Have children curl up like cats, then purr and stretch out as a cat does when it awakens.

- Youngsters can pretend they are witches getting ready for Halloween who can't find their broomsticks. A search around the room can follow.

- Suggest the children be jack-o'-lanterns who lost their smiles and now have only sad faces. They look everywhere to find their smiles. Finally they discover them locked in a big trunk. They open the trunk, take out their smiles, and no longer have sad faces.

  This mime can be accompanied by a finger play:

| Words | Action |
|---|---|
| Pumpkin, pumpkin, big and fat | *Cover your face with your hands.* |
| Turn into a jack-o'-lantern Just like that! | *Remove hands and show a big smile.* |

  (For variety, the children can reveal any kind of jack-o'-lantern expression.)

**Halloween dance.** Dancing with a Halloween theme can be quite effective for exploring shapes and spatial concepts. Show a pumpkin to children and have them describe it. Ask them how this round fat pumpkin would dance. Put on some music (Dukas's *The Sorcerer's Apprentice* is a good choice), and encourage the children to do a pumpkin dance. Have them "think round."

*It's tough trying to walk when you're a pumpkin.*

Next, show pictures of witches. Help the children notice that the witches are straight, angular, and "pointy." Ask how they could make the witch's dance different from the pumpkin's, following up with the dance itself.

Last, show a ghost. A large cloth napkin tied over the fist makes an excellent three-dimensional ghost. Show the children how the ghost glides and swoops. Have them do a ghost dance.

*Pumpkin story.* This dramatic play has great appeal for children learning to stand or walk, who identify with the pumpkin and its difficulties.

- One day, on their way home from school, the children pass a pumpkin patch. They decide to play ball. *(Children can bounce and throw balls to each other in mime to music.)*

- Suddenly, the children hear a moaning sound. They look up, down, and around, but can see only pumpkins.

- They play ball again, but stop when they hear the crying once more. Again, they look and look, but see only pumpkins.

- Finally, they come to a big pumpkin sitting in the field. The pumpkin is crying. *(Have a child play the pumpkin.)*

  - "Why are you crying, pumpkin?" the children ask. "I want to dance because it's Halloween, but I can't, I have no legs," the pumpkin replies.

  - Ask: "What do you think we can do to help the pumpkin?"

The children will come up with various responses, eventually arriving at the idea of using sticks for legs. They search everywhere in the room for things that could resemble legs. They then mime attaching the legs to the pumpkin.

- Say: "Now you all have to count to 10 to help the pumpkin get up." Children count as the pumpkin is helped up. *(Play drumbeats or ascending chords.)* But the pumpkin falls down. *(Play a loud sound on the piano or drum.)*

- Repeat the pumpkin struggling to get up and falling down several times until the pumpkin finally begins to walk.

- Everyone joins hands and dances with the pumpkin. *(Play dance music.)*

**Halloween song.** As Halloween approaches, ask the children what they want to be.

On Halloween *

Marcia Berman

On Hal-lo-ween. On Hal-lo-ween. What are you going to be ———. On Hal-lo-ween On Hal-lo-ween. She's going to be a witch!

If a child answers "witch," play some high-pitched sounds on an instrument. The children practice cackling and speaking in high witch-like voices. Suggest the witch has to get a witchy face ready for Halloween. Talk about what costume and makeup are appropriate for a witch; for example, "What color lipstick would witches wear? What color nail polish? . . . Then let's put some of that color on each finger. And now a wart on the tip of your nose—and some black cheeks—before the little witch goes out."

**Variation:** Mime whatever character each child chooses.

**Witches' brew.** Have the children pretend they are making a witches' brew. Suggest that witches don't like the food we eat: instead, they like the most awful, smelly things. Each child takes the cauldron (large pot or wastebasket) and pretends to throw in something. "Ingredients" could include bugs, worms, smelly socks, old running shoes, frog's eyes, and dirty fingernails, but the possibilities are virtually endless. When we played this, one child "threw in" his little sister via his communication system symbols. Another, not to be outdone, pointed to the word "therapist," and a third pointed to "school."

Pretend taste tests can then be held to determine whether the brew is awful enough for witches. The "Witches' Brew" song can accompany motions of stirring the imaginary brew. (Encourage children to use both hands to stir).

## Witches' Brew*

Stirring the brew. Stirring the brew. Stirring and stirring and stirring the brew.

We will not stop stirring the pot. Ha - ha - ha · ha - ha - ha!

**Variation:** Younger children can watch a witches' brew being made in a large glass jar or aquarium filled with water. Add plastic bats, spiders, frogs, and insects. Cut-up green grapes are a good simulation for cat's eyes. Stirring with a large spoon or dowel decorated with a witch's head adds to the atmosphere. The children will be mesmerized as a few drops of yellow food coloring is added to the water, followed by green, then red, then blue, finally turning the water to black.

**Dress-up corner.** Most children bring their Halloween costume from home to school, but having various hats, wigs, jewelry, purses, old curtains, shifts, fedoras, and ties in the dress-up corner is always a good idea. The corner becomes a resource for dramatic play and provides incentive to create a character.

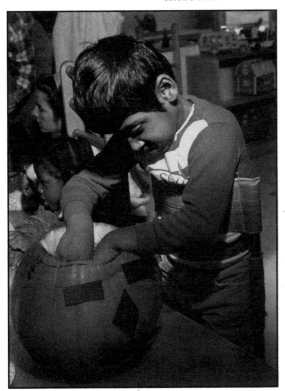

*"It's yucky in here!"*

**Makeup time!** Face-paint crayons are always fun, especially at Halloween time. Makeup is preferable to masks for children with visual-perceptual impairments because it tends to be less disorienting, as well as less likely to interfere with vision.

Always check whether any children might be allergic to the makeup you're using; if so, plan accordingly. Water-based makeup is less likely to cause a reaction than is oil-based makeup. Soft paint sticks are also important for sensitive young skin.

**Pumpkin carving.** Most children will be able to help prepare a traditional jack-o'-lantern by helping to remove seeds and pulp from inside the pumpkin. Children who find this tactile experience too "yucky" may like sorting and cleaning the seeds in preparation for roasting. The seeds, dyed different colors, can be used in collages at another time.

Ask the children for ideas on designing the pumpkin's face. Water-soluble markers allow experimentation. For younger children, preparing a variety of eye, nose, and mouth shapes cut out of black paper provides opportunities to make choices. An adult can then cut the shapes the children have chosen.

*The leg bone connects to the knee bone . . .*

**Scarecrows and such.** To make a scarecrow or jack-o'-lantern person, clothing can be stuffed (for example, with rags, hay, or foam) and propped up in a chair or wheelchair with the jack-o'-lantern on top. Children will be interested in naming and touching body and facial features, which helps them become more familiar with these parts and their functions.

**Skeleton rattle.** A skeleton that wiggles and jiggles as it hangs from the ceiling is a great Halloween prop that the children will enjoy as it moves. Attach string to the center of a dowel and hang the dowel from the bottom of a wire coat hanger, creating a "shoulder bone" for the skeleton (see photo). A head made of cardboard or stiff paper can be attached by string to the front of the hanger and dowel. The children string toilet paper rolls together to make the arms, legs, and body, which is then attached by strings to the dowel. Paper hands and feet can then be added. The longer this skeleton is, the more it will rattle.

**UNIT 2**

# Thanksgiving

Giving thanks for food is an ancient custom. Thanksgiving is closely linked to the harvest, which urban dwellers in particular must make a special effort to experience directly. The Thanksgiving season can give us motivation and a theme for field trips to experience the sights, sounds, tactile feelings, smells, and tastes offered by farms, markets, and greenhouses.

## EXPLORATIONS

*A handprint turkey.*

**"Handprint turkey."** Before the children make a "touch turkey," have a general discussion of turkeys, using whatever pictures and books you may have.

Then give the children construction paper in earth colors. Put within their reach trays with thinly spread tempera paint or water-thinned block printing ink. Show the children that fingers can become tail feathers, the palm resembles the body, and the thumb forms the head and neck; then have them make turkey handprints. Have the children press their hands flat in the paint, then make handprints on the paper. Encourage children with laterality problems to use both hands and to make a line of turkeys walking across the page. Legs may be added by pressing an inked index finger or thumb twice under the body. Other details may be drawn or painted on.

Add a tactile element, particularly for children with perceptual impairments. Kernels of corn may be glued to the paper, as can a bed of straw at the turkey's feet. A granular texture (such as cornmeal, sparkles, sand, flower petals, or confetti) may be sprinkled on the paint while it is still wet.

**Turkey waddle.** The children should now be ready for a "turkey waddle" around the room or yard, looking for corn to the accompaniment of "Turkey in the Straw" and joining in for the "Ah huh haw" chorus.

**Fruit or vegetable prints.** Cut fruit or vegetables in half to make a flat cross section for printing. The child presses the object into tempera, then onto paper. Repeat with different colors. (Some fruits and vegetables must drain cut side down on absorbent paper before they can absorb paint.)

Use fruit or vegetable parts that would otherwise go in the compost pile. The end of celery stalks, when dipped in paint and pressed on paper, yield crescent shapes. The top of a carrot prints circles, green pepper prints an irregular ring, and the top of an apple (cut transversely) prints a ring with a star-shaped center.

**Sharing song.** Have young children cut and paste a Thanksgiving picture showing foods of the season. These may be used as an opportunity to teach quantities (as in one pumpkin, two apples, three ears of corn, four potatoes . . . ).

Afterwards, children can be asked to point to one of the items they would like to share, and sing the "Sharing Song."

## Sharing Song

A - man - da is shar - ing some pump - kin pies, Some pump - kin pies, Some pump - kin pies. A - man - da is sharing some pump - kin pies With you on Thanksgiv - ing day.

2. Sukwinder is sharing some apples red . . .

3. Jenny is sharing some bunches of grapes . . .

Continue asking the children what they would like to share, and with whom.

**Spice book.** This book can help make children more aware of the season. Have them glue various herbs and spices on small sheets of construction paper. Thyme, cloves, nutmeg, and cinnamon are used frequently at this time of year. Adults can staple or clip the spice books together.

**My own garden.** Help the children create and maintain miniature gardening projects, even if only on a windowsill. As mentioned in the "Earth Day" explorations later in Part III, gardening's repetitive tasks, abundant sensory stimuli, and steady incremental progression provide constructive learning experiences.

A garden harvest feast, including vegetables, spices, and table decorations that the children help prepare, will generate enthusiasm and help develop daily living skills.

**Thanksgiving mime.** Tell the children the story of the first Thanksgiving and have them mime the sequences below. All can be mimed by young children. Adding music makes it even more enjoyable.

- The Pilgrims have to make homes because winter is coming. They chop down trees.

- They build their log houses higher and higher, finally adding roofs.

- There are holes between the logs, so mud and clay are stuffed into them.

- Doors and windows are cut and placed.

- One beautiful fall day, the Pilgrims invite their Native American friends to a special party. They want to thank the Native Americans for showing them so many things and for giving them corn to grow.

**Making dyes.** One of the many things Native Americans taught the Pilgrims was how to make dyes from fruits or vegetables to make cloths of different colors.

Many vegetables yield dye when boiled in a small quantity of water, then cooled and strained. Salt is added to help hold the dye. Children (wearing smocks) can help make the dye by cutting the vegetables, pouring the water, and stirring the pot.

Fruits and vegetables that yield interesting colors include:

- Beets (for violet or red)
- Spinach leaves (green)
- Walnut shells (brown)
- Onion skins (yellow or red)
- Blackberries (blue)
- Marigolds, carrots (yellow)

Have the children tie-dye cotton place mats for the feast. Tie the fabric in knots before dyeing, or place string or elastic bands around portions of the fabric to "pucker" and fold it. Then selectively dip or immerse parts of the fabric in their own dyes. Dyeing results are quick, often spectacular, and give a sense of accomplishment.

Children should wear rubber gloves for this activity. For a demonstration, use paper napkins, tissue paper, or paper cloth. The children can drip dye from eyedroppers onto tissues they have folded several times and secured with clothespins. If they cut out segments of the tissue paper in advance, they can make colored snowflakes.

**Thanksgiving decorations.** Colored leaves, gourds, Indian corn, harvested vegetables, and sprigs of bittersweet and other fall plants make beautiful harvest table decorations and help make the children aware of the autumn season.

**Thanksgiving tortillas.** Have the children make modeling clay tortillas with white or yellow clay and a tortilla press. They may then enjoy making real tortillas with cornmeal using a tortilla recipe. Similarly, they can make pasta with a pasta maker, garlic press, or potato ricer. These can be part of the room's harvest decor.

**Cranberry strings.** This sequencing activity is best for older or more adept children. Each child is given a darning needle threaded with light cotton or nylon thread. Put cranberries in bowls and show the children how to pierce them with the needle. When strings are finished, they can be tied together and hung around the room.

**Apple strings.** This harvest treat can be eaten or used for decoration. Apples, with the peel left on, should be thinly sliced, dipped in lemon juice and water, then threaded on a long string. Hang the strings in a warm, dry place for a week before using for decoration or eating.

**Harvest dolls.** Many rural people make these cornhusk dolls. Children can use fresh or dried husks. (Before using dried husks, soak them in warm water for 15 minutes to make them pliable.) Twist a pipe cleaner around the middle of the husk, using the ends for arms. Fray the top of the husk with scissors and

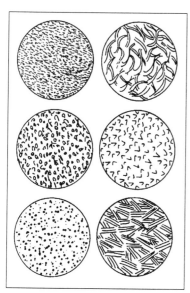

*A harvest texture board.*

flatten down. Draw or add stick-on eyes. Fray the bottom to look like a skirt. The dolls may be used as harvest symbols or strung together to make a harvest wreath.

**Harvest texture board.** Have the children glue various textures to small tagboard squares, which can then be mounted on a large piece of poster board. Materials can include cut-up cornhusks, dried leaves, peanut shells, corn silk, dried grass, wheat, straw, and seeds. The finished texture board can be used in discussions about comparisons and contrasts.

**Variation:** If a double set of texture cards is made, the children can play a matching game.

**Thanksgiving collage.** Materials may include cornhusks, corn silk, used coffee grounds or tea leaves, dried leaves, flowers and grasses, inedible seeds and pods, pine cones, nutshells, or anything the children find outdoors.

**Harvest mural.** Tape a large piece of laminate to the wall with the sticky side facing out. Put a narrow strip of brown construction paper all the way across the laminate, dividing it roughly in half. The strip denotes ground level. A sun in the top half adds to the scene.

Talk with the children about what root crops are and where they should be placed on the mural, as well as where crops that grow above ground should go. Beside the mural, put a basket of pre-cut paper vegetables and fruits, including beets, potatoes, turnips, corn, wheat, tomatoes, and grapes. Have the children attach these in the appropriate half of the mural. This may be difficult for children with poor hand control; they can participate with adult assistance. Fill in the ground area with sand. The work can be preserved by putting a piece of clear plastic shelf paper over it.

**Guessing games.** For this tactile game, make six food cards showing foods eaten at harvest time. Put corresponding fruits or vegetables in a "feelie bag." Each child takes a turn reaching into the bag, guessing what she or he feels by pointing out the matching card, then placing the object on it. Continue the game until the bag is empty.

**UNIT 3**

# Christmas

Christmas is an exciting and joyous time for children who celebrate this holiday, and they love to participate in the preparations. This celebration can engage children in many ways that transcend the commercialism that exerts such an influence in North America. If organized Christmas celebrations are appropriate in your setting, caroling, wishes for peace and goodwill, talking about the birth of Jesus, Santa Claus, and dazzling arrays of food, decorations, and symbols all create a magic time for youngsters.

Some children celebrate this season differently. Find out about their cultures and celebrations, and involve the group in these new experiences. It is important to make young children aware of different cultures and to focus on sharing rather than receiving. Be sensitive to children who may not celebrate the more common holidays by declaring a special day in which they take part.

"Love Is the Word" is a song that crosses all cultures:

Love is the Word

Deborah Dunleavy

Love is the word that brings us to-ge-ther. Love is the word we all can share.

Love is the word that brings us to-ge-ther. Love is the word.

© 1984 by Gabi Music. From "Jibbery Jive" KRL 1015, Kids' Records, Toronto. Reprinted by permission.

2. Peace in our hearts . . .

3. Joy is the song . . .

## EXPLORATIONS

**Reindeer puppet.** Use a brown lunch bag for the puppet head. Make antlers by tracing the children's hands on brown construction paper, then cutting the antlers and gluing them on the bag. Add features such as eyes and a red nose made from shiny red paper or a small pom-pom.

Show the children pictures of reindeer. Talk about where they live and what they eat. You can also describe the mythical reindeer, Rudolph, before singing the song, "Rudolph the Red-Nosed Reindeer."

**Bird feeder garland.** This activity is especially helpful for children who need practice in fine motor skills and general coordination. Have the children use yarn tied to bobby pins to thread breakfast cereal pieces (cereals that have holes or come in large chunks work well). Hang the finished garland in a tree outside a window and watch the birds enjoy their winter treat!

**Clay ornaments.** Use thinly rolled modeling clay and cookie cutters. Let the children press out whatever shapes they choose. A hole is punched through the top of each ornament for attaching yarn or pipe cleaner hangers. Before the clay is set aside to dry, spices (nutmeg, cloves, peppermint, cinnamon) can be sprinkled on and patted into the dough. The spicing creates an appealing fragrance and lasting aroma. Garnish with paint, glue, sparkles, and sequins.

**Pine cone ornaments.** Dry cones in the oven to open them up. The children can then roll the cones in white glue (to cover the tips) before decorating them in trays of glitter, white sand, confetti, or powdered tempera. When the glue has hardened, weave one-foot lengths of thin ribbon, tinsel, or thin chenille throughout the cone. An adult ties a pipe cleaner to the tip for a hanger.

**Gingerbread house.** This activity involves children in stirring, mixing, pouring, smearing, and placing—skills rarely practiced by children who have delayed motor functions.

Use a clean half-pint cardboard milk carton as the form for the house. Make a frothy icing mixture from one teaspoon of cream of tartar, two stiffly beaten egg whites, and one cup of confectioner's sugar. Moisten graham crackers slightly with water so they can be cut to the size of the milk carton without crumbling. Have the children use the icing mixture to glue the graham crackers to the carton, creating the roof and walls.

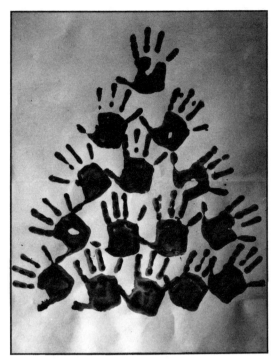

*A tree of hands.*

The children can daub the finished house with the icing to provide a snow-covered look. Decorate the house with sugar sparkles, colored cereals, candies, or cake decorations.

**Making snowflakes.** Put a piece of waxed paper (waxed side up) in front of each child. Spread a generous amount of white glue on the paper. Have the children spread the glue and then use thick wool or string to make snowflake shapes. The glue will make the wool keep its shape. Let the flakes dry overnight. When removed from the waxed paper the next day, the snowflake shapes can be used as mobiles, hung in windows, or put on a tree.

**Tree of hands.** Put a large sheet of paper shaped and cut like an evergreen tree on a table or the floor. Have ready a large tray with just enough green tempera paint to cover the bottom. Show how you can make a handprint by pressing your hand first into the paint, then flat on the paper. Help the children print a tree of hands, making sure each child has the space and time to contribute equally.

**Variation:** Have children trace their hands on green construction paper. An adult then cuts out the hands. When finished, glue the hands together in the shape of an evergreen tree.

**Ornamental balls.** For children who are four or older, making ornamental balls encourages fine motor control and eye-hand coordination. Use foam plastic balls about 2½ to 3 inches in diameter. Cut ribbon of various colors and 1 to 1½ inches wide into squares. Hold the ball steady by wedging it into a cup or the heel of a shoe, or by resting it in a beanbag, pillow, or the child's lap.

Now you need something about three inches long to use as a pin. Blunt toothpicks, hairpins with the ends taped shut, or lollipop sticks work well. Hold a ribbon square against the foam ball while pushing the hairpin or stick into the center of the ribbon square, forcing the ribbon partially into the foam ball but letting the edges show. Children can continue to press in ribbon squares until they are satisfied with the way their ornament looks. An adult then pushes the glue-dipped end of a pipe cleaner into the ball and loops the other end to make a hanger.

**Variation:** Younger or less adept children can drip glue on the ball and then roll it in trays of colored sparkles. A second dripping of glue lets them apply an alternate color. These attractive ornaments are easy to make.

**Pretzel ornaments.** This activity requires fine finger work. Put a piece of foil and some pretzels on the table in front of each child. The children must then arrange the pretzels on the foil so that each pretzel touches another one in at least two places. The child then puts a drop of glue at each point where the pretzels touch. Let the pretzels dry overnight. The next day, add a pipe cleaner as a hanger. Older children may also want to weave ribbon or wool through the pretzel holes as an added decoration.

**Make a Santa.** A cone-shaped drinking cup can be dipped or painted red and, when dry, put on a toilet paper roll. Gluing on pre-cut paper features and fluffed cotton for the beard completes Santa for a jolly window or table decoration.

**Wreaths.** For each child, pre-cut the center out of a small paper plate. Have children glue pastas to the rim of the plate. When dry, they can paint these small wreaths with tempera mixed with glue, afterwards dipping the wreaths in a tray of glitter. The wreaths can be hung anywhere as decorations.

## UNIT 4    Hanukkah

Hanukkah is the Festival of Light that celebrates religious freedom for Jewish people. Light is a universal symbol of freedom from oppression and is central to many celebrations throughout the world, in the form of candles, fireworks, and other manifestations. These joyous celebrations seem designed especially for children, with feasts, gift giving, songs, dances, and family gatherings.

Hanukkah falls sometime from late November to mid-December according to the Jewish calendar. Young children will have limited understanding of the spiritual meaning of this celebration, but it enriches their awareness of cultural diversity. Diversity and tolerance are important concepts for all children to understand; they are especially important to people with disabilities, who are themselves a minority.

The symbols and rituals of ceremonies have personal value to young children. By exposing children to symbols and rituals at an early age, we indicate their potential power and thus move children closer to exploiting that power in their own creative efforts.

In modern Hanukkah ceremonies, most families have their own menorah, which is an eight-branched candelabra. There is a place for a ninth candle in the center or on one side, usually a little higher than the others; this is lit first, then used to light the rest of the candles, going from right to left, on each of eight days. Fresh candles are used each day, so 44 candles are needed in all.

The story of the desecration of the temple in the first Hanukkah can be told. In the story, one day's supply of oil to light the temple's holy lamp miraculously lasted eight days, giving rise to the Hanukkah candle-lighting tradition.

### EXPLORATIONS

**Potato latkes.** Children enjoy making potato *latkes* (pancakes). Food cooked in oil commemorates the lack of oil at the temple in the Hanukkah story.

You can buy potato pancake mix, mixed with fresh potatoes so children can see the whole process:

- Potatoes are washed, peeled, and grated.

- Excess water is pressed out.

- Mix grated potatoes with the purchased mixture.

- Add eggs and water following manufacturer's instructions, and beat everything together.

- Have the children take turns with the stirring.

- Put oil in an electric frying pan. When heated, ladle out spoonfuls of the mixture. Turn once and drain on paper towels.
- Serve with applesauce or sour cream.

**Hora dance.** The Hora is a traditional Jewish circle dance that can be done to the song "Hava Nagila." The dance begins slowly and becomes faster, following the music. You can invent a simplified dance geared to the children's physical abilities.

Here is a simplified version of the Hora:

Children hop and kick once in one direction, then in the other.

Children then walk around in a circle, repeating the hop and kick when instructed.

**What is freedom?** *Freedom* is an idea and abstract, but young children can comprehend it when put in a context they understand.

- Have the children play a dolphin swimming freely in the ocean. The dolphin gets caught and tries to free itself. Music will heighten the scene if the volume is increased to signify the dolphin's being caught and reduced to indicate its escape.
- Have the children imagine a lion creeping through the jungle, only to fall into a hunter's trap, thus needing to figure out how to escape by jumping higher and higher. Children in wheelchairs can use their arms to signify jumping.
- Butterflies can help explore the idea of freedom in the air. Have the children pretend to be butterfly catchers. Each one tries to net or capture a butterfly to some musical cue, such as a piano glissando (rapid notes up or down). Ask the children to hold the imaginary butterflies in their hands and decide whether they will keep them in a jar or let them go.

In one of our sessions with nonspeaking children with cerebral palsy, half of the children set their butterflies free—and were angry with those who did not. The "keepers," feeling the anger of their friends, mimed setting free the butterflies. This example demonstrates how involved children can become in something that captures their imagination, stimulates their understanding, and gives them a choice.

- Children with significant physical involvement often experience significantly greater freedom of motion in water. If you have access to a swimming pool, take advantage of opportunities to involve the children in a simple water dance or other creative movement experience set to music.

**"Hanukkah Song."** The "Hanukkah Song" is fun to sing and increases children's awareness of the Jewish culture.

**UNIT 5** # Kwanzaa

*Kwanzaa* is celebrated by African Americans in the United States. Based on African agricultural festivals, the name *kwanzaa* comes from Swahili for "first fruit of the harvest." The holiday celebrates family and social values and the African American heritage and culture.

The holiday lasts seven days, beginning on December 26. Each day stands for a principle—unity, self-determination, collective responsibility, cooperative economics, purpose, creativity, and faith. Every evening, the family lights a candle in a seven-cup candelabrum, called a *Kinara*—beginning with a black candle in the center and alternating from a green one on the left to a red one on the right until all candles are lit. Then family members discuss how that day's principle affects their lives. The family members often give each other small gifts. On the last night of the holiday, relatives and friends gather for a feast called the *Karamu*.

Local libraries and African American centers at local universities are usually good sources of further information about this holiday. In addition, Eric Copage's *Kwanzaa: An African-American Celebration of Culture and Cooking* (Morrow, 1991) gives information about the holiday, recipes for the Karamu feast, and stories about black history and culture.

## EXPLORATIONS

**Make a Kinara.** The children knead modeling clay or modeling paste to make it pliable, then mold their candelabra into the shape they select. With a pencil or dowel, they poke seven holes in a row, with the center one slightly raised above the others. They can then decorate their Kinaras and help count the days and put candles in place. Use the Kinaras as table decorations at a Karamu.

**Unity mural.** Almost any cooperative art project can be used to talk about working together. One idea is to have the children each make self-portraits in their choice of media, then glue them together into a classroom mural.

**Folktales.** Several traditional African folktales have been published as children's books. One such story with a wealth of creative opportunities is *Why Mosquitoes Buzz in People's Ears*. The mosquito tells a lie that ends up causing chaos in the jungle. A council of animals meets to determine suitable punishment. Once they have heard the story a few times, children will love acting out the animals in the story and adding animal sound effects to the retelling.

**Variation:** Sound effects for the animals can also be explored on various instruments.

**UNIT 6** # Valentine's Day

Big hearts, little hearts, skinny hearts, fat hearts—just a few of the wonderful hearts we see on Valentine's Day!

This popular day gives us a formalized way of helping children learn the language of emotion. Expressing and receiving emotional information are among our most important abilities, abilities we too often think are absorbed without formal learning. However, children with a communication, behavioral, or perceptual disorder greatly need nurturing of these subtle and sophisticated skills. The creative arts provide rich opportunities to enhance understanding of emotional expression.

## EXPLORATIONS

**Sharing time.** Each child brings a favorite toy or small plaything to show and tells the group where it came from, how it is played with, and why it is a favorite.

Pair the children up with suitable partners. The pairs are asked to share their playthings, show each other how they work, and the nicest way to handle, move, or treat them. To compensate for limited vocabulary and experience, rely on the context of familiar toys. (Children's words and concepts are generally better developed here.)

After this sharing, ask each child to create and decorate a home or shelter for their partner's plaything. Have a wide range of materials on hand, such as boxes, fabric, cardboard, and plastic foam containers. Then have the children put the plaything in the finished shelter and present it to their partner as a gift.

**Mending hearts.** This activity is very good for a group with varying cutting and drawing abilities. Each child makes a heart from wallpaper. Children who cannot draw a heart shape can follow a dot-to-dot pattern; some may need to trace a corrugated cardboard template. Those who can handle scissors cut out the hearts. Hearts are then decorated as desired.

Half of the hearts are set aside. The remaining half are given to children who were least able to participate in the previous construction. They rip the hearts in half and put the pieces in a pile. All the children then take a piece from the pile.

Everyone searches through the group to find the person who can "mend their broken heart" (has the other half). When the partner is discovered, the two share a big hug and hooray and mend the heart with cellophane tape. You can repeat the fun with the hearts that were set aside.

**Passing fancy.** Transferring objects from one hand to the other is difficult for many children and should be practiced regularly. To a drumbeat or chime, have the children practice passing a cardboard heart to their neighbor. The tempo should correspond to the children's ability to release the object.

**Variation:** Have children sing "Love Somebody," passing the heart on "you."

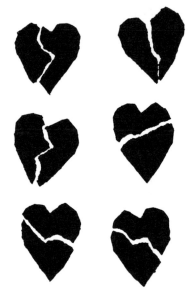

*Who can mend this broken heart?*

*This tree grows valentines.*

**Secret friend.** Explain that each child may choose a secret friend for whom they do something nice that day. Some children will need help keeping a secret and may need prompts in choosing what to do for their friend (perhaps making a small gift, sharing a toy, saying something nice, or helping to clean up).

**Valentine tree.** Put a tree branch in a large pot filled with rocks or plaster of Paris. The tree may be sprayed with white or pink paint. Decorate the tree with valentines made by the children.

**Valentine tree picture.** Paste small hearts onto a painting of a tree trunk for a pretty display.

**Valentine cookies.** Put red sparkles on simple cookies. Children will also enjoy decorating small cupcakes with white and pink icing, then putting red sprinkles on them.

**Valentine train.** Have each child decorate a shoe box and put his or her name on it. Help the children string the shoe boxes together. The children deliver valentines to their friends by dropping the cards into the appropriate "cars."

*A valentine train.*

**Valentine hunt.** Younger children love a valentine hunt to music.

**"Think red" day.** This special day can precede Valentine's Day. Children can go on a "red hunt" for things that are red and have "red snacks," such as red juice, red fruit, and red jam on toast.

***Zillions of Valentines.*** Have the children mime this story by Frank Modell (Greenwillow Books, 1981):

- Two little boys think about valentines. One says, "If I were a big pilot, I'd make a big heart right in the sky."
- Instead they decide to make a zillion valentines on the ground.
- The next day, they put the valentines under everyone's door.
- Everyone is very happy and surprised to get the valentines.
- The boys sell the leftover valentines for a nickel each.
- Then the two boys decide to get each other a valentine.
- They buy valentine boxes of chocolate.
- They eat them all up.

**UNIT 7** Easter

Bunnies, bonnets, and gaily colored eggs symbolize the festive side of Easter. This springtime holiday provides many participatory and creative opportunities for children.

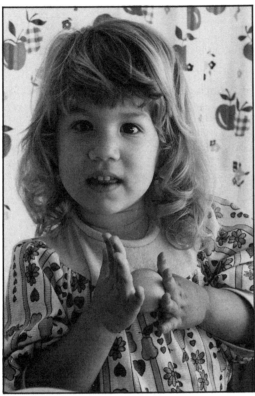

*Getting ready to dye an egg.*

*Children always enjoy an Easter egg hunt, indoors or out.*

## EXPLORATIONS

**Pretty eggs.** This delightful activity encourages careful handling as well as making choices. Put hard-boiled eggs in plastic rings or egg cups so they won't roll. Have the children crayon designs on the eggs. (Some children will need to have an adult to hold and turn the eggs.) When designs are finished, put the eggs in a shallow ladle or spoon and dip them in dyes. The crayon marks will resist the dye and show through when patted dry. More markings can be made before the ends of the egg are carefully dipped in other colors.

For dyes, you can use food coloring or authentic Ukrainian egg dyes, which have brilliant hues and can be purchased at Ukrainian craft stores. The best results are obtained if lighter colors (such as yellow or orange) are used first, and darker dyes later.

**Collage.** Dye broken or unused eggshells and separate them by color. Crush them to produce a colorful and tactile collage medium. The broken eggshells, if thoroughly dry, will adhere to surfaces coated with most varieties of glue.

**Egg hunt.** Children adore egg hunts, whether the eggs are paper or candy. Exploring for eggs is a good exercise for children who must work to orient themselves in three-dimensional space. Frequent verbal hints are necessary and helpful; processing and acting on verbal instructions are substantial skills for these children. Even with the immediate and tangible reward of finding an egg, repeated prompts may be needed, since spatial relationships are complex. In time, we may expect the understanding gained from this activity to be internalized for later applications.

**Variation:** Cut pairs of eggs from the same wallpaper patterns. Give one egg to each child. If the group is small, hide the matching eggs in the room, and have the children search for the matching eggs. For a larger group, give out both sets of eggs and have the children search for their "egg partners."

**Play springtime chick.** Cover the floor with torn newspaper. Hide small treats under the newspaper. The children then pretend to be "springtime chicks," scratching aside the papers with their feet or hands to uncover treats for their baskets. This game can be enhanced with music (such as country or barnyard tunes).

***Jennie's Hat.*** This charming story by Ezra Jack Keats (Harper and Row, 1966) can be the focus for a session using music, story, and art. The hats can be made at any time, but Easter lends itself beautifully to a bonnet parade.

The story is about a little girl, Jennie, who is given a hat by her aunt, a *plain* hat. Jennie begins to put all kinds of things on her head, imagining that they will be more interesting than her hat. They aren't.

The next morning, Jennie peeks out the window and sees ladies with wonderful hats. Later, in church, she thinks that every hat is prettier than hers. On her way home, some birds begin to follow her. Jennie wonders if these are the birds she always feeds. The birds flutter down to her hat, putting on it flowers, leaves, pretty papers, even a nest of baby birds. Jennie feels wonderful. When they reach home, the birds swoop the nest away. Jennie waves goodbye, calling out, "Thank you."

To some pretty music (works by Vivaldi or Mozart are good examples), have the children pretend to be little birds searching for hat decorations. Hide a variety of materials that the children can hunt for and bring to the table to use on their own creations.

To make the hat, take a paper bowl and glue or staple a chin strap (yarn or ribbon) to each side of the rim. Children can paint the hat before pasting on the materials they found in the hunt, plus dyed eggshell fragments, shredded cellophane (Easter grass), or fake fur in pink bunny ear shapes.

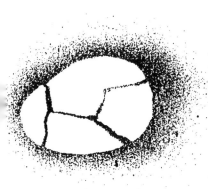

**Humpty Dumpty.** Have the children draw then cut out a large egg shape on an 8½" x 11" sheet of colored poster board. (Provide shapes for those who can't draw and cut their own.) Have the children draw or paint features on their Humpty Dumpty, or indicate to an assistant where those features should go. The finished Humpty Dumptys are cut into four- to eight-piece puzzles and left for later. (Laminating the eggs with clear plastic shelf paper first makes the puzzles easier to cut apart and piece together.)

For a respite from fine motor work, ask the children to move to an open space in the room, preferably carpeted. Have everyone recite the "Humpty Dumpty" rhyme, falling or slumping in wheelchairs on the cue word "fall." Children who have problems with their coordination, vision, muscles or limbs will need to learn how to fall without injuring themselves. This activity provides supervised practice in falling, as does "Ring around the Rosie."

Children with medical problems that prohibit them from falling can recite "Humpty Dumpty" with their limbs outstretched and stiffened. At "fall," they let their limbs fall limp. The designated "King's soldiers" then try to put Humpty together again, miming actions of their choice to sew, glue, or hammer the pieces together.

The children should now be ready to put their paper puzzles together. For those who have difficulty with this, trace all of the puzzle pieces onto cardboard to give the child a visual guide of how the pieces fit into the finished whole.

---

**UNIT 8**     # Birthdays

Birthdays are a great opportunity to focus on a child, reinforcing the child's sense of individuality. Making party hats, preparing treats, and decorating the room can all be part of the festivities.

Birth itself is also very interesting to children, as well as being an exquisite illustration of creativity on a universal scale. Enhance and enlarge birthday celebrations by showing the children pictures and books about babies, both human and animal.

## EXPLORATIONS

***The Hungry Caterpillar.*** This book by Eric Carle (Philomel Books, 1981) shows birth and transformation beautifully and simply.

Have a small green caterpillar puppet peep its head through the pages of the book and the holes of the various foods depicted. The children can add munching sounds as the caterpillar eats more and more food. If you have a larger caterpillar puppet for the last part of the story, so much the better.

Eventually the caterpillar builds its cocoon. The children can mime this with their arms going around and around to a beat on a tambourine—until all is quiet. The caterpillar puppet can be put in a sock for the cocoon stage. Eventually, the sock is turned inside out, and a small butterfly emerges to fly around the room. Any paper or fabric butterfly that will fit into the sock will do.

**Variation:** Have the children burst from eggs and become the hungry caterpillar looking for food. They can mime various aspects of the story. Play some lyrical music as the butterfly bursts forth and flies around. Let the children do their butterfly dance to celebrate its birth.

**Butterfly "births."** If possible, bring in a branch with a butterfly's cocoon. Put it where the children can observe it regularly for signs of the butterfly's emergence. Children take a deep interest in this process and are excited when they first view the butterfly.

**Birthday book.** Young children have difficulty with text, which is normally part of birthday cards. Instead of a card, have the children each contribute a drawing or painting and bind them into a birthday book for the celebrating child.

Using a magic wand, ask the children each to make a wish for or say something they like about the birthday child. This can be done in a circle and written down by the adult as part of the book.

**Past, present, future.** Children need to feel good about their intellectual, social, and physical growth to build self-confidence and their perception of themselves as special people. Ask questions about the birthday child's past and future: "What do you think you were like when you were a baby?" (This may produce lots of giggles.) "What will you be like when you are eight?" "How does it feel to be a year older?"

*A piñata is easily made from a paper bag.*

**Piñata.** Authentic Mexican piñatas are made from papier mâché or pottery and filled with sweets and little presents. When broken open with a stick, piñatas shower their contents into the children's open hands. Instructions for making a papier mâché piñata are given on page 88.

A paper bag piñata is simple to make and adds to the enjoyment of the party. Crush newspapers and use them to stuff a paper bag firmly. Tie the bag's open end with string. The piñata can then be decorated by painting and gluing on shredded tissue paper as well as crepe paper streamers. When decorated, untie the bag, remove the stuffing, and put in candies and treats. Tie the bag up again. Hang it from the ceiling, low enough for a child in a wheelchair to reach with a stick.

Each child is blindfolded and given a stick with which to hit the piñata. Take care to have children sitting well back. Children take turns until it breaks. For a large group, several piñatas will give each child a turn.

**Royal numbers.** Children who are three or four will retain information if they are exposed to it repeatedly. As a number readiness activity, declare the birthday child Queen or King of the Palace of Three (or Four).

You can also have searches to find groupings of three, or stage action and speech games based on the child's age (for example, knock three times, take three steps, say your name three times, or turn around three times).

## UNIT 9    Native Celebrations

Children can begin to learn at an early age about native peoples, the first inhabitants of this continent. Many native people's celebrations are related to seasonal and familial events, such as harvests, birth, lunar phases, weather, and hunting, rather than to a specific day. Activities related to such celebrations should occur outdoors as often as possible. These activities will appeal to the empathy children feel for nature and the people who live close to it.

Learning about people who live in different ways and speak different languages strengthens children's understanding of their world and themselves. The following explorations are designed to celebrate native cultures and draw insight from them. Use these activities to broaden experiences and encourage respect for our multicultural heritage.

### EXPLORATIONS

**Powwows.** These large gatherings include traditional, tribal-social, and spiritual events. Giving thanks is a theme children can adopt in staging their own powwow.

Little children can dance, chant, and provide rhythmic accompaniment. Shakers can be made by placing small pebbles, dried beans, or small nuts in plastic containers with screw-on lids. For drums, children can beat on hard cardboard rollers, drums, or boxes. Encourage them to try and make a strong, steady beat. (In powwows, this beat is meant to echo the pulse of the universe.) Simple dance steps include hopping on one leg slowly in a circle, or twirling and whirling while hopping from one foot to the other and raising arms in the air.

**Button blankets.** The Haida Indians on the west coast of Canada have made and worn button blankets for many years. Buttons are sewn on using traditional patterns for the ceremonial clothes worn at powwows and potlatches.

Children can make their own button blankets using fabric glue to put buttons on a large piece of heavy material. Afterwards, a hole is cut in the middle so that it can be worn as a poncho.

**Potlatch.** This social and spiritual event for Native Americans of the Pacific Northwest includes dancing, rhythmic chanting and drumming, and gift giving.

Show the children pictures of the magnificent sculptural masks, totem poles, and other ritual objects of the Pacific Northwest nations. Then help them make a picture totem using animal and bird pictures and large cardboard tubes or containers. The children can use glue sticks to cover the tubes with glue before pressing pictures onto them.

Another activity is to have the children search a park or open green space for small natural objects, such as a stone, piece of bark, or flower. Seated cross-legged in a circle, children exchange their objects. The children then take turns doing a "thank you" dance in a circle around their partner.

**Sandpaintings.** Show the children pictures of sandpaintings from the American Southwest and of petroglyphs, which are found throughout North America. Then mix tempera paint with sand that the children have filtered through a sieve. Fill plastic ketchup or mustard squeeze bottles using funnels. Designs can be created by pouring the sand from the squeeze bottles onto a smooth soil or pavement surface. (Or squeeze the sand onto glue-covered paper to create a permanent piece of art.)

Have the children do chalk drawings on a pavement, rock, or wall surface (get permission first if necessary). Soaking the surface with water first results in better contrast. Thick sticks of chalk let the children draw freely. They can do a ritual dance as the artwork is completed.

*Rain!*

**Rain dance.** Participants in this universal cultural tradition include the Hopi of the American Southwest, who wear kachina masks as part of their dance ritual. They impersonate the ancestral spirits as they dance and pray for rain and good crops. Impress on children that some parts of the country are very hot and dry, and that rain is precious there.

Give the children rattles that sound like rain when shaken. A simple dance to drumbeats representing rain can be enhanced by having the children wear anklets made of film canisters filled with tiny pebbles and attached to bicycle clips.

**Different peoples, different homes.** Today's children are on the move a great deal—from one place to another, from one group to another, from one city to the next. They always, however, carry with them an image of "home," as a shelter or refuge.

Show children pictures of the homes of different native peoples, suggesting that these shelters are made with materials at hand. For example:

- Igloos in the north, where there is a great deal of snow
- Longhouses of the Iroquois, who lived in heavily forested areas
- Adobe homes, made of mud bricks baked hard by the sun
- Tepees, made of skins and poles
- Different dwellings made by enlarging and adding to natural caves

The children can make models of shelters:

- Big appliance boxes can be made to resemble a longhouse and decorated by the children.

- Igloos call for large quantities of untrampled old snow. Children will be delighted with a circular wall built of several balls rolled in packed snow. For a real treat, heap snow into a large pile. Spraying water on the pile forms a hard icy shell. Hollowing out the insides makes an enclosure the children can actually crawl into.

- Small igloos can be made as outlined on page 141.

- Adobe homes can be made with modeling paste with dry grasses added for texture.

- Tepees can be made by children decorating a piece of brown construction paper, which is then stapled into a cone by an adult.

- Larger tepees can be made by adults. Take four or five long poles or branches, each five or six feet long. Put one end of the poles in a circle on the floor or ground. Tie or tape the upper ends of the poles together, about six inches from the top of the poles. (If you tape, fiber tape works well.)

Wrap blankets, towels, or fabric remnants around the framework. Tie the covering on or hold it together with safety pins. Leave an opening in the covering between poles for an entrance.

On a blanket inside the tepee, arrange nature books or things of interest for the children to observe (such as a bird's nest, birch bark, interesting pebbles, and pine cones). Play Native American chanting or music as a background to tepee play.

**UNIT 10**

# Earth Day

Childhood is a very good time to awaken the environmental consciousness represented by Earth Day. This special day is also an excellent opportunity to show that individual contributions can make a difference in our world. Children enjoy Earth Day activities: they like being alongside others, particularly older children and adults, and welcome the chance to venture into the community as full and valued participants.

Recycling, cleanup campaigns, even public rallies help children develop an awareness of their immediate surroundings. They understand and remember environmental concepts best when activity supports those concepts. Any activity can help, or hurt, our surroundings, so caregivers and teachers can set a positive example by practicing environmental responsibility.

Environmental awareness is acquired gradually; it doesn't "happen" in a day or even a week. If environmental concerns are reinforced as part of daily life, however, children can and will gain this valuable understanding.

## EXPLORATIONS

**Save the Earth.** Get a green balloon or small ball with a representation of Earth on it. Explain that green is the color associated with the environment. Play a game of keeping the ball or balloon in the air as long as possible by hitting it as it gets close to the ground. When it finally hits the ground, explain to the children, "If we don't look after our Earth, it's as though we are hitting it, just as we did when we tried to keep the ball up in the air." Talk with the children about the many things we can do to protect Earth.

**Green finger-painting.** Have children do green finger-paintings. Then cut out letters from the paintings to spell out "Green Earth Day" and put this banner up in the room.

**Green food.** For snack time, make squares of green gelatin dessert, slices of kiwi fruit, and limeade. Children can also put green coloring in cookie dough or put green sprinkles on plain cookies.

**Plant a tree.** Have the children help with the digging, planting, and watering work of planting a tree. Young children will understand and enjoy this activity, which will make them aware that planting helps keep Earth green.

**Rain forest.** Younger groups can undertake this project. If part of a room can be set aside for this for awhile, the children will gain a visual understanding of some of the elements in a rain forest.

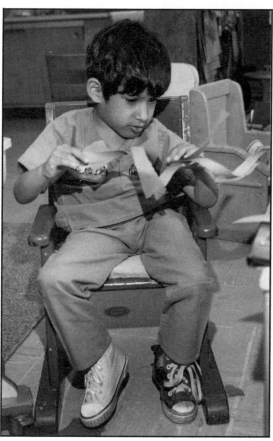

*Making a vine for the rain forest intrigues this young lad as he unwinds his swirl.*

Tell the children that rain forests help keep everything green, and that they can help teach this to others by making one. First, listen to rain forest tapes. Then have the children sponge-print various shades of green on long pieces of mural paper. Use the mural as the forest "walls." Many enhancements can be made to the rain forest:

- Two- or three-dimensional paper images of birds, animals, and insects can be added. Older children might make a papier-mâché crocodile, complete with teeth.

- Strings overhead can hold vines or hanging leaves.

- A background tape of jungle birds and sounds helps bring the whole environment alive.

- A giant spider web can be hung indoors, or outdoors between two large trees. Wind wool, rope, or strong string around the trees at various levels eight to twelve inches apart. (This can be done ahead of time for the group.) Give the children various colored balls of old wool, ribbon, and string, which they weave through the strands to create a loosely woven web. (Let the children weave as they will; there is no "right" way to do the weaving.) Children with limited mobility can weave at one end of the web. Big paper or cardboard spiders can be added when the web is done.

**Garbage totem.** For this recycling project, supervise the children in collecting clean garbage. Broken branches, broken hockey sticks, stakes, or cardboard tubes can become the armature to which the children impale, glue, tape, or staple interesting recycled pieces. When completed, the totems can be driven into the ground, hung from the ceiling or walls, or tied together in a pyramid or tepee shape. Ritualistic dancing and chanting (for example, "Garbage into good things, garbage into good things") sustains the activity.

**Variations**

- Recycled materials can be used in a mural project. A large sheet of stiff cardboard is laced with a network of three- to six-inch stitches in colorful yarn. The resulting yarn loops divide the mural and make a framework on which to hang tie or wedge things that can't be glued.

• Use discarded shells or seeds as part of the recycling program. These can be used as collage elements (see the "Thanksgiving Collage" exploration in the Thanksgiving unit). Gourds, dried for six months, can be painted, varnished, and used as musical instruments.

**Natural homes.** Discovering and examining the homes of animals, insects, and birds can be a prelude to nurturing and creating habitats for them. Learning about taking care of others is especially important to children who are cared for much of the time.

All of the children can participate in attracting birds, which is remarkably easy. Birds need food, water, and a place to raise their young: provide these elements, and birds will come. Bird houses and feeders can be constructed from recycled plastic food or household containers. Simple instructions can be found in most libraries. Decorate with latex or acrylic water-based paint.

**Sea mural.** Have the children paint a huge mural of the sea. Large paper fish of various shapes and colors can then be glued on. Ask the children what the fish might say about keeping their sea world clean. Transcribe the comments onto paper cartoon-like balloons to represent what the fish are saying and let the children glue a balloon to the mouth of each fish.

**Variation:** Younger children can finger-paint or sponge-print a sea mural with green and blue paint. Rolling old tennis balls in paint then printing on paper can create very satisfying variations of color. Again, fish or other sea creatures may be pasted on the mural.

**Treasure boxes.** Recycle plastic berry boxes by letting the children weave shoelaces in and out through the mesh to make solid little containers for their treasures. Children find weaving exciting.

**Composting.** Environmental awareness can be heightened in children through a composting project. It's an excellent starting point for instruction on the environment because it demonstrates the efficiency of nature and the reduction of garbage in home and school.

Dressed in a gardening outfit (hat, gloves, apron, boots), greet the children and discuss gardening with them. Then have children mime various gardening activities appropriate to the season and area of the country—digging, planting, watering, and picking apples and flowers.

Follow with a discussion of the environment illustrated with posters and pictures.

What is the environment? (Living things around us.)

Why is it important to take care of it?

What important things do we get from plants and trees?

For older children, discuss how plants produce oxygen and use carbon dioxide. Healthy plants help clean our air and conserve our soil. Compost helps reduce garbage, produces the best fertilizer for plants, and is free. Tiny living things called bacteria start the process of composting, then other living creatures—such as worms, insects, and animals—help. These things use the compost for food energy.

### Making Compost

### Materials needed:

large bin for mixing

watering can and water

good-quality potting soil

implements for mixing

newspapers spread on table

self-sealing plastic bag for each child

label with child's name on it

organic garbage that the children have brought from home (such as eggshells, crumpled tea bags, coffee grounds, vegetable peels, apple cores, grass, leaves, and bits of sticks).

Each child selects a quantity of each item and puts it into his or her plastic bag. Fill the rest of the bag with soil and water, seal it, and attach the child's name. The bags can be kept in the schoolroom or sent home with instructions to keep the contents moist and to store the bag in a sunny place for the winter. The compost will be ready in the spring.

*Having fun rolling in and crunching leaves.*

**THEME THREE**

# A Special Place—The Spiral Garden

The Spiral Garden is a place at The Hugh MacMillan Rehabilitation Centre in Toronto.

It's also a state of mind.

The place is simple, the state of mind profound. Both can be created anywhere, with the same wonderful and enriching results.

The Spiral Garden itself is a garden of flowers, vegetables, and herbs. Combined with gardening and arts activities year-round, it offers open-ended creative experiences to children in a rehabilitation setting.

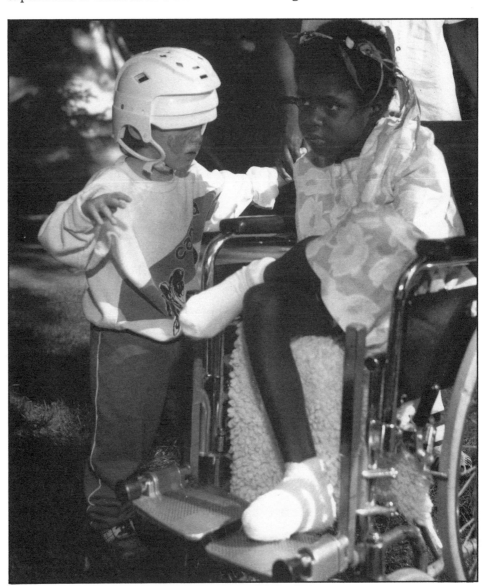

*The Spiral Garden is a special place where children can interact with each other and with various media.*

The Garden is also an integrated place in which children from the community play and work with children from the center. From its inception, the Garden has stressed the value of shared experiences in eliminating attitudinal barriers. Programs may come and go, but meaningful experiences affect the heart and mind long after the experience itself. These positive experiences become building blocks in the formation of children's values and attitudes.

Thus the Garden fosters an environment where interaction is encouraged, the word "disabled" is demystified, and the creative spirit that is in us all can be celebrated. It has become a valued resource for the community at large, offering artists, caregivers, and music therapists an opportunity to observe and participate in an innovative program.

## Activities in the Spiral Garden

The Spiral Garden is in a stimulating outdoor setting that provides many manipulative options. It gives children the opportunity to plant, cultivate, and harvest a garden and to explore the use of natural materials.

Activities may include sand and water play, painting, clay sculpting, movement, mime, music, sculpture, sound poems, and stories. Play is self-directed and self-initiated. Children choose where they go and what they do when they get there. Children who need support in making choices or getting started are assigned assistants.

Many of the ideas and activities used in the Garden can be adapted for other natural settings, but the environment itself can be re-created only by artists and caregivers who have the commitment, energy, and understanding to make it happen.

## Seasons in the Spiral Garden

Children reap the Garden's bounty throughout the year and in many ways. They plant, tend, and harvest the garden; they also celebrate and explore it through the creative arts.

Explorations begin in the spring, when the children plant a vegetable, herb, and flower garden.

Throughout the summer, they help tend the garden, eat salads from the vegetables grown there, and gain an understanding of what makes the garden grow. The summer concludes with an informal piece of theater enacting the season's events and comprised of songs and stories the children help create.

In the fall, a Harvest Festival celebrates the garden's bounty, the creative work of the children and their helpers, and the dying back of the earth into winter.

Each child is given a corn stalk to put on the garden beds for protection from the winter cold. In return, the child chooses gourds and Indian corn for the harvest table. Thus the children carry out a mandate to heal the earth in a very practical, yet thoroughly imaginative, way.

The Spiral Garden is much more than a place where plants grow. It is a place where children and their creativity flourish.

# Special Needs, Special Answers

*A conversation between two three-year-olds playing in a sandbox:*

*Jonathan: Hey, what's that thing around your neck?*

*Evie: It's my brace.*

*Jonathan: Why you got it around your neck?*

*Evie: Cause my back is crooked. It's gonna fix it.*

*The children continue to play. The next morning, at Jonathan's house:*

*Mom: Jonathan, I've been looking all over for you. It's time to go to school.*

*Jonathan: I don't wanna go.*

*Mom: You don't want to go to school? But you love to go to school. Is something the matter?*

*Jonathan: I'm not gonna go to school unless you get me a bracelet.*

*Mom: A bracelet? What kind of bracelet?*

*Jonathan: A bracelet like Evie has around her neck. I want one just like hers.*

Part IV focuses on a number of disabilities and on ways to encourage children with those disabilities to function creatively. We demonstrate these techniques in profiles of individual children. These profiles are inspiring and instructional, showing specific and concrete applications of creative-arts activities.

These activities can, and do, make a difference. The formula for success is always sensitivity, flexibility, patience, and the conviction that no disability should force a child to be a spectator rather than a participant. Children with disabilities need many experiences to discover and adapt to the world. They do not live in a separate world, and they must not be treated as though they do. They must be seen first and foremost as children. They need to be accepted as individuals in their own right and treated with the care and respect we give all persons. They have the right to experience life as fully as possible: to laugh, cry, succeed, fail, learn to make decisions, and develop at their own rate, in their own way.

They do need more understanding and opportunities to grow and flourish than do children who do not have a disability. Children with chronic problems are affected in many ways by their condition. School attendance may be irregular and educational and motivational lags may occur, as may concerns about the future.

If we can use the arts to fertilize these children's expressive activities, enrich their emotional selves, train their senses, and expand their awareness, we will have gone far toward promoting thoughts and feelings that have personal significance for them. Learning to express themselves in a variety of ways is vital to children's well-being throughout their lives. Children also need many tools to survive spiritually and physically, and development of these tools should start as early as possible.

How does one provide for each child's expressive needs? Unique methods must be devised for some; traditional methods can accommodate others. However, no blueprint can be drawn that might cover, or even touch on, the diverse situations generated by a bewildering number of physical, mental, and social conditions.

# Neurogenic Conditions

## Cerebral Palsy

*Cerebral palsy* is a nonprogressive disorder of muscle tone and movement that arises from insult or damage to the brain, before or during birth or anytime up to about the age of three. The distinguishing characteristic of this condition is that it affects the central nervous system's control of movement. Resultant movement disorders may include weakness, stiffness, awkwardness, slowness, and difficulty with balance.

Disabilities in children who have cerebral palsy range greatly; coordination problems can range from slight to severe, and intellectual functioning can range from above normal to severe retardation. There are generally three diagnostic categories. All three—spasticity, athetosis, and ataxia—involve postural control and movement. Some children have "mixed" effects (e.g., athetosis with spasticity).

Most children with cerebral palsy have *spasticity,* which is characterized by increased muscle tone (hypertonicity). Hypertonicity causes tightness in the muscles and a decrease in range of motion in the joints. This condition occurs when the site of the damage is in the motor strip of the cerebral cortex.

*Athetosis* results in infrequent involuntary movements. These movements mask and interfere with the normal movements of the whole body, including the body parts necessary for eating and speaking. Athetosis occurs when cerebral palsy affects the basal ganglia, which are below the cortex in the midbrain. The basal ganglia help to make movement well organized and economical.

*Ataxia* can cause difficulties with balance and a staggering gait. Ataxia results from lesions to the cerebellum, which is located at the back of the brain above the brain stem. The cerebellum helps refine the timing, coordination, and strength of movements initiated in the cortex.

Different body parts may also be involved for different people. The terms most frequently associated with extremity involvement are:

- Monoplegia: One limb is involved (arm or leg)
- Paraplegia: Only the legs are involved with occasional incoordination of the hands
- Triplegia: Three limbs are involved
- Quadriplegia: All four extremities are involved (the arms as much or more than the legs)
- Hemiplegia: Only limbs on one side of the body are affected
- Diplegia: Paralysis of either the arms or legs on both sides (the legs are more typically involved than the arms)

The degree of involvement (extent of impairment) also varies widely. Some children may be so slightly involved that the condition is barely noticeable; more severely involved children may be able to do very little for themselves physically but may function very well intellectually. These children may miss many early childhood experiences because they cannot explore their environments as do children without disabilities. These missed opportunities can interrupt or delay the normal learning process.

Rehabilitation tends to emphasize physical function, individual autonomy, and devices and technologies that enhance independent functioning. This emphasis on the body is necessary, but it is not the whole picture. Professionals who focus only on a child's body or its physical (dys)function will provide a different and less complete service than the person who sees the child as a whole being. Many negatives in the lives of such children have been alleviated or eliminated, but there are times when we forget to accentuate the positive. We forget the strengths the child does have, the creative urges, the ability to respond to the sensory stimulation every child needs to grow and develop. The more the child is exposed to sensory stimulation, the more and deeper the imprints, and the greater and richer the experiences.

*Texture painting
with a lilac brush*

## Living with Cerebral Palsy—Suzanne

Suzanne is a delightful child with an impish grin and a zest for new experiences. She has involvement in all four extremities, but is more affected on the left than the right side. Motor impairment has affected her speech, which is not always clear, and she has a slight drool. She is mobile with a walker, but uses a wheelchair most of the day.

Suzanne enjoys kindergarten and participates in all activities. She attends school in a rehabilitation center, where she can obtain daily physical and occupational therapy. She also sees a speech pathologist once a week. Suzanne is very musical; while her speech is not clear, her intonation usually is. She sings with gusto. Songs with sequential parts or in which a rhyming nonsense word has to be supplied are her favorites.

> What's new at the zoo?
> What's new at the zoo?
> Oh, I saw an elephant
> Who was wrapped up in ___ (cellafint)
> That's what's new at the zoo.

Listening and responding to music is a shared experience, and therefore, a social experience. Through music, children can communicate and share, relate to what they experience in the world, feel free and secure, and have a deeper appreciation of their environment. Music must be fun and immediately related to children's own level of achievement if it is to capture their imaginations. Then, if there is no "price tag" of right or wrong, the music's rhythm and impetus will induce children to participate without fear of failure.

Folk dancing, another social activity, can be done by children in integrated groups. It can involve children using walkers, those in wheelchairs who need to be pushed, and those who are independently mobile in electric wheelchairs. Folk dancing music is especially good for dancing because the rhythm is precise and the melodic line is usually in the foreground, which makes it easy to follow. Suzanne adores dancing and is pleased with her independence in this activity. In dances that are uncomplicated, with in-and-out patterns, simple turning, and sound making, she discovers the exhilaration that all children find through movement. Suzanne dances in her wheelchair and, though she is slow in her responses, she wants to do them on her own.

This need to assert herself is clear when Suzanne undertakes an art project. She insists that the art materials be put before her and that she be allowed to work on her own. It is therefore very important that each project be thoughtfully designed so that she can use the creative part of herself fully.

One can use the visual strengths of these children to design art projects that do not require fine motor control. Suzanne reacts strongly to color and expresses definite preferences. In addition to finger-painting and collage making, she enjoys painting with cold water dye powders. She selects colors to sprinkle on absorbent paper. She applies the powder by shaking small plastic containers of Dylon® cold-water dyes punctured with a needle so that only a small amount of dye goes on the paper. The dye containers are held in Suzanne's hand by an elastic strap taped to the container. The powdered dyes are barely visible until Suzanne spatters them by bringing her arm down on a plant sprayer handle that has a dowel attached for better leverage. The water hits the dye, which bursts into life and mixes to form richly colored spattered patterns.

### Nonspeaking Children with Cerebral Palsy

Children with cerebral palsy vary greatly in their communication abilities. To communicate meaningfully, some may need an augmentative or alternative communication device, containing letters, words, or graphic or picture symbols.

Communication is a fundamental human need. It binds people together in a cultural and social milieu. It lets us share thoughts and feelings, express fears, and draw closer to those around us. Those unable to communicate will be forced to exist on the fringe of the community, passive and dependent.

This was the role that children with cerebral palsy found themselves in for many years. Because of their accompanying disabilities, nonspeaking children—children whose communication difficulties prevent understandable self-expression through speech, hand movements, or facial gestures—are severely restricted in the kind and number of early social and learning experiences they can have. This, of course, limits opportunities for communication.

Because communication is both verbal and nonverbal, we must assist these children in exploring their feelings, learning to express those feelings, and finding release in that expression. Music is one of the most effective tools for this work. It is possible to impel these children at a very early age to become avid participants, to pique their curiosity, lengthen their attention span, and stretch their horizons by encouraging them to travel through the world of imagination.

### A Nonspeaking Child Living with Cerebral Palsy—Anna Marie

Six-year-old Anna Marie's shy grin lights up her face when she is trying to express her pleasure with things or people. She has virtually no speech due to severe quadriplegic involvement. Anna Marie is scarcely able to make any sound at all, and the severity of her cerebral palsy eliminates any communication through gestures or pointing. With much work, she has learned to signal a clear "Yes" by looking upward, and a "No" by looking toward that word on her communication tray.

*A voice-activated computer promotes vocalization in children.*

Anna Marie will play with adapted materials with some pleasure when she can manage them. She enjoys working with sponge blocks on her wheelchair tray. Both ends of the blocks are covered with hook-and-loop fastener (such as Velcro®). When placed on a board with hook-and-loop fastener strips glued to it, the blocks remain upright and can be built up without toppling over, thus allowing Anna Marie the possibility of creating structures in designs she chooses.

Another activity that appeals to Anna Marie is to sit in front of a voice-activated computer that displays a colored kaleidoscope. If Anna Marie makes even a weak "Aaahh" sound, the picture changes. It is very difficult for her to make the sound, but the visual impact of the color and design provides a strong motivation to try.

But it is music that touches this little girl like nothing else in her environment. She tries to respond to whatever is suggested and becomes totally drawn into the experience. A music therapist asks Anna Marie how she is feeling and shows her pictures of faces expressing various emotions; Anna Marie indicates which picture describes her mood at the moment. The therapist then improvises a song describing how Anna Marie is and what she is wearing. Here's one song:

> Anna Marie is feeling good,
> She is very happy today.
> She is wearing a dress,
> With little pink flowers.
> Hooray! Hooray! Hooray!

Then it's time for "Stump the Therapist," which is a good exercise in concentration. Every child gives the therapist a word, which must be incorporated into a story-song. Each week the children try to get words that are more and more unusual and are delighted when their word is mentioned, at which point they make a noise or motion to indicate they have heard it. *Alligator, bus, baseball, cheese sandwich, rabbit, Batman,* and *dinosaur* are examples from a recent list.

The therapist tries to reinforce any communication the children bring to the session and to give them ample opportunity to exercise their imaginations. An example: the book *Jump, Frog, Jump!* by Robert Kalan (Greenwillow Books, 1981) repeats the phrase "Jump, Frog, jump" many times. The music therapist told the story and showed the pictures to a group of young children in Anna Marie's class, having them take turns using a flap switch to make a toy frog jump. (Children with more hand control can use this toy by squeezing a rubber bulb attached to a thin air tube.) When the frog "jumped," the children were to make a vocal or banging sound. As the story progressed, the enthusiasm for making sounds grew and the laughter increased.

Throughout, the therapist improvised music to heighten and describe the story action. Each youngster, no matter how limited in movement, was able to actively participate in a joint adventure with classmates. This participation is extremely important; for Anna Marie, it is a passageway out of the isolation she so often feels. Music has become a significant resource for her, one that she is able to explore on her own terms.

## A Nonspeaking Child Living with Cerebral Palsy—Justin

Justin is a charming little lad with an infectious smile and many winning ways. He has serious involvement in all four limbs. His speech musculature is also affected; he can make some sounds and articulate a few words. He is highly motivated in trying to communicate with others and takes responsibility for creating and sustaining clear interaction, using mime, symbols, and printed words to accompany his very limited spoken vocabulary.

Justin attends school in a rehabilitation center, where he receives physical and occupational therapy. He is also learning to use an augmentative communication system in a class where he is learning to communicate and print on a computer. He is always eager to get to the computer to write stories about his favorite characters (such as Batman and Hulk Hogan). His stories are becoming more interesting and detailed as he explores his ability with technology.

In music sessions, the music therapist reinforces what Justin has written by improvising an appropriate musical backdrop that reflects and emphasizes Justin's efforts. Here is one of Justin's stories (written entirely by himself), which the group enjoyed acting out to music:

"Batman"

I am Batman.
You are Robin.
Batman beats up bad guys.
BOOM . . . BANG
The bad guys go away.
AHHHHHH . . . BOOM . . . OUCH
Batman goes home.
The End

*Can you hear the ocean?*

Music can be combined with art, thereby using children's visual strengths. One day, Justin's music therapist brought a basket of seashells, starfish, and coral for the children to listen to, see, and touch. After an explanation of how these creatures live in the sea, the lights were lowered and, with eyes closed, the children listened to selections from Hap Palmer's "Seagulls" (Educational Activities Record No. ar584). As the music played, the children were asked to imagine a picture of the sea. Gradually, the sound was turned down and the lights turned up, and the therapist began to draw a seascape on the chalkboard as the children indicated what elements the drawing should contain.

Therapist: Show me what color the sky should be in our seascape.

(The children indicate that the sky should be blue.)

Therapist: Is there anything in the sky?

Justin: (indicates a balloon)

Therapist: What color is the balloon?

(Justin points to red, yellow, blue. Other children request birds and a big kite.)

Therapist: Tell me about the sea. What do you imagine is in the water?

Justin: Me.

Therapist: What are you doing in the water?

(Justin mimes swimming. Others suggest adding fish and starfish; one girl who is unable to point indicates shells by looking at them on a nearby table.)

Therapist: Is there anything else in the sea?

Child: (indicates a boat)

Therapist: What kind of boat?

(The child mimes blowing.)

Therapist: Do you mean a sailboat?

(Child nods.)

Therapist: There is a beach at the bottom of this picture. What happens at the beach?

(Various replies, from hot dogs to children playing in the sand.)

Now the mural is complete, but another dimension is added to the session by dramatizing various aspects of the mural. The music comes on again, and the youngsters are encouraged to be seagulls gliding in the breeze before landing on the sand to look for food, children building tall sand castles (which tumble down when the music gets louder), or the waves of the sea itself, rolling in and out to the rising and falling music. A huge piece of blue chiffon stretched over the children's heads enhances their enjoyment of the dramatization.

Acting out stories to music is always the high point of the session, for here the youngsters can try on new roles. Each child, no matter how limited in motion, can mime characters in the story and experience the feelings and behaviors of those characters. These explorations help children work toward the primary goal: to know each other better and to appreciate themselves as viable human beings.

## Music and Communication

Children with physical impairments need to learn dramatic play to acknowledge and act out their feelings. They cannot "run their anger off," and feelings that are denied or suppressed eventually may take a toll. Dramatic play that highlights inner feelings emphasizes emotional attitudes. In the story *David Was Mad,* by Bill Martin, Jr. (Holt Rinehart and Winston, 1967), a boy goes through the day feeling very angry and lashing out at everyone. Children dramatizing the story use a great deal of vocalization and gross motor movement. Afterwards, when discussing anger, they are encouraged to indicate whether they sometimes get angry. The therapist then improvises songs to support their communication.

Listening and responding to music is a shared experience that can help children discover a bond with others. We can help children communicate their awareness of this bond and bring them out of the isolation created by their disabilities. When children are allowed to move and create in ways that express their feelings, they can visibly grow in power and self-possession.

## How to Facilitate Better Communication

Remember: it takes two to talk. The adult working with a nonspeaking child must avoid dominating the conversation and causing the child to slip into a passive role. The adult must also be attuned to the child's most fragile initiative, supporting it in any way possible.

- Give the child an opportunity to initiate topics or to give a cue about the topic he or she wants to pursue.

- Ask questions that call for more than a "Yes" or "No" response.

- Be sensitive to the child's needs to organize his or her thoughts. Allow time to finish: don't interrupt with interpretations, finish sentences for the child, or put words in the child's mouth.

*For a child to communicate, she must have*
- *something to say*
- *confidence in the way she communicates*
- *sufficient praise, encouragement, and satisfaction to make the effort worthwhile.*

- Speak slowly and clearly, and use short sentences, when giving instructions; some children process information slowly.

- Follow the child's lead whenever possible. Unless given the opportunity, a child with a disability may not fully exercise abilities to provide information, express feelings, and make requests.

- Make sure that praise and encouragement are part of the interaction so that the child feels that it is worth the effort.

### Resources for Coping with Cerebral Palsy

**United States**
Medical Director
United Cerebral Palsy Association
66 East 34th Street
New York, New York 10016
(212) 481-6300

Executive Director
National Easter Seal Society
2023 West Ogden Avenue
Chicago, Illinois 60612
(312) 243-8400

**Canada**
Canadian Cerebral Palsy Association
55 Bloor Street East
Suite 301
Toronto, Ontario M4W 1A9
(416) 923-2932

## Spina Bifida

*Spina bifida* is a defect in the spinal column; the spine fails to close properly, resulting in an opening or protrusion that may expose the nervous system. The severity of disability varies considerably, depending on where on the spinal column the lesion occurred. Some children show few or mild disabilities—occasionally the only symptom is an abnormal x-ray, with no disability present. Others have more severe symptoms, which may include:

- Paralysis or spasticity of the trunk or lower limbs

- Little or no bowel or bladder control

- Loss of sensitivity to pain, temperature, and touch, resulting in problems such as burns and pressure ulcers

- Bone deformities such as scoliosis (spinal curvature), lordosis (swayback), kyphosis (humpback), club foot, dislocation of hips, and hip and knee contractures

- Weak fine motor skills or eye-hand coordination

- Hydrocephalus, or excessive fluid in the brain. If the fluid is allowed to accumulate, the child's head enlarges and brain damage occurs. To prevent this, pliable plastic shunts are inserted surgically to drain the excess fluid from the brain. The fluid is then absorbed by other areas of the body.

Many of these children are hyperverbal; their tendency to learn language well by rote can mask their actual level of intellectual functioning. They present with a range of intellectual capabilities, and even those with average intelligence may experience a number of perceptual and language-learning disabilities.

Two aspects of visual perception that seem troublesome for many children with spina bifida and/or hydrocephalus are spatial judgments and figure-ground discrimination. These difficulties may explain why some of these children have problems making sense of pictures, staying inside the lines when coloring, or paying attention to relevant letters and digits on a page with a great deal of distracting information.

There may also be indications of difficulties with laterality and directionality, which may be due in part to:

- Considerable delay in the preferential use of one hand
- Delayed ability to distinguish right from left
- Much higher proportion of left-handedness and mixed-handedness among children with spina bifida with hydrocephalus

Children who have spina bifida with or without hydrocephalus may need to use wheelchairs, braces, walkers, crutches, and other apparatus for mobility. Some younger children may stand in a standing frame to free their arms and hands and allow for a change in position. Bracing children with a short ankle-foot orthosis or longer knee-ankle-foot orthosis may be the primary means of ensuring continued independent ambulation. This type of brace has a built-in base that allows standing or sitting without the need for other support, thus giving the child a different view of the world and giving others a more normalized perception of the child. Such a brace provides other advantages for upright posture, such as increasing bone strength, possibly improving cardiovascular and respiratory functioning, and improving kidney functioning by allowing the bladder to empty by gravity.

Every effort should be made to help these children meet typical developmental milestones in a sequence that resembles normal (although perhaps delayed) motor development. Assistance with personal care probably will be required until the children are mature enough to take on such tasks independently.

Achieving independence can be greatly assisted by exposure to creative opportunities. All children who have spina bifida with or without hydrocephalus can participate in programs designed around their social, educational, and physical needs.

## Living with Spina Bifida—Nicole

Nicole is a cheery, energetic, sociable four-year-old with spina bifida. She enjoys engaging adults in conversation and play, and is enthusiastic about activities in her nursery school.

Nicole is paralyzed from the waist down and uses a wheelchair, although crawling is her preferred mode of mobility. She can easily scoot across the floor on her tummy and thus can explore her environment and participate in many activities. For a period each day she is put in a standing brace and can engage in many play and art activities from this standing position. She is also learning to "walk" in her brace.

Nicole likes to take on a leadership role and decide on play situations for her and her friends (she is encouraged to involve others in decision making). She has a lively imagination and shines during dramatic role-playing activities in the doll center and with the doctor's kit. When playing on her own, she needs assistance and direction to persist in and complete an activity.

Her readiness skills indicate that she can identify colors and shapes and sort objects by whether they are the same or different. She holds large crayons in various grasps and can make marks on paper in targeted areas.

Distractibility is a major concern for Nicole. In music, we use sequential activities to help her improve concentration. Nicole is asked to duplicate the therapist's rhythm sequence. Beginning with very simple exercises (such as clap two times, then ring the chime) the sequences will become more complex as her attending improves. She is also delighted (as is her nursery group) when asked to touch body parts, point to various objects in the room, say specific words, or follow the therapist's commands for a rhythm accompaniment on the drum or other instrument. She has markedly increased the number of items she responds to before her concentration lapses.

Nicole also enjoys manipulative art activities, such as wood sculpture, modeling clay work, painting, and finger-painting, but has difficulty cutting with board-mounted scissors (see Appendix A) and needs support to stay with the task. She is encouraged in scissor activities by cutting and duplicating fringes on paper, cloth, and leafy vegetables (such as cabbage leaves).

Nicole's real strength lies in expressive language. She can answer you and comment on other persons or objects, and demonstrates a good memory for names and events. She has become familiar with a wide variety of songs and finger plays, which are used to help her stay on task.

Dramatizing stories verbally as well as through movement and mime can be an asset to all children, allowing them to stretch their imaginations and lose inhibitions as they discover the joys of fantasy. Initiating this process is simple: make sure that children are allowed to function freely in a relaxing and accepting atmosphere. Praise every attempt by a child, for we are concerned not with the result but with the process. Ask the children if they can be, for example, a chick hatching out of an egg; a snowman melting in the hot sun; a baby crying for her bottle; or a little mouse being chased by a cat. Playing in this way widens a child's perspective while contributing to self-esteem.

Nicole adores participating in such activities. In a recent enactment of *The Three Billy Goats Gruff,* Nicole insisted on being the smallest goat because she was the smallest child in the class. A contoured gym bolster was used as the bridge, and Nicole was helped to the top of it. When confronted by the troll, she told him why he shouldn't eat her up, elaborating extensively and using a variety of voices. Throughout the story, she was able to stay with her role as the smallest goat, and when the story was done, she wanted to play the game again and again. Adding music expands and extends her developmental growth in these experiences as well as encouraging her to take turns, stay on task, and not interrupt others.

## Living with Spina Bifida and Hydrocephalus—Connie

Connie is a playful and personable six-year-old with spina bifida and shunted hydrocephalus. Because she is such a good conversationalist, she appears brighter than she actually is. Connie displays the "cocktail party" syndrome characterized by endless chatter that is frequently lacking in substance and makes inappropriate or repetitive use of words. Sometimes she talks so much that she fails to pay attention to the task at hand, which hinders her ability to follow directions and to learn.

Connie uses crutches and wears additional splints for support. Her arms and hands are strong, and she has no difficulty with most daily activities. She labors to print, though, and her printing tends to be illegible and limited in quantity. This fine motor immaturity is characteristic of many children with spina bifida and accompanying hydrocephalus, and should be addressed regularly. As a child matures, poor handwriting often becomes an increasing handicap, manifesting in problems in spelling and arithmetic as well as in language arts. (These symptoms may also be due to learning disabilities, which are often seen in such children.)

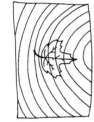

*Simple figure-ground puzzles.*

Helpful art activities include drawing large circles on a chalkboard, then advancing to large letters. It is important to teach the child the right direction of the strokes for a letter; many children with perceptual and visual-motor learning difficulties do not automatically pick this up. Some children with spina bifida and hydrocephalus who are not taught to form letters correctly tend to regard handwriting as pattern copying. Because such children often have visual-spatial problems and consequent directional confusion, they often have difficulty when they attempt cursive writing. Many are now being exposed to computers as an augmentative method to enhance speed and quality of written communication.

Make sure these fine motor activities are short in duration so that the child will not get fatigued or frustrated. Colored chalks enhance the exercise, and background music aids relaxation. Cutting, pasting, modeling, printing, and drawing in various media should also be used. Activities that Connie finds helpful include finger tracing raised tactile letters of various materials (such as sandpaper, felt, or cardboard) or drawing in sand, in the air, or on soapy surfaces; this work helps her become more aware of shapes. Paper tracking (with a teacher sitting in front of Connie and slowly drawing a line pattern from left to right) as Connie tracks and follows with her finger bolsters visual acuity. Finding, tracing, and coloring figures hidden in puzzles helps figure-ground discrimination.

Connie's ability to remember lyrics, mimic sounds, and repeat rhythms supports her enthusiasm for musical experiences. She does folk dancing with determination and joy. Her outgoing personality, imagination, and involvement in mime and dramatic play help offset the frustrations she feels in other areas while contributing toward her acceptance by peers.

### Resources for Coping with Spina Bifida

**United States**
Spina Bifida Association of America
343 South Dearborn
Room 317
Chicago, Illinois 60604
(312) 663-1526

National Hydrocephalus Foundation
Route 1, River Road
Box 210A
Joliet, Illinois 60436
(815) 467-6548

### Canada
Spina Bifida Association of Canada
633 Wellington Crescent
Winnipeg, Manitoba R3M 0A8

# Orthopedic Conditions

## Arthrogryposis

*Arthrogryposis* is a congenital condition characterized by poorly developed muscles and stiff or dislocated joints. Deformities are apparent at birth, although their cause is unknown. A mild form of arthrogryposis is evidenced by a child with club feet and possibly some other stiff joint. Other children may have various joints affected, including those of the hands, arms, elbows, and shoulders, all of which may be straight or bent. Serious involvement may include the hips, trunk, and even the head. If the trunk is involved, there may be spinal deformity or weakness of the respiratory muscles.

Arthrogryposis does not affect the child's general intelligence level, speech, feeling, or balance. The child learns to compensate for the weakness and stiffness; with rehabilitative therapy considerable independence is possible, including attendance at a regular school. Thus, it is important to encourage academic achievement while at the same time directing these children toward goals that do not involve advanced hand skills or (if the legs are affected) general mobility. The rapidly developing technology of our time is leading to advances in aids for many children with disabilities. Children with arthrogryposis have the drive to take full advantage of these new developments.

*A sponge print says, "I love you."*

### Living with Arthrogryposis—Darryl

Darryl is a five-year-old boy whose arthrogryposis has affected his shoulders, arms, elbows, and hands. His legs are unaffected and his breathing is normal, but his arms and hands look like withered stalks. At the age of three, Darryl had surgery on his elbows, which were fixed in extension. As a result, he now has limited range of motion in his elbows.

Darryl attends kindergarten in a school setting within a children's rehabilitation center, where he works out in a daily stretching program to maintain the maximum range of motion possible and prevent the formation of permanent contractures. For part of each day, Darryl needs to wear splints on his hands and wrists for additional support. The splints do not intrude on his activities. He plays hard and is highly motivated to do what others in his class are doing. Darryl is not shy about asking for adult approval and support, and adults respond wholeheartedly to this determined and appealing boy.

Darryl loves art despite the difficulties he has in this area. To paint, he stands before a low table so that he can raise his shoulder and bring his arm over the paper, which is taped to the table. His favorite art activities are dye painting (see page 177) and printing, where he can hold a dowel glued to sponges of various shapes.

Dramatic play also gives Darryl satisfaction. His verbal skills make for some interesting dialogue with his play group. He prefers to be the doctor who "fixes kids up," directing his peers to have specific maladies. In this role, he dominates the proceedings and will brook no interference.

Darryl: You are very sick now, go to bed.

Sara: Well, I wanna play.

Darryl: I am the doctor, and you gotta get a operation so I can fix you up.

Sara: Okay.

Darryl: Now be sick, sick, sick. Sandra has to get me.

Sandra (knocks on door): Doctor, Doctor, come quick. Sara has a sick leg. I think you gotta cut it off.

Darryl (examines Sara's head, ears, arms, and legs): I think I can fix her up. She just needs my special medicine.

In music activities, Darryl is able to beat a drum by wearing a mitten that has a drumstick glued to it and is fastened at the wrist with a strip of hook-and-loop fastener (such as Velcro®). Most instruments have to be adapted for him; he occasionally experiments with using his feet to explore other instruments. Darryl demonstrates skill in simple folk dancing, which he does with flamboyance and a good sense of rhythm.

### Resources for Coping with Arthrogryposis

**United States**
Avenues
National Support Group for Arthrogryposis Multiplex Congenita
P.O. Box 5192
Sondra, California 95370
(290) 928-3688

**Canada**
Canadian Rehabilitation Council for the Disabled
45 Shepherd Avenue East
Suite 801
Toronto, Ontario M2N 5W9
(416) 250-7490

# Osteogenesis Imperfecta

*Osteogenesis imperfecta* literally means "imperfect new bone formation" (osteo = "bone" + genesis = "new beginning"). The common term is "brittle bone disease." Its cause is unknown, but the condition is known to be inherited. It is seen in both males and females; no racial predominance is evident.

A baby born with this condition will have short deformed limbs, numerous broken bones, and a very soft skull. Other associated problems are a face that appears triangular due to the bone formation of the skull, scoliosis of the spine, a barrel-shaped chest, teeth that are easily broken and prone to cavities, joints that are excessively mobile and often regarded as double-jointed, and a pale blue coloring to the whites of the eyes.

Children with this condition have normal intellectual abilities, are usually very verbal, and learn easily. Because their bones are fragile, it is important to guard against situations that might result in falls and fractures. Physical education is out of the question, so developing skills in social games and creative endeavors helps these children make and maintain normal relationships.

## Living with Osteogenesis Imperfecta—Charmaine

In her 5½ years of life, this charming little girl with blond hair, very blue eyes, and a dimpled smile has had more than 20 fractures. Despite the number of hospitalizations this has meant, she demonstrates a realistic self-concept and an independence unusual for a child of her age. Frequent hospitalizations have provided her with the opportunity and the need to learn to get along with adults. Her large vocabulary, coupled with her ability to initiate and maintain a meaningful conversation, has contributed to adults' acceptance of this bright little girl.

Charmaine also interacts well with her peers in kindergarten, often taking on the role of leader during play. She assumes many roles and can mimic voices, gestures, and postures to play a mother, therapist, teacher, witch, even an imperious fairy or queen. She delights in seeing other children in the class get involved in her dramatic moments.

Charmaine uses an electric wheelchair because she is unable to walk. She loves dancing in her chair and eagerly awaits movement explorations in music sessions. Her strong verbal ability helps her remember the lyrics of many songs, which she sings with enthusiasm. She is also learning to accompany herself on the Suzuki Omnichord® electronic keyboard (see Appendix A). Music provides a challenging creative outlet for Charmaine; it gives her the freedom to explore herself and her world.

## Resources for Coping with Osteogenesis Imperfecta

### United States
American Brittle Bone Society
1256 Merrill Drive
West Chester, Pennsylvania 19380

Osteogenesis Imperfecta Foundation
P.O. Box 245
Eastport, New York 11941

### Canada
Canadian Rehabilitation Council for the Disabled
45 Shepherd Ave. East
Suite 108
Toronto, Ontario M2N 5W9
(416) 250-7490

# Amputations

Limb deficiencies include the complete or partial loss or absence of one or more limbs. A child born with such a condition is said to have a *congenital amputation*. Congenital amputations are the most common form of amputations in children. Other causes include trauma and malignancy. Defective or partial limbs may also be amputated to permit the use of prostheses (artificial devices that substitute for missing body parts).

The design and fitting of prostheses plus training for their use is the usual treatment prescribed for children with amputations. How well the prostheses fit, how functional they are, and the children's attitude toward them often determine how well they will be managed and worn.

The age at which a child loses a limb is often significant in the acceptance of a prosthesis. It is generally thought that the earlier the loss, the more likely the child will accept and cope with the prosthesis. Some children adjust to functioning without their prosthesis, but many professionals think that children are better off learning to use their device. It is therefore important to know the child's levels of competence with and without the artificial limb. Some devices are more cosmetic than functional, but all need regular adjustment and replacement as the child grows.

## Living with an Amputation—Rebecca

*The earlier a child is given a prosthesis the easier it is to adjust to.*

Three-year-old Rebecca is typical of many children with limb deficiencies: she is missing part of one arm below the elbow. At six months, Rebecca was fitted with a passive hand strictly for cosmetic purposes. Later on she tried a mechanical hand with a complicated harness fitting. When she was 16 months old, she was fitted with a myoelectric arm which she still uses.

This precisely molded and crafted arm-hand unit slides snugly onto Rebecca's residual arm. No straps are required. Her hand movement is powered by a battery-operated microcomputer within the arm. The motor is switched on and off by the muscles in her natural forearm, where two surface electrodes (smooth metal discs inside the myoelectric unit) are in tight contact with her skin. The nickel-cadmium battery in the arm is rechargeable.

Because of her age, Rebecca has a simplified version of the arm. When she tenses her muscle, the hand opens; when she relaxes, it closes. As she becomes more adept, a more sophisticated and versatile prosthesis will be fitted. At this time, however, the arm gives her an opportunity to have two-handed function, is cosmetically beneficial, and makes social acceptance easier.

Rebecca's skills include holding a paintbrush in her hand, pasting with a glue stick, stringing large beads on a shoelace, coloring on an egg in her hand, and pouring liquids from one vessel to another. In music, she is encouraged to hold two drumsticks and beat them together or separately in a "Mama, Papa" pattern. She loves to play with the Suzuki Omnichord® electronic keyboard (see Appendix A) using her left hand to press down the chord and her myoelectric hand to glide along the touch bar. She also loves dancing and uses both arms for balance and for interpretation of the music.

In all other aspects of play and movement in her nursery school, Rebecca manages with ease. One can see that a marvel of engineering has given her a chance to lead an ordinary life.

## Living with an Amputation—Earl

Earl is a chubby, freckled, blue-eyed boy who looks and acts like an imp. He was 5½ when he entered kindergarten in the middle of the school year, enrolling late because his family had just moved to town.

On his first day, the other children in the class each brought something for "show and tell." Each child took a turn, After they finished the session, the teacher said that next time Earl could "show and tell," too. Well, Earl said, he did indeed have something he could show right then and there, and with the teacher's permission, he did:

*My name is Earl the Pearl. That's what everybody calls me. What I got to show you is my leg (he then rolled up his pant leg). I got one good leg and this one (he showed his prosthetic device). Now when I was borned, this bad leg was shorter and the foot was on backwards. So the doctor decided to cut it off because I couldn't walk on it or anything. Then when the leg got better, I got this artificial leg and they had to teach me how to walk on it. At first, it was kinda hard but I kinda got used to it and now I don't even know that I got it on. I can run and walk just like everybody else. That's all.*

The children responded to his spunky story with many questions, which Earl answered very well for his age. His matter-of-fact approach to his problem contributes greatly to his ability to cope with other aspects of daily living.

## Resources for Coping with Amputations

### United States
National Easter Seal Society
22023 West Ogden Avenue
Chicago, Illinois 60612
(312) 243-8400

March of Dimes Birth Defects Foundation
1275 Mamaroneck Avenue
White Plains, New York 10605

### Canada
War Amputations of Canada/National Headquarters
Child Amputee Program
2277 Riverside Drive, Suite 207
Ottawa, Ontario K1H 7X6

*This prosthetic arm allows for two-handed function and better balance.*

Also contact local veterans' organizations and hospitals for information on prosthetic limbs.

# Sensory Conditions

## Visual Impairment

Being *visually impaired* means one's eyesight is not good enough to allow participation with ease in everyday activities. Children who are considered visually impaired fall into one of two categories: blind and partially sighted (low vision). Education for these two groups differs; children who are blind must learn to read using braille, whereas the children who are partially sighted will read large print and often require special glasses.

Adaptations to sensory loss have profound personal, social, and educational implications. Every effort must be made to give these children programs that involve all areas of development and adjustment. Fortunately children who are

*Touching the strings to feel the vibrations.*

visually impaired need not be excluded from most creative activities. Tactile features can be included in painting and other visual activities (such as finger-painting, collage, mosaic, modeling, and relief printing). Activities requiring auditory or tactile sensitivity obviously benefit these children. With little or no adaptive requirements they can participate in vocal explorations, music making, sculpture, dramatic play, and movement exercises.

The remaining senses do not automatically enhance themselves. Each sense must be trained and exercised to compensate for sight loss. As with all children, but more critically with children who are visually impaired, sensory-motor experience is the crucial basis for explorations of space and time. These explorations, in turn, are necessary to establish concepts of motion and form.

Children who have limited vision should be provided with materials that are large in scale and strong in contrast. Lighting should be adjusted to maximize visibility while eliminating glare. It is important to arrange seating so lighting in the room is favorable for those who need it most. When teaching, remember not to sit or stand with your back to the light source. When reinforcing the children's behavior or accomplishments, talking and touching must replace smiles and body gestures.

Because these children depend more on listening skills to deal with and understand their environments, it is essential that they learn to localize as well as identify and discriminate among sounds. It is difficult to do this in a large or noisy classroom. If the noise level can be toned down, the children have a better chance of picking up the auditory cues they need.

Children who are blind need even more accommodations to function in a setting that includes sighted children. It is essential to eliminate clutter and unnecessary obstacles in the room. Encourage children to put toys away as soon as they finish playing with them. It is also important not to rearrange the room, but to build in tactile, auditory, and olfactory cues that help the children get a sense of where things are located. A bubbling aquarium, a section of carpeted floor, and dried eucalyptus in a vase are examples of measures that can indicate various locations and encourage independence. You can also help by using consistent sound cues when changing activities, telling the children what is happening in an ongoing activity, and passing around small replicas of objects talked about in a story.

Visually impaired children usually respond well to creative arts experiences because of their capacity for expression and sensory involvement with materials. Appreciation of their efforts will be heightened if one remembers that one does not have to see to create.

## Living with Visual Impairment—Sara

Sara is a delightful five-year-old who is partially sighted. She can distinguish light from dark. At times, she seems to be awkward, stumbling over small objects. Sara loves music and spends many hours listening to tapes of her favorite singers and to the radio. Her whole body responds to the music's rhythm, particularly when she is seated. Like many children who have visual impairments, Sara is reluctant to move in space and must be urged to do so.

To help overcome her fear of movement, she is offered many kinds of movement experiences. These experiences range from slow undulating rhythms to bouncy, vigorous music, and always include spatial contrasts. Movement experiences always begin with work on the floor because children like Sara frequently feel

disoriented in space. The floor provides a firm, safe base while minimizing the chance of falling or colliding with others or with things, thus promoting a feeling of security.

Sara usually begins with a degree of uncertainty, looking for direction. "Sara, pretend you're sitting on a lovely pink cloud and it is moving softly and gently around you," the music therapist says. "Touch it, reach out with all your body as the cloud wraps you up in its mists." Another time, the therapist tries suggesting that Sara pretend to be "a beautiful bird flying through the sky. You are sweeping up and away then down and around with swooping wings." As the music continues, Sara becomes caught up in the exhilaration of the moment and begins to move with greater abandonment, using the space around her.

Sara always enjoys moving with props in her hands. Scarves and hoops give her something concrete she can use to identify space. Because others in the group have small bells attached to elastic bands around the wrists, Sara is able to dance with more ease, knowing that she will be able to tell how close they are.

Sara enjoys music sessions where the group plays percussion instruments, sings songs, learns finger plays, does listening games, and dramatizes stories to music. Her listening skills are well developed and she has a real flair for imitating voices and rhythm patterns. Because music is genuinely interesting to Sara, it can become a meaningful activity for her and provide for growth in other areas. Here she is not disadvantaged but is able to excel and gain in self-esteem, body awareness, confidence in movement, and peer relations.

### Living with Visual Impairment—Jamie

Jamie is a five-year-old boy who has been legally blind since birth. Like many blind children, he has a limited degree of light perception, which is valuable to his mobility. He attends kindergarten with children who are not visually impaired, but needs a good deal of support in several of his daily routines.

Jamie's mother has spent a great deal of time with him in play and in helping him learn to be as independent as possible in the home environment. She is a warm, understanding woman who provides substantial support for her son's initiatives, yet consistently stresses that he must do for himself whenever possible. Her matter-of-fact attitude has contributed to Jamie's feeling of self-worth and to his healthy attitude in peer relationships.

Jamie's father is separated from his wife. He sees Jamie on weekends and takes him many places, painstakingly describing each experience so that Jamie learns from each outing. The father answers questions patiently and helps Jamie establish a tactual, olfactory, or aural sense of where they are and what is exciting about the place. Thus visits to the zoo, to a farm, to a sculpture exhibit in an art gallery become significant and real, mitigating against the isolation many children with visual handicaps experience.

Jamie's father is a commercial artist who tries to give his son opportunities to experiment with various art media. From the time he was a toddler, Jamie has been playing with modeling clay, modeling paste, sand, and clay. He has learned to derive a great deal of pleasure from these manipulative materials, making interesting shapes that have become more and more sophisticated as his tactile abilities mature.

At school, Jamie enjoys finger-painting, especially on a tabletop because it's less confining than a piece of paper. Gluing pieces of wood together is another favorite activity. Playing with blocks or other three-dimensional toys holds his interest for a long time. Jamie also enjoys listening to stories, either live or recorded. He is curious and asks many questions as the story unfolds. He can get frustrated when he doesn't understand what is happening in the story or if he becomes confused about his immediate environment. At such times, it is important to help him sort out the situation so that he can diffuse his anger and regain his composure.

Jamie's parents have given him much of the support he needs to function well, so well that he is now attending first grade in a mainstreamed school.

## Living with Cerebral Palsy and Visual Impairment—Andreas

Andreas is a four-year-old boy with cerebral palsy that affects all four limbs. He also has only peripheral vision, which means he can see only outside the direct line of vision. Because of his defective vision, he often tilts his head or raises or lowers his eyes to see pictures in a book, numbers, and letters of the alphabet. This impairment in vision and his severe spasticity affect his mobility and collection of information in the environment.

Andreas enjoys being with the other children in his nursery group. He engages in parallel play and attempts cooperative play with adult assistance. He is aware of the routines in his school, but needs encouragement and prompting to move from one activity to another. Andreas works best when limits and expectations are carefully set out. Tasks must be broken down and taught in sequence so that he has time to work things out for himself and to discover and examine with his limited vision. A specific goal of his education is to improve his senses of touch, hearing, smell, and taste.

Staff who work with Andreas believe that his vision fluctuates daily a great deal, depending on his physical and emotional health and motivation to concentrate. He tires of most learning activities easily and must often be supported to complete what he has started to do.

To offset his frustration in so many areas of his day, music and daily listening activities are provided to improve orientation and auditory awareness, sound discrimination, word recognition, comprehension, and retention. Andreas demonstrates real strength in the auditory and verbal modes and is encouraged to explore in these areas. He particularly enjoys finger plays and songs and stories put to music. In circle time, he volunteers information and speaks well, using complete sentences and descriptive words.

He is very inventive in making up songs as he plays. He will sing about things that are happening to him or that he is thinking about:

> Now Mellissa goes boom boom,
> Now Mellissa goes boom boom,
> Boom boom goes the drum,
> Boom boom on the big big big big drum,
> Boom boom boom.

He can chant this song, and change it as he sings fragments over and over.

Andreas also enjoys making things with his hands. He is becoming more adept at gluing wood constructions, uses large round crayons for artwork, and loves to make things with modeling clay imbued with odors, such as perfume, cinnamon, cloves, and oregano. Making bread-dough sculptures that are baked before he paints them gives him immense satisfaction even though the sculptures are primitive in form.

**Resources for Coping with Visual Impairment**

**United States**
Association for Education of the Visually Impaired
919 Walnut Street, 7th Floor
Philadelphia, Pennsylvania 19107

National Association for Parents of the Visually Impaired
P.O. Box 180806
Austin, Texas 78718
(512) 459-6651

**Canada**
Canadian National Institute for the Blind
1929 Bayview Avenue
Toronto, Ontario
Canada M4G 3E8
(416) 486-2500

**Local**
Hospital eye clinics
Local chapters of organizations serving people who are visually impaired

# Hearing Impairment

There are several kinds and degrees of hearing impairment. Some children have mild hearing difficulties, are able to pick up most sounds, and with training will have little difficulty in communication. Greater difficulties are experienced by children with severe to profound hearing losses who exhibit deficits in receptive and expressive language and speech production. The extent of deficit depends upon the degree and the type of loss. Depending on its cause, the impairments may be temporary or permanent. The word "deaf" can be misleading; only about 10 percent of persons who are hearing impaired are totally without hearing.

The complexity of the hearing process itself makes it important to be aware of the specific nature of the child's hearing problem. *Sensitivity* (the ability to detect sounds at various pitches) is important, especially with respect to the audibility of conversational speech. Hearing aids increase the sensitivity of hearing by making sounds louder and, we hope, improving the audibility of conversational speech.

Some children can't hear the difference, for example, between the words "book" and "took." This aspect of hearing is called *discrimination*. Because all sounds are amplified equally, a hearing aid is of little help in sound discrimination. Other children have problems interpreting sounds or recognizing and comprehending words, known as an auditory processing disorder. Sound is heard but can't be interpreted effectively.

Children must be taught to use their residual hearing via good and appropriately prescribed hearing aids and aural rehabilitation. Aids do not immediately improve the level of learning; instead, their use begins a slow and tedious process of learning language. It is difficult for a child who is using a hearing aid to focus on one sound source while excluding others, particularly because most hearing aids will amplify the signal and background noise equally. Consequently, distracting noises and other sound sources, which compete for attention, should be eliminated.

As with other children with sensory defects, the child with impaired hearing needs individual attention. The teacher should be alert to every opportunity to provide individual help to fill the gaps stemming from the child's hearing defect. Children with impaired hearing listen with their eyes as well as their ears; therefore, it is best to have them sit with their back to the light, not more than five to ten feet from the teacher.

Numerous problems arise from a child's difficulty in perceiving auditory stimuli. To be unable to hear the conversation of family and others is an enormous loss and frustration. Adding to such a personal loss is the inevitable delay and difficulty in acquiring language and social competency, which further impedes the child's progress in many other areas of development. Communication starts at birth. Without the capacity to communicate ideas, thoughts, and feelings, we cannot grow to our full potential. Early diagnosis of hearing loss and accompanying early intervention increases the opportunity for progress.

A child whose communication resources are restricted by hearing impairment can expand and develop existing skills by experiencing the communication potential in the arts. It is easy to overlook the importance of the hearing person's continuous experience of self in a spatial environment. A loss or reduction of such feedback weakens a child's ability to orient the body in space and time and accurately discern movement and form. The body and sensory awareness activities found in Parts I, II, and III can help compensate for some of the information the child lacks.

It is common for the child who is hearing impaired to feel isolated and become withdrawn and self-centered. Creative activities should be scheduled to allow for a period of free expression right after a stimulating experience, thus allowing the child to share, ventilate, and express feelings about the experience.

Some general principles should be followed when interacting with someone who has a hearing impairment:

- If a hearing aid is used, it must be regularly checked for adjustment and repair.
- A person speaking should face the listener at the listener's eye level and make ample use of facial expression, lip movement, and body gestures.
- Attract the child's attention before speaking (for example, call the child's name, tap a shoulder, or flick the lights). Do not speak until eye contact has been made.
- Create a favorable hearing environment with small-group work in rooms that are acoustically dead with doors and windows closed, shutting out distracting noises.
- Use illustration, demonstration, dramatization, mime, and sign language to communicate information to the child.

Almost any activity can be adapted for children who are hearing impaired by supplementing the auditory components with visual cues. Making everyone part of the adaptation is in itself a creative exercise. The goal is to help the child develop the ability to function as independently as possible in the most normal living and learning environment.

## Living with Hearing Impairment—Sol

One morning when Sol was two-and-a-half, he woke up listless, not at all his usual bubbly self. By midmorning he crawled onto his mother's lap; as she held him, he cried out, "Mommy," became rigid, and stared out into space. His father, a physician, immediately came into the room, looked at Sol, and realized he might have meningitis. His diagnosis was later confirmed at the hospital.

Sol was in a coma for ten days, and it was several more weeks before he could go home. He had lost 15 pounds and regressed to bottle feeding and diapers. He could not walk, talk, sit, or hold up his head without support. There was little movement on his left side. He could not turn his head or straighten out his elbows or knees.

For three months Sol was exercised hourly to strengthen his muscles. He often screamed from the pain and fear of what was happening to him. He had tantrums when he was frustrated. He no longer said words or responded in any way to what was being said to him. An ear, nose, and throat specialist diagnosed a severe to profound hearing loss.

Following considerable research, his parents decided on a program of auditory-verbal therapy. This approach is based on the theory that even minimal amounts of residual hearing, if stimulated, can lead to the development of spontaneous oral speech and language. The child learns to process language through amplified hearing, thus acquiring language adequate for mainstreaming.

Most children who are hearing impaired can learn to listen and speak. The auditory-verbal program Sol is in teaches the child to maximize the use of residual hearing by using two well-maintained hearing aids and by immediate and ongoing intervention that follows developmental models. Parents observe and participate in the sessions to learn techniques and methods for continuing at home daily.

Through exercises and reinforcement of language acquisition and understanding, Sol was taught to listen to sounds. He learned to associate such sounds with words and objects; thus began the long journey toward learning to listen and speak. Little by little, Sol made gains. He began to walk again. It took eight months, but he began to wake up with a smile rather than a scowl. He resumed eating table foods, giving up his 18 bottles of milk a day. At the age of four, he was once again toilet trained.

The family bathed him in the sound of their voices and spent hours playing games and reading to him. It took about a year before he could say "Mom," and words continued to come slowly. Eight more months were needed to learn colors and numbers or to answer a simple question like "What's your name?"

Finger and hand puppets were often used to enhance the proceedings and to keep Sol focused on the task at hand. His mother made a large puppet apron (see page 124) and would ask Sol to put his hand into a pocket to see which puppet was hiding there. Each puppet had its own name, and Sol was encouraged to greet it and to talk to it. The puppet served as a strong visual motivation for Sol to participate in verbal exchanges.

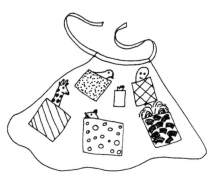

*A puppet apron.*

Sol's mother also started a diary of daily events. A picture was drawn into his diary each day of something that was important to him. If they went for a walk and had ice-cream cones, his mother immediately drew an ice-cream cone, which Sol could then perceive was the same as what he was eating. When his siblings and father came home, Sol would run and show them the day's picture, and was encouraged to tell them about it. Being talked to during the day and talking with other family members was one of the most important aspects of helping Sol develop understanding of speech. The important thing was not correcting Sol's efforts at speech, but encouraging his acquisition of language to express himself in ways satisfying to him.

As Sol's frustration lessened, so did his tantrums. Sol's mother found that when he was particularly upset and difficult to handle he could often be diverted by coloring. She kept a large supply of pastels, crayons, and markers on hand and would encourage him to make pictures of feelings when he was upset. Sol sometimes started out with angry scribbles, but as he became more involved in the process, his markings became more deliberate. This nonverbal outlet diluted his anger, allowing him a more appropriate way of handling difficulties.

Sol works at grade level in his first-grade class. He has an itinerant teacher for an hour four times a week, plus a weekly one-hour session with an aural rehabilitation therapist. He wears an FM system during school hours. Sol works and plays hard; his teacher's only complaint is that he talks too much!

## Living with Hearing Impairment—Allison

Allison is an awkward, hesitant little girl with moderate hearing loss. Her sense of balance is impaired by frequent inner ear infections; she loses her footing sometimes and feels unsure of herself. Allison needs more practice than others in developing balance. Exercises such as starting and stopping, or changing directions while maintaining balance, are important in helping Allison feel more sure of herself.

Giving Allison props such as a hoop or scarf for dancing helps her concentrate on the activity while alleviating some of her tension. A dancing partner encourages her participation. If a person is not available, a life-size puppet or doll substitutes. (Allison's favorite is "Henrietta.") Elastic bands attach the doll to the child's ankles and wrists.

Allison has difficulty hearing conversational speech and therefore seems to ignore or confuse spoken requests or directions. Such a child frequently displays poor listening skills, tilting the head to favor the stronger ear. Allison has trouble understanding the speech of others if they are far away, not facing her, or speaking in groups. Speaking clearly, simply, and loudly is essential to communicating with Allison.

Children like Allison react well to sounds of musical instruments because they generally are more audible than conversational tones. "Dialogues" with percussive instruments are Allison's favorite musical activity. She can imitate rhythms and carry out simple improvisations with the music therapist for several minutes. (They take turns making and responding to a musical statement.) Allison's ability to see and imitate rhythms with her hands, on a percussion instrument, or in movement helps her respond to auditory cues.

The young child with hearing loss must come to terms with many frustrations. Particularly acute are feelings of isolation that are accentuated by seeing others communicating but not being able to understand what is being said. The child should be encouraged to express feelings through sound as well as movement. Laughter, anger, and fears need to be expressed; in miming, however, accuracy should be stressed to facilitate communication.

Children who are hearing impaired get a great deal of satisfaction from singing with others if the tempo is suitable. Most recordings of children's songs are too fast for children in general and especially for those with auditory difficulties. Live music is best. Keep the tempo moderate so the words come through clearly. Allison is encouraged to sing along with the rest of her kindergarten class and to try to do all the movements that the song suggests. Participation helps her develop self-confidence and the skills necessary to take part in mainstreamed education.

## Living with Hearing Impairment—Brendan

Brendan is a four-year-old boy with a rare congenital syndrome that left him with a severe-to-profound sensorineural hearing loss. He wears bilateral hearing aids with much difficulty, as do many young children who need to wear them. The hearing aid mechanisms are delicate, and it is sometimes difficult to know if they are functioning properly. Sometimes they seem to aggravate Brendan.

During storytime or music sessions, the adult working with Brendan wears a wireless FM microphone to amplify sounds. The music therapist alters some activities to include experiences that will be more meaningful for him. Many visual cues (such as hand clapping, finger snapping, foot stamping, and thigh slapping) as well as work on instruments are made with deliberate gestures so that Brendan can sense the rhythm. He is also encouraged to feel the vibrations of the piano by putting his hands or bare feet on the wood. (Many people can sense vibrations in this way.)

Brendan's parents chose an educational philosophy called "total communication" designed to teach children to communicate by all possible means including speech. This approach uses auditory, visual, and tactile senses in combination, verbalizing while signing, finger spelling, or gesturing. Brendan has good manual dexterity and is making progress with this approach. His dexterity is also useful when he works on the computer, which he will use at every opportunity. He takes similar joy in playing with a Suzuki Omnichord® electronic keyboard (see Appendix A); through experimentation, he could see the cause and effect of pushing various buttons on the instrument. He appeared to enjoy the sounds he was making and giggled when he made the rhythm go faster. Clearly, he was managing his environment—a positive step with the promise of more to come.

## Resources for Coping with Hearing Impairment

### United States

Alexander Graham Bell Association for the Deaf
3417 Volta Place, NW
Washington, D.C. 20007
(202) 337-5220

American Society for Deaf Children
817 Thayer Avenue
Silver Spring, Maryland 20910
(301) 585-5400 (Voice/TDD)

### Canada

The Canadian Hearing Society
271 Spadina Road
Toronto, Ontario M5R 2V3
(416) 964-9595

Voice for Hearing Impaired Children
360 Bloor Street West
Suite 412
Toronto, Ontario M5S 1X1
(416) 928-1006

### Local

Hospital audiology and speech clinics
School districts and special-education consultants

# Neuromuscular Disorders

## Spinal Muscular Atrophy

*Spinal muscular atrophy* is a disease characterized by degeneration of the motor nerve cells of the spinal cord. This degeneration, the cause of which is unknown, results in atrophy of the muscles that control movement of the limbs and decreases movement of the breathing muscles.

Characteristic features of this condition include progressive muscular weakness, causing difficulties in walking, and sitting, and climbing stairs. The child may have an unsteady gait and frequent falls. The muscle weakness and immobility create the possibility of contractures and joint deformity. Weakness in the shoulder muscles makes it difficult to raise one's arms, lift objects, even to brush one's teeth. Loss of bone substance leads to brittle bones and the possibility of arrested growth.

This condition does not affect intellectual capacities, and most children will use these capacities, particularly as their motor strengths diminish. They need modified educational programs that let them be in control or increase the control they exercise. Because it is easy for these children to become dependent, adults must encourage independence whenever possible. Plan open-ended activities that do not require excessive time or energy to complete.

### Living with Spinal Muscular Atrophy—Jordy

Jordy, a fair-haired boy of four, was diagnosed with spinal muscular atrophy two years ago. He uses an electric scooter for mobility, controlling it with a joystick. He is often weak and fatigues easily.

Considered bright for his age, Jordy is very verbal and particularly articulate with adults. His curiosity and memory contribute to his appeal. He enjoys being in junior kindergarten and is careful in selecting the activities in which he becomes involved. He especially likes to look at books and "read" the pictures to make up a story. Painting, drawing, listening to records, and playing with puppets are among his other interests.

For Jordy, as for all children, developmental growth depends on emotional growth. One of the most useful skills here is the ability to identify, understand, and communicate thoughts and feelings. This can be very difficult for a youngster of four. One very effective method for eliciting a child's response is "puppet talking" (see the "Talking through Puppets" exploration on page 124). Through puppet talking, a child like Jordy is able to see, listen, imagine, and express. The puppet can be the child's spokesperson or a nonthreatening, nonjudgmental friend.

For Jordy, puppet talking provides a much-needed avenue for expression, as well as an opportunity to vent his anxieties about hospitals and separations from his family. Growing fears about his diminishing abilities were brought out in the following exchange:

Puppet: Hey, Jordy, I've been looking for you. What have you been doing?

Jordy (looking down): I been here.

Puppet: Did you do any painting today?

Jordy: No, I don't wanna paint.

Puppet: That's okay, Jordy. Is there something else you'd like to do today?

Jordy (still looking down): Nope.

Puppet: Are you feeling kinda yucky today? (Jordy nods his head and starts to cry.) Gonna tell your old pal Nikolas Rabbit why you're crying? Maybe, just maybe, Nikolas can help.

Jordy: 'Cause the tears are falling out of my eyes.

Puppet: Yup, I can see that. Sometimes it feels good to cry when we feel sad or scared or just mixed up. It's okay to let the tears come out then. Are you feeling scared of something?

Jordy (hesitating): . . . Mommy says I gotta go back to the hospital . . . I don't wanna go. I get all alone there. . . . They give me needles.

Puppet: Yes, Jordy, it's hard to be alone in a big hospital and to get needles. I can see why you are upset about going there.

Jordy: Yeah, and those stupid needles hurt, you know.

Puppet: Yeah, they sure do hurt . . . Hey, I got it! Let's make up a Jordy Box!

Jordy: What's a Jordy Box?

Puppet: A Jordy Box is really neat. It can hold all your favorite things in the whole wide world. Think of something special that you'd like to put in your box. Because it will only be for you, you know.

Jordy: Can I put in my teddy bear?

Puppet: What a good idea, Jordy! You can put in your favorite tapes, too. Hey, and what about some books?

Jordy: Yeah, and can I take my snookie (blanket)?

Puppet: I'm sure you can.

Jordy: Are they gonna fix me up? I want them to fix me up.

Puppet: I think the doctors will try to do their best, Jordy, but I think that's something you will have to ask them.

Jordy (beginning to look tearful again): Will it hurt? Will they give me the needles?

Puppet: I don't know, Jordy, . . . but the things in your Jordy Box will help you when you are there. Now let's go find your box so you can start painting it.

## Resources for Coping with Spinal Muscular Atrophy

Refer to resources listed under muscular dystrophy.

# Muscular Dystrophy—Duchenne Type

There are many types of muscular dystrophy; Duchenne is the type most often seen in children. This progressive disease always occurs in boys, developing between the ages of two and six. It is marked by wasting and progressive weakness and atrophy of the skeletal muscles (which control movement).

Deterioration usually is rapid. Within a few years, the child has difficulty walking, begins to waddle, has difficulty climbing stairs, falls more easily, and has trouble getting up from a fall. Trying to get up from a sitting position requires walking the hands up the legs to gain support until upright. The child is frequently seen walking on his toes, an early sign of weakness in the muscles that pull the foot up.

Children with muscular dystrophy have normal sensation in their limbs, although they cannot move them at will. Once the dystrophy appears, there are no remissions, and the course of the disease is steadily downhill. There is no cure or specific treatment for muscular dystrophy at this time, although recent and promising developments may lead to successful management of the disease in the future. In general, medical treatment focuses on preventing, correcting, and minimizing contractures in conjunction with maintaining functional activities.

A psychoeducational assessment should be completed on all children with muscular dystrophy. Because the condition is progressive, the child will present a gradually changing disability, and numerous adjustments will be required. The major educational aim should be to provide creative opportunities, fulfillment, and enjoyment within the framework of the child's limitations.

## Living with Muscular Dystrophy—David

When David entered kindergarten at five, he had already been diagnosed as having Duchenne-type muscular dystrophy. He stumbled frequently but was still able to walk with a waddling, awkward gait. The calf muscles in his legs appeared enlarged (this is caused by fatty deposits but is often misinterpreted as muscle tissue). David had poor posture with a protruding abdomen and a swayback (lordosis), resulting from weakness of the muscles of the abdominal wall.

At that time, David was becoming aware of his progressively worsening motor skills. It was important that the teacher not press him into situations that would expose his limitations and perhaps increase self-consciousness. However, activity and exercise, unless overdone, do not hurt such a child, and David was encouraged to do as much as he could comfortably. When he tired, he rested until he was ready and able to participate again.

David was hesitant to try out any of the apparatus in the outside play area. Instead, he headed for the sand table each day and played there until it was time to go into the playroom. David loved the feeling of the sand on his fingers and hands; it was an ideal tactile and kinesthetic experience for him. The sand table had pails filled with plastic animals and people, imaginative creatures, and seashells. Sometimes David buried these objects in the sand; sometimes he stood them up and had imaginary conversations with them.

As time went on, he started playing with plastic dinosaurs. He chose one as his friend, naming it "Ma-koo" and taking it with him everywhere. David began to create an environment for Ma-Koo, using small branches, twigs, pieces of moss,

and a round piece of blue plastic material as a lake. He poured water over the plastic material to give Ma-Koo a drinking hole. Other children at the sand table got caught up in the scenario and would help create Ma-Koo's environment for the day.

The dinosaur play eventually turned to something more prosaic: making mud pies, then collecting flowers, grass, and leaves to decorate the pies. Much deliberation took place as David and friends arranged their decorations.

David could not compete with his peers in more active areas, but he clearly initiated a way to gain acceptance from them through play.

### Resources for Coping with Muscular Dystrophy

**United States**
Muscular Dystrophy Association
3300 East Sunrise Dr.
Tucson, AZ 85718
(602) 529-2000

Families of Spinal Muscular Atrophy
P.O. Box 1465
Highland Park, Illinois 60035
(708) 432-5551

**Canada**
Muscular Dystrophy Association of Canada
150 Eglinton Avenue East
Suite 400
Toronto, Ontario M4P 1E8
(416) 488-0030

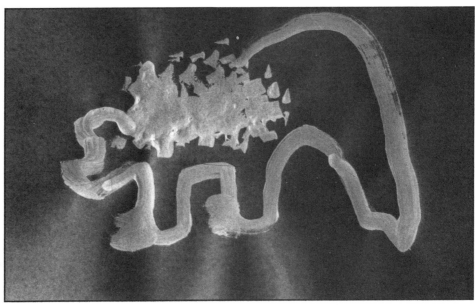

*David's picture of Ma-Koo.*

# Blood and Immune System Disorders

This section covers developmental concerns associated with a number of serious chronic illnesses: sickle cell anemia, hemophilia, leukemia, acquired immune deficiency syndrome (AIDS), juvenile arthritis, and asthma.

Intellectual functioning is not directly affected by most of these conditions, but frequent bouts with the illness may delay social and educational development. Certain common emotions and behaviors emerge in such children; lack of experience may diminish self-esteem, and they become very hesitant in trying new activities. These children may be shy and introverted because they are so frequently overprotected by family members, both because of their condition and the related susceptibility to other infections.

*Music, movement, storytelling, and dressing up provide a focus for a child's imagination and energy.*

Children with these conditions often become fearful and anxious, always awaiting the next crisis or the next attack of pain. They may suffer from loneliness, boredom, or depression. Teachers and therapists can help these children become aware of their feelings, helping them learn to express themselves and providing opportunities for them to work through emotions and experiences. The children should be given every opportunity to do as much for themselves as they can. It is essential to avoid focusing on the disability, which adds to the feeling of being different from peers and lessens opportunities for psychosocial experiences.

Participating in creative endeavors lets these youngsters regain opportunities to make choices and practice decision making. Children are encouraged to choose where they want to be and what they want to do when they get there. They can be assertive within a carefully designed environment filled with clues and possibilities that will help them make rewarding choices.

The challenge, then, is to provide expressive activities that will effectively meet such a child's needs. To do so, teachers and therapists must learn to use themselves expressively, especially when stimulating creativity. They must use their voices, gestures, and movement to communicate a commitment to play, to experiment, to try new ideas. In this way, they can begin to answer some of the needs of these very fragile children.

## Sickle Cell Anemia

Sickle cell anemia is a painful, inherited blood disorder that primarily affects the black population. There is sickle cell trait and sickle cell anemia; those with the trait carry the disease but suffer minimal effects from it, while those with anemia are seriously affected. A child who has one parent with the disease will have the trait; a child who inherits the trait from both parents will have anemia.

The condition can be diagnosed in the early years. An abnormality in the hemoglobin that carries oxygen in the blood, this condition causes chronic fatigue, weakness, abdominal pain, and various kinds of infections. Painful swelling of the hands and feet may also occur. Periodic transfusions may be necessary to replenish red blood cells destroyed by the disease. To date, no cure has been found.

*"Pooh Bear" in a happier mood.*

### Living with Sickle Cell Anemia—"Pooh Bear"

"Pooh Bear" is the nickname hospital staffers gave four-year-old Jerry, who wanted to be named after his favorite story character. Jerry has been in the hospital about four times a year since being diagnosed with sickle cell anemia at the age of six months. These hospitalizations are needed to stabilize and monitor disease-related pain and dehydration and to check levels of healthy red blood cells versus abnormal blood cells.

Pooh Bear is small for his age. He speaks to staff in broken three-word phrases and a very timid voice. He often has to be encouraged to go to nursery school, play on the ward, or get involved with activities, preferring to stay in his room and wheel around in his cart. Much of the time he just wants, and needs, to sleep.

Pooh Bear was referred to music therapy because he needs more socialization and to resolve his fear of needles and of the person in the "white coat" who draws his blood. The therapist slowly gained rapport with Pooh Bear, who shows much musicality and a good auditory memory. She sees him every time he is in the hospital. Their relationship is enhanced by her absence from the painful medical interventions he has to undergo; she is, therefore, perceived by Pooh Bear as a safe person.

One hospital stay came about because Pooh Bear had painful ulcers all over his face and legs. Eight hospital staffers tried, one by one, to put an IV needle in his arm. As each staffer approached, Pooh Bear screamed, flailed his arms, and tried to avoid their grasp. His crying could be heard throughout the hospital floor for more than an hour. Finally, a desperate head nurse summoned the music therapist.

Upon entering the room the therapist saw a whimpering little boy with a sheet pinning him down at the waist. She asked whether he would like to do something with her or sing some songs together. He nodded and replied, "Sing and puzzle." He indicated a "Mr. T" puzzle, then completed it, fitting in all 15 pieces.

Therapist: Why do you like Mr. T?

Jerry: Mr. T is strong. Mr. T not scared.

Therapist: Is Pooh Bear scared? (Jerry nodded.) Would Pooh Bear like to be big and strong like Mr. T? (Again, a positive response). Shall we sing a song about Mr. T? (Again, a nod.)

Together, the therapist and Pooh Bear sang:

Mr. T, he's my man.
Big and strong, not a lamb,
*He* can help me make it through the day.

Therapist: When the doctor comes over, will you be brave and strong? (Jerry nodded.)

Therapist: Now, what would you like to tell the doctors and nurses?

Jerry (holding out his left arm): I want this vein.

Therapist: Pooh Bear, is this what all the fighting was about? (He nodded.) Why didn't you tell them that?

Jerry (tears rolling down his cheeks): I tried. . . . No listen.

Therapist: Shall we sing the song for them, and then you'll tell them what you want? (He agreed.) Will you tell me which doctor and which nurse you want to come in?

The designated staff came in, were sung to, and the needle was inserted without further difficulty. After that, the therapist prepares Jerry for any painful treatment or blood drawing using puppets, singing, or drawing. Now, he is losing his fear of needles and goes to other children on the ward he thinks need help and says to them, "Be brave like Mr. T and me."

### Resources for Coping with Sickle Cell Anemia

National Association for Sickle Cell Disease
4221 Wilshire Blvd. #360
Los Angeles, California 90010-3503
(800) 421-8453
(213) 936-7205

# Hemophilia

Hemophilia is an inherited blood disorder marked by a permanent tendency for profuse, spontaneous bleeding. This bleeding is due to a defect in the clotting ability of the blood. A child with hemophilia may bleed internally as a result of bruises or bumps, or from extra stress on certain muscles. Even a small scratch can lead to heavy bleeding that does not stop by itself.

There is no known cure for this condition. Hemorrhaging (bleeding) can be treated with a clotting factor derived from plasma, but this is not a permanent solution. Bleeding in the joints can have a crippling effect. Children with this condition also have severe pain, but aspirin is contraindicated because it further reduces the blood's ability to clot.

Many youngsters with this condition already know their limitations; however, it is extremely important to alert them to possibly hazardous areas on the premises. Visual markers for these areas help the child. It is also necessary to tell other youngsters in the group that this child has a few special needs and that they should not jostle or play roughly with the child.

If the child is experiencing considerable pain or becomes fatigued, let him or her lie down or go home early. The condition may cause the child to miss a great deal of school, but it is essential to take every measure possible to ensure the fragile health of a child with hemophilia.

## Living with Hemophilia—Carlo

Carlo is a five-year-old boy with hemophilia. He is small for his age and appears overanxious most of the time. He has been in the hospital many times, with stays ranging from a few days to several weeks. The loneliness and fear of these hospitalizations and of being separated from his family have contributed to his apprehension. He always wears a bracelet that says he is a hemophiliac.

Carlo attends a regular kindergarten in his neighborhood. The teacher has checked the environment for any sharp corners on furniture, padding them for his protection. She has also helped him become aware of potentially hazardous areas on the playground by painting small colored circles in those areas. Because Carlo's condition is severe, he wears protective clothing, such as a helmet and sponge-rubber knee pads, when playing outside.

Because a child with hemophilia can bleed internally from bumps and bruises, constant supervision is necessary in the classroom as well as on the playground. Safe activities such as cognitive and creative experiences, felt-board work, puppets, and playhouse fun are used as alternatives to help Carlo relate to his peers.

Carlo demonstrates a budding musical flair, which is encouraged by his teacher. He has good auditory memory and a definite feeling for rhythm, singing in pitch with a clear small voice. Carlo loves percussion instruments and constantly asks for various listening and rhythm games. One of his favorite games is playing the "good" and "bad" drums. Two drums are put side by side, and Carlo is asked to beat out all the things he likes on the "good" drum and all the things he doesn't like on the "bad" drum. Carlo beats out school, Mama's cooking, rainbows, and baby sister on the first drum. On the "bad" drum he beats out spiders, needles, hospitals, bleeding, falling, cuts, being alone, and being scared.

The teacher tries to give Carlo an opportunity to develop a feeling of control. Controlling his environment is not always possible for him, but it is important to strengthen this feeling as much as possible. Carlo is a responsible little boy who is very fearful of being hurt. Because of this, the emphasis during the school day is on relaxation and helping Carlo gain a sense of freedom.

## Resources for Coping with Hemophilia

### United States
National Hemophilia Foundation
The Soho Building
110 Greene Street, Room 406
New York, New York 10002
(212) 219-8180

**Canada**
Canadian Hemophilia Society National Office
100 King Street West, Suite 210
Hamilton, Ontario L8P 1A2
(416) 523-6414

# Leukemia

Leukemia refers to several diseases involving an uncontrolled proliferation of white blood cells. It is a malignancy that attacks the tissues in the bone marrow, spleen, and/or lymph nodes. Children with leukemia can be in very poor health; pale, tired, with aches and pains in the joints, and highly susceptible to infections. They may exhibit sleeplessness, weight loss, excessive bruising, and swollen glands.

Medication, chemotherapy, and/or radiation therapy may be used to halt the progression of this disease. Chemotherapy may cause hair loss, which can be devastating to a child. It is essential that teachers explain to other pupils that this hair loss is due to special treatment the child needs, that eventually the hair will grow back, and that it is important to accept the child as the person she or he is.

There can be many bouts of illness for such a child, and caregivers and teachers should try not to lose heart. The best attitude to adopt is that the child's life should be filled with enjoyment and creativity, not merely hospitals and treatment.

## Living with Leukemia—Lauren

Lauren, a shy five-and-a-half-year-old, has just returned to her kindergarten group after a three-month bout with leukemia. An individualized intervention plan was designed to help her adapt to hospitalization during her long stay.

The plan has been worked out by a child development specialist with Lauren's parents, teachers, and other hospital professionals. The plan centers on Lauren's emotional, cognitive, social, and self-help skills, and focuses on her behavioral adjustment and on creating a therapeutic environment.

During Lauren's hospitalization, her parents were encouraged to bring some of her clothing, toys, family photos, and other meaningful objects to the hospital to make her room more homelike and familiar. Hospital staff brought in a rocking chair and a cot for her mother to rest on during the long hospital days. Daily routines were established to make Lauren aware of the special times she would spend with the child development specialist and the creative-arts therapist. These therapy sessions were scheduled before medical procedures and around stressful routines.

To reduce stress and opposition to routine care, the therapist fostered Lauren's understanding of medical procedures by using play materials, conversations, puppetry, books, music, and various art media. Lauren particularly liked to work with her hands. The therapist would bring materials to manipulate when Lauren was lying in bed; she particularly liked bread dough permeated with cinnamon, cloves, and lemon rind.

Most of all, Lauren enjoyed painting, and this was provided whenever possible. Most children's painting occurs on the symbolic level, with little conscious awareness. Expressive arts seem to tap directly into the unconscious mind, where feelings are frequently expressed as images, and healing occurs directly through expression and play.

Another project Lauren undertook with the creative-arts therapist was a pictorial schedule and wall calendar for her room. They put predictable routines and special events on the calendar. This activity anchors a child in time and provides a connection to events in the outside world.

Lauren also wanted the calendar to describe what she had felt like on the previous day. She determined which symbols would represent her feelings. This activity was an excellent opportunity for the therapist to work with Lauren on some of her feelings and fears. When Lauren felt poorly, she asked the therapist to draw for her; at other times, she preferred to do her drawing herself.

As Lauren began to feel better, the therapists worked with the whole family to make the transition from hospital to home and school as smooth as possible. Play combined with experiences in the expressive media are important components in the recovery process because they sustain emotional health through the rigors of a long and difficult hospitalization.

### Resources for Coping with Leukemia

**United States**
Leukemia Society of America
800 Second Avenue
New York, New York 10001
(212) 736-3030

**Canada**
Canadian Cancer Society (National Office)
130 Bloor Street West, Suite 1001
Toronto, Ontario M5S 2V7
(416) 961-7223

**Local**
Local cancer society and leukemia association chapters

## AIDS (Acquired Immunodeficiency Syndrome)

AIDS is a new and frightening disease causing major concern around the world. The condition is thought to be caused by human immunodeficiency virus (HIV). This virus attacks and seriously disrupts the immune system, leaving the body vulnerable to many infections and cancers. It is these opportunistic infections that cause death, not the HIV virus itself.

Evidence indicates that AIDS is transmitted only through the exchange of semen or blood. Transmission methods include sexual contact, use of nonsterile hypodermic needles, or via HIV-contaminated blood. (Since 1985, developed countries have been testing blood for HIV. However, blood was not screened before that time, and many persons, including children, received HIV-positive blood, with symptoms occurring several years later.) Some children with AIDS are believed to have acquired the condition while in the uterus or through their mother's milk. (The mother must be infected for a baby to be born with HIV; the father's status does not affect the fetus.)

Current research demonstrates that the HIV virus is *not* passed on by casual contact—not by breathing the same air, not by touching, not by hugging or kissing—and that the virus dies quickly when exposed to air. There is also *no* evidence to indicate that HIV is transmitted through minor cuts, sharing toilets, coughs or sneezes, or by living with a person who has HIV disease.

There are generally three stages of HIV infection: being infected (HIV positive) but not showing any symptoms; showing some symptoms, an imprecisely defined stage known as AIDS Related Complex, or ARC; and the presence of specified opportunistic infections, or AIDS. The term *HIV disease* is now preferred by the medical community because it recognizes the progressive nature of the condition, rather than creating artificial divisions. It also acknowledges that HIV can have debilitating effects before advancing to AIDS. (In fact, some people die without ever contracting any of the infections that qualify for an AIDS diagnosis.)

Children with HIV disease have a shortened life expectancy and are plagued by infections that can be difficult to control. Extreme fatigue is a common effect, and there may be failure to thrive. Other serious complications include kidney or heart problems, as well as the probability of developmental delay. Because HIV is capable of crossing into the brain, these children are also vulnerable to numerous infections and complications of the central nervous system. AIDS also brings the cruel burden of stigma, largely because in North America the syndrome originally was associated with gay men and thus called up societal prejudice and bigotry against homosexuals. Thus special attention must be paid to the psychosocial effects stemming from this stigma, as well as to altered social experiences and to painful regimens that create complicated scenarios between child, parents, and health-care providers.

HIV disease has emerged as a major illness of childhood, and children with AIDS may rarely be well enough to attend school regularly. However, they have the right to the same educational opportunities accorded other children. Schools, though, are having problems accommodating children with AIDS while dealing with misunderstanding and fear about the syndrome. Some communities have reacted with fear and hysteria when an HIV-positive child attends day care or school, whereas others have rallied to support child and family. In 1991, Zidovudine® (AZT) was approved for use with pediatric HIV. While we await development of other effective therapies for this syndrome and the opportunistic infections that make it so painful, we have the tools and knowledge in hand to support the child with AIDS.

## Living with AIDS—Eric

Eric, a small six-year-old with hemophilia, contracted the HIV virus through blood transfusions when he was only an infant.

Eric was frequently absent from kindergarten. Midway through the year his symptoms decreased, and he began to attend school regularly. Now an additional, serious problem for Eric is stigma: before the teacher could meet with parents to help them gain an awareness of HIV/AIDS, one parent refused to allow her child to attend school. Talk spread rapidly, and Eric soon became isolated from most of the other children.

The teacher addressed this matter first with the parents and caregivers. She informed them that quarantine is applied only with infectious diseases that are spread through ordinary daily activities. She stressed that HIV is not spread this way and that it is very difficult for a child to become infected. Parents were reassured by this frank talk, which was supported by literature made available to all of them.

With support of the parents, the teacher next worked with the children to help them reestablish rapport with Eric and to help him feel part of the group again. She declared a "Moneto Day," a lovely concept from the Philippines meaning "secret friend." Although it is difficult for young children to keep a secret, she hoped this day would be a stepping stone to reaching out and touching this isolated little boy. The children, in a circle, discussed some of the things they might do to surprise their Moneto.

Each child was given the name of another in the room who was to be their secret Moneto person. They were to think up nice things to say or do for their secret friend throughout the day. Materials were provided for the children to make necklaces and other little gifts. The teacher helped them get started.

They made cereal ring necklaces that could be nibbled on all day. Other necklaces were made out of pastas, buttons, beads, or paper clips. As another gift, each child was encouraged to draw a picture with an inscription to their friend transcribed by an adult.

As the day progressed, the children gave their gifts away, hiding the presents where their Moneto would find them. At the same time they were encouraged to say something nice to their Monetos. The children were exhilarated by the experience, and friendliness pervaded the atmosphere as they sang songs and talked about being friends.

The following day the children were each given a 12" x 12" piece of colored material and a choice of fabric paint, crayons, or nontoxic permanent markers. They were asked to make a picture for their friend. The finished pictures were fabric glued to a large sheet and the wall hanging was put up for all to see and for the children to remember.

One of Eric's gifts—a drawing from his Moneto friend, Leah.

This was only the beginning, but Eric is delighted with the Moneto days and the feeling of acceptance they sponsored. A child with HIV needs the affirmation and acceptance that group activities can provide, although intervention may be necessary to mediate crises.

Children with full-blown AIDS probably will be tired and listless, in part due to loss of appetite. Visual art projects are ideal because the children can participate (perhaps on a reduced scale) without being drained of energy. They may not be able to sustain an activity for long without becoming tired or distracted, so it is best to involve them in projects that can be finished in a short time.

If a child prefers musical or storytelling tapes, he or she can make selections when it is hard to sleep or when distraction from pain is needed. A music or play therapist can also use music to help the child get involved or vent distress.

Dramatic play offers children the chance to leave behind difficult or painful circumstances, entering a world of their own where they make the rules and control events. A child with HIV may perceive a pattern of events that overwhelms even adults, who had seemed omnipotent. Dramatic play can be directed and altered to follow the child's initiative and imagination.

Puppet play also gives children the opportunity to "try out" some of the fears and anger they feel in the more neutral territory of dramatic play. This play can make adults aware of the child's concerns that were previously submerged or inexpressible due to limited verbal capabilities.

Other valuable activities include planting seeds and watching them grow, keeping insects (for example, in an ant farm), and caring for fish or other pets. All of these broaden a child's concept of the life force. Such activities shared by friends may help the child feel motivation and a sense of belonging and companionship. They also allow opportunities to be in control at a time when the child may feel control ebbing away.

## Resources for Coping with HIV

### United States
World Hemophilia AIDS Center
2400 South Flower Street
Los Angeles, California 90007-2697
(213) 742-1354

Immune Deficiency Foundation
P.O. Box 586
Columbia, Maryland 21045
(301) 461-3127

National Pediatric HIV Resource Center
Children's Hospital of New Jersey
15 South 9th Street
Newark, New Jersey 07107
(800) 362-0071

National AIDS Hotline
(800) 342-AIDS
(Operators have a national directory of local AIDS service organizations and medical professionals knowledgeable about HIV.)

### Canada
National Advisory Committee on AIDS
c/o Laboratory Centre for Disease Control
AIDS Centre, Health and Welfare Canada
Ottawa, Ontario K1A 0L2
(613) 993-7711

## Juvenile Arthritis

Juvenile arthritis is an inflammation of one or more joints, causing pain, swelling, and a general feeling of malaise. The condition is chronic; the cause is not known. Pain and stiffness may be worse in the morning, and the severity may vary from day to day. Stiffness also occurs with prolonged sitting or with staying in any given position. Because of this, it is best to allow fairly frequent movement from one area, seat, or activity to another. Attendance at nursery or school may be irregular or reduced in hours, depending on the child's stamina and ability to cope with pain.

Treatment is directed toward improving and maintaining mobility in the joints during flare-ups, thus preventing fixed-joint deformities. Medication is given to reduce inflammation, pain, and swelling. Children with severe arthritis may be given a steroid, which can delay growth, cause obesity, and result in a characteristic moon-shaped face.

Juvenile arthritis can go into remission (disappear, or seem to disappear). The first remission may be permanent. If the arthritis does come back, subsequent remissions tend to last longer. Most children with juvenile arthritis have an excellent prognosis and, with proper therapy, 80 percent will grow up without deformity or arthritis in adult life.

Pain may make the child irritable at times. The child may want to avoid some activities and should not be forced to participate. The physician or therapist may be able to suggest activities that are particularly useful such as motion or joint-stretching exercises. These exercises can then be incorporated into group activities.

Children with arthritis need support in coping with their disability and the accompanying fear of pain, long hours of treatment, and possible limitations in their ability to do things and have fun. As with all children, it is very important that their lives remain as normal as possible. Parents, teachers, and therapists must think in terms of what the children *can* do to encourage them to find their own limits right from the start.

### Living with Juvenile Arthritis—Tammy

Tammy showed signs of Still syndrome (a type of arthritis) at the age of three. By the time she was five, she was so seriously affected that she had to be hospitalized for ongoing physical therapy. Steroid medication was also prescribed to bring her arthritis under control. She had to wear hand splints designed to hold her joints in the proper position. Her classmates were curious about the splints, so it was explained to them in a matter-of-fact way that splints, like braces on the teeth, are used temporarily to ensure that the body grows as it should.

Even with splints, Tammy needs paintbrushes, markers, and pencils built up with foam so she can grasp the marking instrument firmly. She is a creative little girl and relishes most expressive experiences as long as her tools are adapted to let her use them without too much difficulty.

Tammy has a sweet voice and enjoys singing with her classmates. The music therapist showed her how to play the Suzuki Omnichord® (see Appendix A), which facilitates arm extension. She enjoys the Omnichord® and is also learning to play an electronic keyboard to keep her fingers supple. The electronic keyboard lets Tammy produce a chord with just one finger, which means she doesn't have to stretch her left hand beyond its current range of motion to produce a chord.

Tammy also enjoys working with her hands, doing modeling and sculpting. If her hands are stiff, she asks for soft material, such as bread dough. Otherwise, she prefers a more resistant material, such as modeling clay. The soothing effect of manipulating these tactile media helps to improve Tammy's control of and strength in the small muscles of her joints and fingers. She is also encouraged to use a rolling pin and blunt plastic knife in working with these materials.

## Living with Juvenile Arthritis—Nella

Six-year-old Nella had her first bout of arthritis when she was five. At first, her illness was nothing more than a recurring high fever. She didn't feel well, but could not say why. She had countless tests and was hospitalized for several days in an isolation room because the doctor was concerned that her fever might be due to an infection. After much testing, it was finally determined that she had juvenile arthritis.

Nella was put on a regimen of therapeutic exercise and aspirin to control inflammation in the small joints of her fingers, hands, wrists, knees, and ankles. She responded well to this combined approach. With support from her family, she has been learning to cope with a new style of living—balancing exercise (to keep her joints flexible) with rest (to avoid possible painful stresses on arthritic joints).

For the past two months, Nella's arthritis has been in remission, and she has been able to attend first grade for the full day. She still tires easily and needs to rest when fatigued. Her therapy and medication have been reduced, although she maintains an active exercise program to gradually strengthen her muscles and keep her joints supple.

Because young children are extremely curious, mobility is important psychologically. A tricycle is excellent for exercise: it can strengthen hips, knees, and ankles when walking has become too stressful and weight-bearing needs to be avoided. Swimming is a must for every child with arthritis because it is the best way to improve muscle tone and movement of large joints. Nella has participated in such activities since she developed arthritis.

Each child with arthritis is an individual with unique needs and reactions. The attitudes and emotional responses of the child and family can often determine how that child meets the problems connected with this condition. Helping the child bring his or her feelings out into the open can be a constructive way of dealing with emotions. One activity that helps accomplish this goal for Nella was to have her make a book called "Feelings." Each page started with an incomplete phrase that Nella completed with her own ideas and drawings. Some of her phrases follow:

Love is . . . wen everybody fels good and dont yell or fite.

I feel afraid when . . . I no its gonna hirt me to walk.

I feel lonely when . . . I go to hospital and jest me in room.

I feel sad when . . . my budgee dide.

I feel mad when . . . I goota get needels.

I wish I could . . . fly in the sky.

What I like about myself is . . . I got nice long hair.

I wish my arthritis . . . wood go away and not make me scairt.

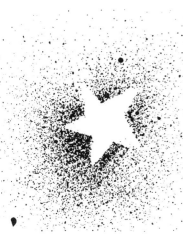

Completing unfinished sentences is an excellent way for children to make declarative statements about themselves and get in touch with their wishes, ideas, needs, and disappointments. For Nella, it opened discussion of her feelings about arthritis.

### Resources for Coping with Juvenile Arthritis

**United States**
Arthritis Foundation
1314 Spring Street N.W.
Atlanta, Georgia 30309
(404) 872-7100

**Canada**
The Arthritis Society, National Office
Suite 401
250 Bloor Street East
Toronto, Ontario M4W 3P2
(416) 967-1414

**Local**
Arthritis associations
Occupational and physical therapy clinics

# Asthma

*Asthma* is the most common disease of childhood, and it's increasing in both severity and incidence. The reasons for this are not clear. The disease is not new: it was known to the ancient Greeks, who called it "asthma," meaning panting or breathing hard. Childhood asthma is caused by inflammation of the airways that results in hyper-reactivity to a variety of stimuli. This hyper-reactivity in turn results in shortness of breath, incessant coughing, and wheezing that frequently require medical attention.

During an asthma attack, the airways are constricted, the smooth muscles around the airways tighten, the linings of the airways swell, and excess mucous is secreted. Of the many factors that can trigger an asthma attack, the most common are:

- Allergies
- Exercise and active play
- Colds and respiratory or viral infections
- Inhaled irritants
- Emotions

Although attacks can occur at any time, the more troublesome ones tend to come during the night or early morning. If acute, such attacks necessitate a trip to the emergency room and probably a hospital admission. As a result, many children with asthma are excluded from everyday childhood experiences by restrictions placed on them by their parents, the school, the community, and even themselves.

Parents of such children are frequently torn between concern for the child's health and fear of being overprotective, encouraging a child to be spoiled, whiny, and dependent. Siblings often resent the attention given to the child with asthma. All of this increases family tension, which may create anxiety and guilt in the child. Prolonged absences can also lead to educational problems that necessitate additional assistance to acquire basic skills.

For the teacher of a child with asthma, it is important to avoid bringing into the classroom things that might trigger an attack: pets, plants, and foods should be checked in advance with the parents. Sprays, glues, paste, and paints should be approved by the school nurse and all substances to be avoided listed in the school records and classroom. Apart from these precautions, the child should be accepted as an ordinary member of the class who has a few special needs.

### Living with Asthma—Johnny

At first, this six-year-old looks much younger than he is. Johnny is small, underweight, and pale. He has had asthma since the age of three, and his attacks have become more frequent and more severe with age. He is allergic to pollens and grasses in the spring and summer, when he has a dry hacking cough, itchy eyes and nose, and wheezing. When he has a severe attack, he doesn't talk, smile, or eat; even lying down can be distressing.

Johnny is beginning to respond to medication administered in both a mask and spray forms, and his school attendance is improving. During earlier absences, he missed whole blocks of readiness skills work. To catch up, he needs remedial work and much encouragement.

Johnny's creative strengths lie in plastic arts. He particularly likes working with clay, the malleable feel of which can provide a bridge between a child's senses and feelings. A child who is fearful and insecure can feel control and mastery over clay. Johnny feels little control over his asthma at this point, and he uses clay with much satisfaction. He makes elaborate villages complete with rivers, gardens, hills, huts, and trees. He chooses a theme and goes with it. Sometimes he takes an idea from a story, other times he says something like, "Today I'm gonna make an Indian village." He works very hard on his villages, using pine cones, pebbles, acorns, moss, sand, and twigs. He particularly likes it when broccoli with dip is brought in for snacks, hoping for leftovers that can become green trees for his village.

At this time, Johnny's exercise-induced asthma keeps him from competing in sports with his peers, but the admiration they show for his artistic work gives him gratification and self-confidence.

### Living with Asthma—Maria

As a baby, Maria had very severe eczema, constant respiratory infections, and marked allergies to foods such as nuts, chocolate, eggs, fish, and milk. She had several very acute asthma attacks when she was five years old that resulted in a three-month stay in the family asthma unit of a rehabilitation center. This hospitalization was considered necessary to adjust her medication and build up her stamina. While there, Maria was placed on a routine that involved a physical fitness program, swimming, music therapy, and kindergarten.

Various music therapy activities were used to help Maria with her breathing. In the first activity, the group sat in a circle and blew on an imaginary feather or a magic candle that never went out. This was followed by an exercise in which each child sang a note until he or she ran out of breath, then touched the neighboring child, who continued the singing. The children enjoyed keeping track of how long they could sustain the sound in the circle.

A similar task was to sing a song, holding the last note of each phrase for as long as possible. Measuring the seconds that a note is held, either by clock or counting, adds to the fun.

> My Bonnie lies over the ocean, (count)
> My Bonnie lies over the sea, (count)
> My Bonnie lies over the ocean, (count)
> Oh, bring back my Bonnie to me. (count)

Maria had a real flair for drama and movement. She loved dancing to music, simple poems, or descriptive words. She enjoyed a sense of release when she could move to familiar ideas. A little poem about popcorn, for example, ("It just pops and bursts all over/And I can too!/Yes, I can too!") inspired her to curl up, then "burst" forth.

Little rhymes give children a special pleasure. The following poem plunged Maria into an imaginative world as she became the fluttering, twirling butterfly. Her nimble feet and lithe, expressive body enhanced the interweaving of dance, music, and rhythm.

### The Butterfly

by Fran Herman

> Darting here,
> Darting there,
> The butterfly is everywhere.
> From a flower
> Red and bright
> It flies away—out of sight.

Maria had been dealing with so many negatives in her life that it was especially important for this creative approach to enhance her self-confidence. Creative opportunity helped divert her feelings of being different and helpless to an awareness that there was something very special about her and the way she responded to movement and music. She is now beginning to understand that she does not wheeze after strenuous dancing if she relaxes by lying down, breathing deeply, listening to music, or drawing. All this is experienced on a very simple level, yet Maria responds with childish delight. Her improved health is apparent in her total abandonment while she dances.

## Resources for Coping with Asthma

### United States
Asthma and Allergy Foundation
19 West 44th Street
New York, New York 10036

### Canada
Canadian Lung Association
75 Albert Street
Ottawa, Ontario K1P 5E7

### Local
Local asthma and lung associations
Hospitals and clinic

# Developmental Delay

Developmental delays in children can be traced to a wide variety of causes. They can also be accompanied by any number of physical and perceptual difficulties. These conditions generally occur in the developmental years, hence their term. Despite the diversity of conditions, these children have many qualities in common. Their development generally is slower than other children's and marked by limited intellectual potential.

Children with developmental delays find it difficult to retain information and often are unable to follow simple routines. They can become upset by changes in routine or by having to cope with new situations. They are often unaware of their surroundings and hesitate to explore their environment. Delay may be seen in their social behavior and in adaptive skills such as sharing and turn taking.

Experience has shown, however, that many children who are developmentally delayed respond surprisingly well to a rich variety of activities, such as those found in good nursery schools. Because these children are weak in academics, the arts can be very helpful in ensuring that they make the most of their nonacademic endeavors. The emotional and adaptive strengths demonstrated by the child usually indicate the level of mental functioning and are therefore a guide for the music therapist. The fine and gross motor capabilities of many of these children are unaffected, and their tireless enthusiasm often yields high levels of accomplishment.

Music is important in these activities: through active and enjoyable participation, children learn to coordinate mind and body, manipulate language, listen, and become more aware of their environment. Music is one of the best tools to exploit sensitive communication, which is a basic need of all human beings. Music making can be used to improve age-appropriate self-help skills, as well as to help these children participate in and enjoy group activities.

Creative activities should present the opportunity to explore concrete practical applications using existing basic skills. Material should be presented slowly and sequentially in a highly organized manner. Larger motor skills, crucial to the discovery of form and space, should be emphasized. During creative periods, the children can receive valuable sensory stimulation by handling many different art materials and by taking in a variety of visual experiences. Even if the children do not end up with a finished product, the multisensory experiences provided by these sessions enrich the children's existence, adding to their knowledge and growth.

## Living with Developmental Delay—André

When he was two, André had a severe case of measles that resulted in a developmental delay. He is now six, but functions at a level two years younger. A likeable little chap, André enjoys kindergarten, especially music and puppetry.

Puppets are a strong visual focus that help motivate André to participate in new experiences. They can also stimulate imaginative responses. If an adult puts on a puppet and signals André to do likewise, he can be engaged in puppet talk. André can be encouraged to exercise his budding ability to make conversation, to talk about the things he likes to do and about his world. He also enjoys participating in stories that are acted out very simply with puppets. Recently, he was one of the pigs in "The Three Little Pigs," a production done with puppets made from old cereal boxes. Music added much to the production's dramatic impact.

Initial music experiences for children with significantly slower learning ability often focus on encouraging them to respond vocally or on an instrument to a physical or auditory cue. André is learning to respond to "stop and go" games by following the sound of an instrument, reacting to raised red or green signals, or responding to a wand waved up and down or from side to side. He is also learning to center his attention on a moving sound (such as a maraca, a hand-held gourd filled with beans for shaking) as it comes near his face, then moves away and goes in different directions, but always on a plane level with André's face. At all times, the teacher describes the maraca's movement to help the child stay focused. ("It's going up, it's going away, it's coming closer to you, it's being very quiet now.") Tone of voice is important: the child may not grasp all the words, but their sense may well be understood.

Singing is also a favorite activity for André. If the tempo is not too fast, he manages quite well in singing words to simple songs. Repetition is vital for him to remember the words. Material presented in a song should be repeated in many ways to ensure overlearning. André seems to require more repetitions of an experience or an association to retain it. Once André has learned the song, he sings with a robust voice. He finds it easier to relate and attend to one instrument or voice rather than to many, and he has a tendency to prefer a single musical source. This preference is common and should be kept in mind when working with such children. Far too many recordings or tapes have too busy an accompaniment, which makes it difficult for children who are developmentally delayed to integrate the array of sounds they hear.

André likes songs that have either a visual component or a very bouncy rhythm. His favorite songs are ones about farms; he enjoys choosing a plastic animal, holding it up on cue, and saying or singing the appropriate sounds. Songs about cars, buses, and trains are his next choice, and he enjoys singing them repeatedly. Physical actions to songs are very important and can eventually lead to simple mimes without music. André responds to "pretend" activities if they are about familiar things, such as eating an ice-cream cone, washing face and hands, combing hair, brushing teeth, or patting a puppy.

These children have short attention spans and usually remain with one activity for only brief periods of time. Nevertheless, they respond to music; they can benefit from exposure to and involvement with music, and they learn from such experiences.

## Living with Developmental Delay—Amanda

Amanda is a winsome three-and-a-half-year-old girl with Down syndrome. She has a lovely smile and an affectionate nature, which is one of her unique qualities. She attends an integrated nursery school three mornings a week and, though she does not actively play with the other children, appears to enjoy being with them.

Amanda is in the tactile exploring stage. She will play with textured balls and playthings, clutch toys, and shapes as an adult helps her identify the sensations as fuzzy, soft, smooth, hard, cuddly, silky, and so on. Textured cloths are held up to her face in like manner. Other attributes are explored, such as wet/dry, hot/cold, or hard/soft, using materials and food. She uses her mouth to explore objects and foods, which stimulates chewing, sucking, and biting.

Various tables are set up for exploring the feeling of cereals, food-colored pastas, and puddings of assorted colors. Amanda's desire to finger the textures of things and put them in her mouth tempts her to try new activities, but she first needs prompting or modeling by an adult. After some hesitation, her hands go out to the new experience; with encouragement she can stay with such explorations for some time. When she paints with pudding, Amanda is encouraged to use not only fingers and fingertips but also the entire palm of the hand. This emphasis is particularly important because Amanda was tactile defensive when she was younger and has needed considerable encouragement to participate in such activities willingly and without alarm. Water play, modeling clay, and sand are also valuable tactile experiences for children like Amanda.

Amanda responds well during music circles, trying to bring her hands together to clap, stamping her feet on cue, and touching parts of her body during songs. She can receptively and expressively identify the face, hands, legs, tummy, fingers, feet, hair, knees, and chest. She is sometimes able to sing a few words but does not remember entire songs. If she's not singing words, she makes sounds when the music captures her attention. She responds to her name in a song, and hearing her name sung increases her self-esteem and sense of belonging.

The concept of "fast and slow" is also being presented to Amanda in a variety of ways: by walking, jumping, rolling, clapping, slapping legs to a definite tempo, or playing a drum or other instrument to a changing rhythm. Like many children with Down syndrome, Amanda is hypotonic, which means she has floppy muscle tone. It is therefore important to provide gross motor activities, such as skipping, jumping, crawling, and moving to music. She sometimes needs prompting to become involved, but usually does whatever the other children do to the music.

All children in the nursery wear only pants or diapers and go around in bare feet. In this way, they can experience sensations through their feet of textured surfaces, such as carpets, rubber floor mats, grass, sand, and cold and warm water. Water play with hands and face is also encouraged. Amanda likes to pour water from one vessel to another in a plastic tub, amusing play that is also a good visual-spatial exercise.

Concrete experiences with objects are critical for a child like Amanda and should be repeated frequently to increase security and reinforce learning skills. By working on auditory, tactile, visual, and taste discrimination and identification, Amanda is expanding the use of all her senses in new learning experiences.

## Resources for Coping with Developmental Delay

### United States

Down Syndrome Congress
1640 West Roosevelt Road
Room 156E
Chicago, Illinois 60608

National Association for Retarded Children
2709 Avenue "E"
East Arlington, Texas 76011

Joseph P. Kennedy, Jr., Foundation
1350 New York Avenue N.W.
Suite 212
Washington, D.C. 20005
(202) 393-1250

### Canada

Canadian Association for Community Living
4700 Keele Street
Toronto, Ontario M3J 1P3
(416) 661-9611

# Appendix A

## Adaptations for Success

To minimize problems in the use of creative equipment, media, and instruments, special consideration should be given to techniques that will compensate for a specific disability.

This could be as simple as offering children a choice of instruments or tools that complement their functional capabilities. In other circumstances, specific devices must be obtained or devised to compensate for a child's disability. An occupational therapist's assistance can be helpful in these circumstances; if this help is not available, a common-sense approach should produce satisfactory results.

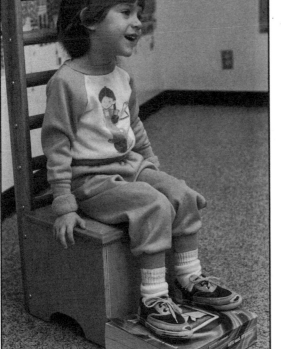

*Correct positioning helps children feel more comfortable and exercise greater control of their arms and legs.*

Children should be encouraged to attempt their own ways of adapting physically, perhaps by doing an activity in a slightly different way. Making adaptations independently leads them to generalized problem-solving strategies that can be applied to any creative task.

Similarly, it is essential to include children when equipment is being chosen, set up, or adapted. Trial and error, based on close observation of a child's range, strength, control, and pattern of movement, will usually lead to improved functioning. If in doubt, ask the child what feels most comfortable.

## Adaptations for Play and Work

**Correct positioning** of the child ensures that the work or instrument is within easy reach while the child is seated or supported as comfortably as possible. Feet should be squarely on the floor or on footrests. Backs, chests, and sides may be supported with hook-and-loop-fastener (such as Velcro®) belts, folded towels, foam, or pillows. Work should be on a tray or table adjusted individually to the best height or angle.

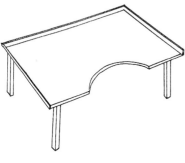

*A cutout table.*

**Cutout tables.** Cutting a semicircle out of a table allows children to sit closer to the work space. The tabletop on either side supports the children's arms and keeps objects from being easily knocked off the table.

**Paint containers** should have a wide mouth and low profile. Prevent upsets by setting the containers on wooden trays with discs cut into them that match the diameter of the containers' bottoms.

**Paint** should be thick enough so that it won't drip if a child hesitates or doesn't have a steady hand. Cornstarch, white flour, wallpaper sizing, and tempera powder can be used to thicken water-based paints.

**Brush substitutes** can often be manipulated more easily than brushes. Foam-tipped paint sticks are available at paint and hardware stores. Another alternative: pop the ball out of a roll-on deodorant dispenser, fill the container with paint, and replace the ball. Fingers and hands can be used to apply paint with a sophistication much greater than is normally associated with fingerpainting.

**Three-sided trays** with raised edges keep objects from being knocked out of reach.

**Minor grasping difficulties** can sometimes be overcome by the use of large-diameter pencils, crayons, brushes, markers, or pastels.

**Stabilizing** the free hand promotes control of the hand grasping the art tool.

*Stabilizing the free hand gives this child better control.*

**A dowel** inserted in a board and clamped to the table is another way to provide a handle the child can grip to stabilize the free hand.

**Rubber ball grips** accommodate those who can best manage an overhand grip, which reduces the need to rotate the wrist. A short pencil, brush, or marker is inserted in a hole drilled in a rubber ball of an appropriate diameter.

**Foam tube grips** (available from occupational therapy supply catalogues) or a segment of foam hot-water-pipe insulation (available at hardware and building-supply stores) can be used to help a child with weak grasp as well as for control of small-diameter objects. To use, wedge a marker into the hollow center of the tube.

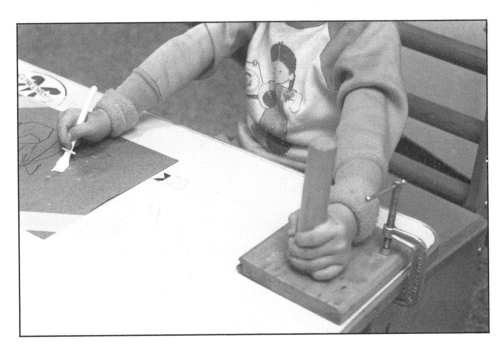

*A dowel board is inexpensive and easy to make.*

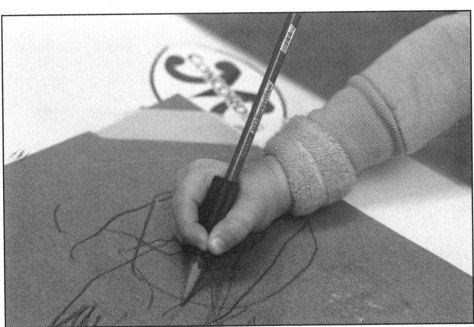

*Building up the pencil aids in grasping it.*

**Grasping Knobs.** Replace the knobs on wooden puzzles and toys with larger knobs from the hardware store.

**Rubber band or tape grips** can be wrapped around tools to create a "stop" on the lower end. This keeps fingers from slipping down too close to the drawing surface if the hand muscles have uncontrolled spasms or if weakness occurs. Triangular rubber grips are also available from most primary school catalogues.

**Transverse grips** can be fashioned by fixing the drawing tool in a dowel. Use a set screw in the form of a screw eye that clamps the tool in a hole drilled in the dowel. The hand then grips the appropriately sized dowel while the tool is held at a right angle.

**Involuntary muscle contractions,** such as those experienced by many children with cerebral palsy, pose a danger if the hand holding a pointed object is pulled back toward the face. To avoid injury, cover the upper end of the object with tape, foam, or modeling paste.

**Hold work materials in place** with clamps, tape, rubber-backed matting or place mats, or clothespins. These measures help children who can't steady materials and work on them at the same time. For other children, it may be best to encourage them to steady their own work, thus increasing use of a poorly functioning hand. The child should keep the hand in his or her sight.

**Distinguishing left from right** can be encouraged by placing a strip of masking tape down the center of the working surface. Left and right labels can be pinned on the child's sleeves.

**Work size** should be scaled to each child's circumstances. Those with better fine motor skills excel at smaller projects; those with better gross motor skills perform more comfortably on a larger scale. Children should be eased into work in a scale they are less comfortable with.

**Scissors with double finger holes** let a helping hand guide the child's hand as it becomes accustomed to scissor movement.

**Left- and right-handed scissors** should be available, with the thumb hole marked with tape or paint.

**Easy-grip loop scissors** are available from most primary school supply catalogues. The handles are connected with a plastic loop that causes the scissors to open when pressure on them is released. These scissors can be mounted in a slot between two boards to create a miniature guillotine-type cutter for children who normally are unable to operate scissors.

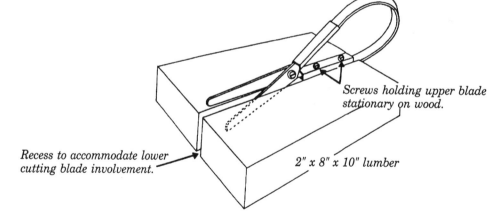

*Spring-opening loop scissors.*

*Screws holding upper blade stationary on wood.*

*Recess to accommodate lower cutting blade involvement.*

*2" x 8" x 10" lumber*

**Glue sticks** reduce spillage of liquid glues and increase control for those who have difficulty with liquid glues.

**Clay and other modeling media** should have the moisture content varied to meet the strength and motor skills of the child. Increased moisture in the clay demands less strength to manipulate.

# The Use of Instruments

People often ask about using instruments with preschool children who are severely disabled. Unless used with care, instruments can be a source of frustration rather than joy. Whatever instruments are used should have good, clear sounds, as opposed to sharp-sounding tin drums, jangly maracas, or high-pitched whistles that may irritate or overstimulate some children.

A special note concerning children with cerebral palsy is that children diagnosed as spastic sometimes respond best to stimulating music, while those diagnosed as athetoid relax and respond better to soothing music, in terms of their movement abilities. This consideration is important to keep in mind especially when working in groups with children diagnosed as athetoid. Be sensitive to children who show distress and agitation when a loud or fast piece of music is played, when someone uses an instrument with a sharp sound, or when there is a sudden or unexpected sound. Children should see the whole activity so that they will not be easily startled.

The following instruments are recommended for young children.

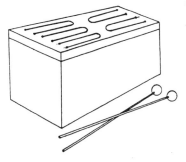

*A tongue drum.*

**Willow reed rattles** are excellent for sound and have a good handle for grasping. They may contain bells, small pebbles, or nuts. A variety of these rattles can make an interesting sound collage.

**Tongue or slit drums** are three-dimensional wooden drums with different slits on the top part which form the "tongues." Each "tongue" has a different tone. All children respond well to the mellow sounds they achieve when hitting the different parts of the drum with a rubber-tipped mallet. The drums can be placed on a flat surface or held in a position for a child who may have difficulty hitting the top area.

**Clappers** can be managed by small children.

**Bells with handles** are useful. If the child is not able to grasp, a simple adaptation can be made. Bells attached to a band of hook-and-loop fastener (such as Velcro®) can be put around the child's hand or foot. A mitten with bells can also be effective.

*A large hitting area, plus a handle built up with foam, allow this child to play the drums.*

**Drums** should have a large hitting area. A flat drum is best if the child is sitting on the floor or in a wheelchair with a tray. A tongue or slit drum may be enjoyed but has to be positioned. If a child is unable to hold a drumstick, build up the handle with sponge and masking tape, or fasten it to the hand with an elastic band. Another adaptation that works well is to have the child wear a mitten with hook-and-loop fastener (Velcro®) placed on both the mitten palm and stick.

**Finger cymbals** will be easier to play if they have elastic attachments that go around the hand instead of knobs.

**Suzuki Omnichord® electronic keyboards** can delight a child of any age. This unique instrument's design lets even a very young child produce a beautiful harplike sound merely by touching the instrument with a hand, wrist, or arm while the other hand (or another person) presses a button. This instrument gives immediate gratification to children whose disabilities prevent them from satisfactorily using other instruments.

*The Suzuki Omnichord®, a touch-sensitive instrument, makes beautiful harplike sounds and can be played by children with severe physical involvement.*

# Appendix B

## Additional Readings

### On Children with Special Needs

Barnes, E., C. Berrigan, and D. Biklen. 1978. *What's the difference? Teaching attitudes toward people with disabilities.* Syracuse, NY: Human Policy Press.

Blackford, P., and A. King. 1985. *Count me in: A resource on disability awareness.* Toronto: IS Five Press.

Canfield, J., and H. C. Wells. 1976. *100 ways to enhance self-concept in the classroom: A handbook for teachers and parents.* Englewood Cliffs, NJ: Prentice-Hall.

Deiner, P. L. 1983. *Resources for teaching young children with special needs.* New York: Harcourt Brace Jovanovich.

Furuno, S., K. A. O'Reilly, C. M. Hosaka, T. T. Inatsuka, T. L. Allman, and B. Zeisloft. 1985. *Hawaii early learning profile (HELP).* Palo Alto, CA: Vort Corporation.

Herman, F., and J. C. Smith. 1988. *Accentuate the positive: Expressive Arts for children with disabilities.* Toronto: Jimani Publications.

Manolson, A. 1992. *It takes two to talk.* 4th ed. Toronto: The Hanen Early Language Resource Centre.

Paasche, C. L., L. Gorrill, and B. Strom. 1990. *Children with special needs in early childhood settings.* Don Mills, Ontario: Addison-Wesley.

Schwartz, S., and J. E. Miller. 1988. *Heller: The language of toys.* Kensington, MD: Woodbine House.

Segal, M. 1988. *In time and with love: Caring for the special needs baby.* New York: Newmarket Press.

Wirth, M. J. 1976. *Teacher's handbook of children's games—A guide to developing perceptual-motor skills.* West Nyack, NJ: Parker Publishing Company.

## On Music

Bitcom, C. 1979. *Alike and different—The clinical and educational use of orff schulwerk.* Santa Ana, CA: Rasha Press.

Cass-Beggs, B. 1990. *Your baby needs music.* 2d ed. Toronto: Addison-Wesley.

Glazer, T. 1972. *Eye winker, Tom tinker, chin chopper—50 musical fingerplays.* Garden City, NY: Doubleday and Co.

Nocera, S. 1979. *Reaching the special learner through music.* Morristown, NJ: Silver Burdett.

Robbins, C., and C. Robbins. 1980. *Music for the hearing impaired.* St. Louis, MO: Magnamusic Baton.

Seeger, R. 1948. *American folk songs for children.* Garden City, NY: Doubleday and Co.

Ward, D. 1979. *Sing a rainbow, hearts and hands and voices.* London: Oxford University Press.

## On Puppets

Camplin, C., and N. Renfro. 1985. *Story-telling with puppets.* Chicago: American Library Association.

Currell, D. 1980. *Learning with puppets.* New York: Plays, Inc.

Hunt, T., and N. Renfro. 1982. *Puppetry in early childhood education.* Austin, TX: Nancy Renfro Studios.

Sullivan, D. 1982. *Pocketful of puppets.* Austin, TX: Nancy Renfro Studios.

## On Movement

Gerhardt, L. A. 1973. *Moving and knowing—The young child orients himself in space.* Englewood Cliffs, NJ: Prentice-Hall.

Green, G. A. 1977. *Teaching the three R's through movement experiences.* Minneapolis, MN: Burgess Publishing.

Lynch-Fraser, D. 1982. *Danceplay: Creative movement for the very young child.* New York: New American Library.

Nelson, E. L. 1978. *Dancing games for children of all ages.* New York: Sterling Publishing Company.

## On Art

Krone, A. 1978. *Art instruction for handicapped children.* Denver, CO: LOVE Publishing.

Lindsay, Z. 1966. *Art for spastics.* London: Mills and Boon, Ltd.

Lowenfeld, V., and L. W. Brittain. 1964. *Creative and mental growth.* 4th ed. New York: Macmillan.

Rodriguez, S. 1984. *The special artist's handbook—Art activities and adaptive aids for handicapped students.* Palo Alto, CA: Dale Seymour.

Silborstein-Storfer, M., and M. Jones. 1982. *Doing art together: Discovering the joy of appreciating and creating art at the Metropolitan Museum of Art parent-child workshop.* New York: Simon and Schuster.

Uhlin, D. 1972. *Art for exceptional children.* Dubuque, IA: William C. Brown.

Zubrowski, B. 1979. *Bubbles: A children's museum activity book.* Boston, MA: Little, Brown and Company.

## On Discovery

Kendall, F. E. 1983. *Diversity in the classroom: A multicultural approach to the education of young children.* New York: Teachers College Press.

Lowenfeld, M. 1967. *Play in childhood.* New York: John Wiley.

Moyer, I. D. 1983. *Responding to infants: The infant activity manual.* Minneapolis, MN: T. S. Dennison and Co.

Segal, M. 1988. *Your child at play.* New York: Newmarket Press.

# Index

## A

Ability, 1
AIDS, 205, 210-11
  living with, 211-13
  resources, 213
Amputations, 190-91
  living with, 191
  resources, 191
Art
  adaptations, 18, 223-26
  bathtub, 59
  computer, 79
  positioning for, 78-79
  support, 2-3
  and visual awareness, 77-78
Arthritis, juvenile, 205, 214
  living with, 214-16
  resources, 216
Arthrogryposis, 46, 187
  living with, 187-88
  resources, 188
Asthma, 205, 216-17
  living with, 217-18
  resources, 218
At risk babies, 11-13
Ataxia, 175
Athetosis, 175
Attention, 92
Auditory acuity, 71-74
Auditory awareness
  in babies, 12, 20-22
  in formative years, 69-71
  in toddlers, 24-28
Auditory concentration, 71-74
Auditory discrimination, xvi
Auditory memory, 74-76
Auditory sequencing, 74-76

## B

Babies
  at risk, 11-13
  difficult, 9-11
  distressed, 10-11
  medically fragile, 11-13
  tactile defensive, 9-11, 13
Baths, baby, 7
  tactile defensive babies, 9
Behavioral difficulties, xv
Bells, 28
Birthdays, 161-63
Blowing, 90-92

Body awareness
  in babies, 7-8
  in formative years, 50-53. *See also*
    Spatial and kinesthetic awareness
  in toddlers, 14-16
Body image. *See* Body awareness
Body language, 61
Books, for toddlers, 19

## C

Cerebral palsy, 16, 46, 57, 91, 135, 156,
  175-76, 227
  in babies, 9
  living with, 177-81, 195
  resources, 185
Chanting, 90
Christmas, 152-55
Circles, 60-61
Clapping, 14, 75, 90
Clothes, for tactile defensive babies, 10
Cognitive appetite, in babies, 6
Color awareness, 83-86
Communication difficulties, in toddlers,
  42-43
Computers, 79
Concentration, 92
Control, 77
Coordination, 7-8, 77, 153
Creativity, 1

## D

Dance play, 125-29
  elbow dancing, 51
  hand dancing, 19
Developmental delays, xv, 11, 47, 219
  living with, 219-21
  resources, 222
Difficult babies, 9-11
Directionality, 66-68, 184
Distressed babies, 10-11
Dramatic play, 115-19, 182
Drums, 27, 227

## E

Earth Day, 165-68
Easter, 160-63
Environmental awareness, 165
Expressive language, 39
Eye-hand coordination, 19, 154

*Additional creative resources for enhancing your students' self-expression . . .*

## SENSEABILITIES
### Understanding Sensory Integration
*by Maryann Colby Trott, M.A., with Marci Laurel, M.A., CCC-SLP, and*
*Susan L. Windeck, M.S., OTR/L*

> Educate parents and teachers about sensory integration with this easy-to-understand training resource. Give them practical information they can apply to real-life situations. Activities encourage children to move across all sensory domains without realizing it! Reproduce all or part of the material including chapters on the tactile and vestibular system, therapy session, school, and more. **Catalog No. 4283-Y    $59**

## LEARN TO CUT
### A Structured Program of Cutting Tasks with Reproducible Patterns
*by Robin R. Wolfe*

> These developmentally sequenced, reproducible activities help children learn and develop fine motor skills, and practice visual discrimination and shape recognition as well. Each skill step focuses on specific aspects of cutting and presents different cutting tasks for children to complete. With tracking sheets and recordkeeping forms to follow your students' progress. Instructional objectives make it ideal for home carryover, too. **Catalog No. 7401-Y    $29**

## KIDS IN MOTION
### An Early Childhood Movement Education Program
*by Pamela J. Gilroy*
*Foreword by Marsha Dunn Klein, M.Ed., OTR*

> Encourage movement exploration in children who have developmental delays with this book of fun activities! Youngsters discover and build on gross motor skills with games and stunts like "Row a Boat" and "Backward Dog." You'll like the week-by-week developmental program that includes objectives and warm-up exercises. **Catalog No. 7227-Y    $15**

## DISCOVERY IN MOTION
### Movement Exploration for Problem Solving and Self-Concept
*by Pamela J. Gilroy*

> Provide your students with physical challenges to sharpen their critical thinking skills while increasing their self-esteem. Thirty-seven sequenced movement exploration activities will help students, individually or in pairs, develop better spatial and relational awareness of their bodies. For use in your regular classroom, general physical education, and adaptive physical education classes. **Catalog No. 7609-Y    $20**

## KIDS IN ACTION
### Developing Body Awareness in Young Children
*by Pamela J. Gilroy*

> Provide your 3- and 4-year-old children with a variety of activities to develop body awareness. Here are complete 20-minute lessons for each school week, September through June. You can begin this program at any time. Lessons are taught from a movement exploration approach, with no "right" or "wrong." **Catalog No. 7323-Y    $15**

## LOOPS AND OTHER GROUPS
### A Kinesthetic Writing System
*by Mary D. Benbow, M.S., OTR/L*

> Help your second-grade children learn the formations of all lower-case letters in just six weeks! This writing program develops systematic steps for letter analysis and provides easy-to-remember motor and memory cues. Students learn by using four groups of letters which share common movement patterns—Clock Climbers, Kite Strings, Loop Group, and Hills and Valleys. **Catalog No. 4189-Y    $39**

## SOURCEBOOK FOR CHILDREN WITH ATTENTION DEFICIT DISORDER
### A Management Guide for Early Childhood Professionals and Parents
*by Clare Jones, Ph.D.*

Learn practical information you'll need to manage attention deficit disorder—an area of growing interest and concern in early childhood education. This nontechnical manual discusses issues of the disorder in terms family members and the entire disciplinary team will understand. Within easy-to-read sections you'll find resources and many reproducible materials, including—home carryover activities, ideas for teachers in management and curriculum, computer-assisted curriculum ideas, normal development scales, fact sheets, and more! **Catalog No. 7696-Y     $35**

## FINE MOTOR DYSFUNCTION
### Therapeutic Strategies in the Classroom
*by Kristin J. Levine, M.S.Ed., OTR*

These remediating and compensating strategies help you adapt regular classroom programming and materials for your preschool and school-age clients. You'll have extensively illustrated instruction sheets that are completely reproducible and ready to use—an ideal supplement to your program. Activities are arranged in 15 skill areas. This task-specific approach enhances children's self-image by helping them participate in school activities with greater success. **Catalog No. 4704-Y     $69**

## MOTOR DEVELOPMENT PROGRAM FOR SCHOOL-AGE CHILDREN
*by Jeanne Shanks Sellers, Ed.D., PT*

Use this graded program to assess a child's level of motoric development and create an individualized program. You'll have sequenced activities for eight motor activity stations including perceptual motor, manipulation, body awareness/stunts, and more! **Catalog No. 4143-Y     $29**

## PRE-SCISSOR SKILLS (3rd Edition)
*by Marsha Dunn Klein, M.Ed., OTR*

This expanded, versatile workbook gives you a variety of activities to teach creative scissor skills in your classroom, home, clinic, or hospital. Brand-new features include illustrations, principles of normal progression, lists of adaptive scissors, presentation of adaptive techniques, and more. You'll be able to understand the developmental stages of scissor use and teach at each child's skill level. **Catalog No. 3101-Y     $24**

## PRE-DRESSING SKILLS
*by Marsha Dunn Klein, M.Ed., OTR*

This manual presents the developmental sequence of learning specific dressing and undressing skills. It offers practical methods for teaching these skills to your clients. Also includes adaptive techniques and equipment available for handicapped children and adults. **Catalog No. 4689-Y     $23**

## PRE-WRITING SKILLS (Revised)
*by Marsha Dunn Klein, M.Ed., OTR*

This revised version incorporates current principles of movement learning—with emphasis on development of mobility from stability. Learn what prerequisite skills are needed for writing and the developmental stages children go through to learn pre-writing skills. Clear guidelines are given to help you with individual pre-writing programs. **Catalog No. 2089-Y     $24**

## MOTIVATE TO COMMUNICATE
### A Pragmatic Game for Users of Minspeak™ and Other Augmentative Systems
*by Houri Kaloustian Vorperian, M.A., CCC-SLP, and Patricia Winn-Kirk, M.S., CCC-SLP*

Teach and encourage 4- to 8-year-old children's use of augmentative communication systems with this innovative game. While moving around a stand-up gameboard designed like a house, players answer questions about the home and other subjects related to daily life. Children become more adept at retrieving information from their systems and gain confidence in initiating conversation with peers and adults. Help your clients and their parents, siblings, and caregivers explore and build reciprocal communication relationships as they master the use of the augmentative communication system. Play this game with users of the Touch/Light Talker™ with Minspeak™, or easily adapt it for use with other picture or letter-based augmentative communication systems.　**Catalog No. 7806-Y　$79**

## LISTEN AND DRAW
### An Integrated Skills Activity Program
*by Laura Grey, M.S., CCC-SLP, and Michael Goudket, M.A.*

Young clients draw delightful dinosaurs and other cute creatures in this unique sound-symbol association program. Develop auditory-visual integration skills using children's love of drawing. You'll have 12 art projects which involve children listening to step-by-step directions on audiotapes, following those directions, and ultimately producing a drawing.　**Catalog No. 7744-Y　$39.95**

## SEMANTICALLY SPEAKING—FOR EARLY INTERVENTION
*by Elaine Burke Krassowski, M.S., CCC-SLP*

This board game is similar in format to the others in the *Semantically Speaking* series—but for your PK, kindergarten, and first-grade children. Students will improve their abilities to receive, organize, and convey information in five word categories: food, clothing, animals, tools, and household items. You'll also be able to teach a basic vocabulary students need for successful daily communication, and expressive and receptive language skills as well.　**Catalog No. 7675-Y　$45**

---

# IMPROVE YOUR THERAPY PROGRAM AND SAVE MONEY WITH MORE THAN 700 IDEAS IN ONE RESOURCE!

## EXTRAORDINARY PLAY WITH ORDINARY THINGS
### Recycling Everyday Materials to Build Motor Skills

*by Barbara Sher, M.A., OTR*

**IDEAL RESOURCE FOR A LIMITED BUDGET**

*Extraordinary Play with Ordinary Things* shows you how to recycle materials in a broad variety of games and therapeutic activities. Use for home visits, in the clinic and regular classroom, and with mainstreamed special needs children. These versatile activities require little preparation and your students **4 to 12 years old** will love them!

**PRACTICAL TIPS HELP YOU LOCATE MATERIALS FOR USE IN THE GAMES**

Each chapter lists ideas for games to play using different types of reusable items. Students can collect these objects from their own home or neighborhood. Chapters include Games to Play With—

- Newspapers
- Hoses and Pipes
- Cardboard Boxes
- String and Rope
- Cans
- Paper
- Unmatched Socks
- Milk and Other Cartons
- Lids
- Wood

Also includes adaptation chapters of Games to Play With—
- People Who Are Hemiplegic
- People Who Are Wheelchair Bound

**TARGET SPECIFIC SKILL DEVELOPMENT EASILY**

Individualize each game for one person or a group. Each chapter is divided into sections according to skill development. Address these skills—

- Gross Motor
- Spatial Sense
- Flexibility
- Imagination
- Eye-Foot Coordination
- Fine Motor
- Motor Planning
- Rhythm
- Eye-Hand Coordination
- Laterality
- Balance
- Group Play

*Reduce your preparation time with more than 140 helpful illustrations!*

**IDEAL FOR TRAVELING THERAPISTS**

This resource is a must for itinerant therapists who have to have an assortment of equipment. Clinic or school therapists who have limited funds for a variety of expensive equipment will find it very useful.

*165-page manual, 8½" x 11", softbound.*

**Extraordinary Play with Ordinary Things**
**#4738-Y**          $39